THE NEW KEY TO
COSTA RICA

Beatrice Blake
Anne Becher

Publications in English S.A.
San José, Costa Rica

Cover and illustrations: Deirdre Hyde
Maps: Huberth Monge
Drawings, p. 87-8: Anabel Maffioli
Photos: Dennis Moran
Proofreading: Sally Pearson

Published and distributed by:

Publications in English
Apdo. 7-1230, 1000 San José, Costa Rica
(506) 34-3789
Fax: (506) 23-1609, attn. Beatrice Blake, 34-3789

Distributed outside Costa Rica by:

Bookpeople
2929 Fifth St.
Berkeley, CA 94710, USA
1-800 999-4650
Fax: (415) 848-6322

Bradt Publications
Chalfont St. Peter, Bucks.,
England
Ph/fax: 02407 3478
Fax: (0) 734 509262

ITMB Publishing, Ltd.
Vancouver, BC, Canada
(604) 687-3320
Fax: (604) 687-5925

Distribution Ulysse
4176 St-Denis
Montréal, QC, Canada
(514) 843-9447

917.286
B636n   Blake, Beatrice
The New Key to Costa Rica/Beatrice Blake--10.
ed.--San José, C.R.: Publicaciones en Inglés,
S.A., 1991.
272 p. ; 21 cm.

ISBN 9977-9961-1-3

1. Costa Rica - Descripciones y Viajes. 2. Costa
Rica - Geografía. I. Título.

For
peace with justice
in harmony with nature

ACKNOWLEDGMENTS

Each year brings many changes to tourism in Costa Rica. Interesting new projects develop, but at the same time the dilemmas involved become more challenging. I want to thank all the people who are thinking and working hard to make sure that tourism does not run rampant over the very environment and native cultures which attract people to Costa Rica in the first place. My dear friends Paula Palmer, Bob Mack and Sergio León are constantly involved in this struggle, as well as Juanita Sanchez and Gloria Mayorga of the KekoLdi Reserve, Francisco Soto, Anabel Maffioli and Carlos Coles of Arbofilia, and the members of Tsuli Tsuli, the Costa Rican branch of the Audubon Society, to name just a few.

The ecological and social awareness of Anne Becher set the course for this book when we rewrote it together five years ago. Even though life has taken her all the way from Costa Rica to Maine to Argentina and back to Colorado, her thoughts and suggestions are still a vital part of the *Key*.

Deirdre Hyde is another fighter for environmental issues and uses her wonderful artistic talent to bring those issues to life. We are proud and happy to have her delightful cover and illustrations. Jerry Ruhlow is just as avid about saving Costa Rica's sportfishing resources, and we are honored to have his contribution to the fishing section. It is always a pleasure to work with Hubert Monge of the Servicio de Parques Nacionales. We are grateful that his beautiful maps grace our book. Many thanks to Alvaro Gomez and Rafa Vargas for making it possible for me to learn about computer typesetting, and to Isabel Macdonald for enthusiastically confronting the mountains of research that had to go into this new edition, as well as for her very helpful editorial comments.

Thanks to all the people who have written with suggestions, corrections and feedback, and to the Audubon Society of Costa Rica for formulating, and allowing me to reprint, their Code of Environmental Ethics for Nature Travel (p. 36-8). Special thanks to Ronnie Cummins of the Asociación Talamanqueña de Turismo y Conservación for his ideas on new directions for the book in the future.

None of my research would have been possible without the partnership of my husband, Dennis Moran. For the first time, we are including photographs in the book--Dennis's best shots from his eleven years in Costa Rica.

Anyone who has ever traveled with a two-year-old and a newborn will know that at some points this year we seriously questioned whether this was the right line of work for us, but we all survived. Our son Danny has matured into a seasoned traveler of three, and our sweet baby Elizabeth seems none the worse for wear. Luckily, Anne Becher and her husband Joe flew in, did the Tortuguero update and trekked through the Southern Zone writing poetry, trips that would have been impossible for our family.

Sincerest thanks go to my assistant, Adita Molina for her constant, loving support, and to her father, Fernando Molina, for helping us out when we really needed him. Essential too has been the kindness of our neighbors, Martina Alvarez Gutierrez and family.

And deepest love and gratitude go to the strong, generous and joyful spirit of my mother, Jean Wallace, who started the original version of the *Key* in 1978, in honor of this special little country in which she finally found her home.

Beatrice Blake
San José, Costa Rica
February 1991

TABLE OF CONTENTS

Fold-out maps of Costa Rica and San José: Inside back cover

COSTA RICA
DISARMED DEMOCRACY

At one point in its history, Costa Rica produced more bananas than any country in the world, but it is far from being a "banana republic". Armyless, democratic, conservation-minded-- people in many developing countries are fighting for what Costa Rica has had for years. How did this come about?

Costa Rica acted progressively long before that was the general trend. The establishment of free, obligatory, tax-financed education in the constitution of 1869, the elimination of the death penalty in 1882, and the abolition of the army in 1948, all testify to Costa Rica's unique character and vision, and all laid the groundwork for the present social order.

Historically, Costa Rica has almost always remained uninvolved in the conflicts that have shaken her sister republics. John L. Stephens, a North American archaeologist who visited in 1840, mentioned even then that Costa Rica was an island of tranquility compared to the rest of Central America. Although the national character tends to ignore or imagine itself above the problems of its neighbors, former president Oscar Arias (1986-90) took a decisive and responsible role in waging peace, especially in relation to Nicaragua. His unflagging efforts to bring warring parties to the conference table won him the 1987 Nobel Prize. At the same time, many Costa Ricans resented his concentration on international issues and wished he would pay more attention to the economic problems at home.

Family trees show that 75% of the leading figures in Costa Rica's history were descended from only four *conquistadores* and, of course, their indigenous consorts. The native people of

Costa Rica were never completely dominated by the Spanish colonizers, so the class divisions that exist to this day in other Latin American countries were not developed to the same degree. The few indigenous groups not decimated by war and disease moved away to isolated mountain regions where they still live. Costa Rica's poverty and isolation led colonial families to fend for themselves, establishing more egalitarian values than in other Latin countries.

When it was discovered in the 1830's that coffee grew well in Central American highlands and fetched a high price in European markets, the powerful elites of most of the newly-independent nations on the isthmus forced *campesinos* from the land in order to make large coffee plantations. Not so in Costa Rica. Small farmers were encouraged to grow coffee and sell the beans to central *beneficios* or processing plants, owned by wealthier farmers who would prepare the beans for export. Thus rich and poor participated together in the coffee-growing process, each small farmer caring for his bushes in a personal way. Coffee plants demand a lot of attention, and Costa Rican coffee has always been known as one of the finest on the international market. The *beneficio* policy gave stability and importance to the small farmer, and allowed him to grow subsistence crops for his family.

The development of the educational and electoral systems during the late 1800's provided the basis for a participatory democracy. By the end of the 19th century, political violence began to decrease and the budget of the police force began to exceed that of the army. When the victorious forces of the 1948 civil war decided to constitutionally abolish the army, a *de facto* situation that had been developing from the beginning of the century was legally ratified.

For Costa Ricans, abolishing the army had several functions: it inhibits the formation of a military group capable of gaining autonomy; it frees public funds for development; it makes elections the only route to power; it establishes Costa Rica's neutrality in the region--a country which is militarily weak cannot be attacked without provoking international condemnation of the aggressor; it shows the illegitimacy of armed opposition to a state which has renounced the use of force.

The pragmatic thinkers who brought about the abolition of the army recognized the United States as the dominant super-power of the region, and their ally and friend. Implied in the abolishment is the belief that the US would come to Costa Rica's rescue if it were attacked. During the years of Sandinista arms build-up in Nicaragua, many Costa Ricans longed for the United States to invade and put an end to the regime. Ex-president Arias faced as much internal opposition to his peace plan as he did external. In fact, it was not until he won the Nobel Prize in 1987 that his critics started to let up a bit. Similarly, the vast majority of Costa Ricans lauded the US invasion of Panamá. So in this case, disarmament does not imply pacifism. Costa Ricans, by nature, seek to avoid conflict, so being army-less fits in with the national character. But more practically, abolishing the army just means the removal of a force that, allied with powerful economic interests, has wreaked havoc on democracy in developing countries for centuries.

Costa Ricans view the military as an encumbrance to their political and social life as well as to the public budget. They prefer to channel their national resources to health and education. Because of their nationalized medical and social security systems, Costa Rican health is on a par with that of in-dustrialized nations. In an attempt to ensure the well-being of future generations, 27% of Costa Rica's territory is legally set aside as national parks, biological reserves, forest reserves and buffer zones, wildlife refuges and Indian reserves.

Even without an army, finding the money to pursue goals of social justice and ecological balance has become well-nigh impossible. Costa Rica is fighting an uphill battle against her tremendous deficit, the largest per capita in the world. The International Monetary Fund demands austerity from a govern-ment whose bureaucracy employs 20% of the workforce. The developed countries pump in millions of dollars of aid, but the largest chunk of the country's budget--almost one third--goes to service the same foreign debt!

Costa Rican currency is worth about one twelfth of its value ten years ago, and is devaluated monthly. A respectable middle-range salary is still under US$300 per month, and the national average is about $150 per month. Recent studies show that the average family has to spend $125 per month on food alone. A third of Costa Rican families are below poverty level.

Despite all this, Ticos, rich and poor, actively support their democracy. On election day they honk horns, wave party flags, dress up in party colors, and proudly display their index fingers dipped in purple indelible ink to show they have voted. The Communist parties, which have played an important role in Costa Rican history, won less than 1% of the vote in the last election.

Even with the enthusiasm that turns their election day into a national fiesta, Costa Ricans are skeptical about politics and politicians. Their roots are still in the soil and in the unity of their families. Babies are the acknowledged rulers of the household. Mothers' Day is one of the biggest national holidays. Foreigners complain that it is hard to make deep friendships here because family ties are so strong. The united family that made it possible for early poverty-stricken farmers to survive is perhaps still the real basis of Costa Rican stability.

At the same time, women are a solid 50% of the workforce, and are rapidly increasing their numbers as doctors, lawyers and government officials. Dr. Victoria Garrón became the first woman Vice-President of the Republic in 1986, and Dr. Rosemary Karpinski the first woman president of the Legislative Assembly.

Costa Ricans' love for the beauty and freedom of their country is almost palpable. At 6:00 pm each September 14, the eve of their Independence Day, everyone drops what they are doing to sing the national anthem. In corner stores and homes across the country, everyone joins in. It's a rousing hymn in tribute to peace, hard work, and the generosity of the earth, but it also warns that if these things are threatened, Costa Ricans will "convert their rough farming tools into arms", as they did when William Walker tried to invade in the 19th century.

Now Costa Rica faces another kind of invasion. The increasing popularity of "eco-tourism" has opened the country to a huge influx of visitors, attracted to her incredible ecological diversity. Convinced that the "clean industry" of tourism will be a source of much-needed foreign exchange, the government is offering incentives for large tourism projects that will provide hotel rooms to keep up with the demand. No one is listening to the voice of the *campesino* who still has not been paid for his land which was made part of a biological reserve, or the dairyman who cannot afford to buy more pasture for his animals because the price of land has gone up due to foreign and local speculation, or the coastal dweller that suddenly finds there's no room on the bus to town because it's filled with surfboards. A more serious threat is the kind of touristic development which regards local people as a pool of potential maids, waiters, gardeners and laundresses and nothing more. The traditional values of the small independent farmers who are the backbone of Costa Rican democracy could be lost in the process.

On the other hand, most Costa Ricans are proud to share the beauty of their land with visitors, and know how to make foreigners feel at home. Some programs are trying to incorporate native skills into tourism and ecology: young men who were raised hunting turtles are now being trained to help visitors understand the ancient ritual of turtle nesting; sharp-eyed *campesinos* are learning to be taxonomists in the national parks; men and women from the dry Guanacaste region are reviving the ancient pottery-making techniques of their ancestors; indigenous women from Talamanca have written a book to explain their beliefs about conserving the forest and its wildlife.

Even though the campesino and the oxcart are powerful symbols in Costa Rican life, almost half the population of the country now lives in urban areas. Cramped housing developments cover the fertile soil of the Central Valley. As happens everywhere, the city dwellers quickly forget their roots. Hopefully, visitors like you will take time to meet rural people and learn to value their knowledge, cultures and lifestyles, as well as supporting the small businesses they have created.

If you find any truly Costa Rican places or services not mentioned in this book, we'd like you to tell us about them. Often visitors can see and appreciate things that are overlooked by those of us who live here.

Beatrice Blake
Anne Becher
February 1991

15

HISTORY

PRECOLUMBIAN COSTA RICA

The largest and most developed precolumbian population in Costa Rica was that of the Chorotegas, whose ancestors had migrated from Southern Mexico to the Nicoya Peninsula, probably in the thirteenth century. They were running away from enemies who wanted to enslave them; their name translates as "fleeing people."

Much of the information we have about the Chorotegas was collected by Gonzalo Fernández de Oviedo, a Spanish explorer who lived with them for a short period in 1529.

Outstanding farmers, they obtained three harvests of corn per year. They also grew cotton, beans, fruits, and cacao, which they introduced to Costa Rica. They used cacao seeds as currency. Land was communally owned and the harvest was divided according to need, so that old people and widows with children could be cared for. They lived in cities of up to 20,000 people. The towns had central plazas with a marketplace and a religious center; only women could enter the market. Women wore skirts, the length of which depended upon their social level. Men could go naked but often wore a large cloth or a woven and dyed sleeveless cotton shirt.

Women worked in ceramics, producing vessels painted in black and red, decorated with plumed serpents (the symbol for unity of matter and spirit), jaguars, monkeys, and crocodiles. They carved stylized jade figures in human and animal shapes. The figures could have been used in fertility ceremonies or to bring good luck in the hunt. They wrote books on deerskin parchment, and used a ritual calendar.

War was institutionalized. There was a permanent military organization that fought to obtain land and slaves. Slaves were used as human sacrifices. Eating someone who had been sacrificed to the gods was a purification rite. The Chorotegas would also sacrifice virgins by throwing them into volcano craters. The Chibcha Indians from Colombia migrated to the South Pacific part of Costa Rica. They lived in permanent, well-fortified towns. Their concern with security could have arisen from their possession of gold--they fashioned it into human and animal figures (especially turtles, armadillos and sharks). Both women and men fought for the best lands and for prisoners, whom they used as slaves or human sacrifices. They believed in life after death; vultures eating corpses performed a vital role in transporting people to the other world.

These people probably made the granite spheres that lie in linear formations in the valley of the Río Térraba and on the Isla del Caño off the coast of the Península de Osa. They range in diameter from 7.5 centimeters (the size of an orange) to 1.8 meters. Their almost perfect sphericity and careful placement make their meaning one of Costa Rica's precolumbian mysteries.

Indians from the jungles of Brazil and Ecuador migrated to the lowland jungles of the Costa Rican Atlantic Coast. They lived semi-nomadically, hunting, fishing and cultivating *yuca, pejibaye,* pumpkin and squash. Their chief's nobility was hereditary, passed down through the female line of the family.

Social prestige was gained by good warriors. Apparently, decapitated heads of enemies were war trophies. Their stone figurines represent warriors with a knife in one hand and a head in the other.

They worshipped the sun, the moon and the bones of their ancestors. All things had souls. During religious festivals there was a ritual inebriation with a fermented *chicha* made from *yuca* or *pejibaye.* The burial mounds of these people have yielded the greatest number of precolumbian artifacts in the country.

COLONIAL COSTA RICA

On September 18, 1502, during his fourth and last voyage to the New World, Christopher Columbus anchored in the Bay of Cariari (now Limón), after a violent tempest wrecked his ships. During the 17 days that he and his crew were resting and making repairs, they visited a few coastal Indian villages. The

17

Indians treated them well and they left with the impression that *Veragua* (a name that Columbus used for the Caribbean Coast between Honduras and Panamá) was a land rich in gold, whose gentle and friendly Indians could be easily conquered. A few years later, in 1506, King Ferdinand of Spain sent a governor to colonize Veragua. Governor Diego de Nicuesa and his colonizers received a different welcome. First, their ship went aground on the coast of Panamá, and they had to walk up the Atlantic shore. Food shortages and tropical diseases reduced the group by half. Then they met the Indians, who burned crops rather than feed the invaders. The Spanish realized that their task was not going to be easy. There was no centralized Indian empire to conquer and sack, and the scattered tribes were at home in a climate and terrain that the explorers found devastating. This first attempt at colonization was a miserable failure.

After Vásco Núñez de Balboa discovered the Pacific Ocean in 1513, the Spaniards started exploring the west coast of Veragua. In 1522, an exploratory land expedition set out from northern Panamá. Despite sickness, starvation and tropical weather, the survivors of the long, hazardous trip called it a success: they had obtained gold and pearls and their priest claimed he had converted over 30,000 Indians to Catholicism between Panamá and Nicaragua.

More explorers and would-be colonizers arrived. There were attempted settlements on both coasts, but they ended in tragedy for the settlers who died of hunger, were driven out by the Indians or fought among themselves and dissolved their communities.

Juan Vásquez de Coronado arrived as Governor in 1562. He found a group of Spaniards and Spanish-Indian *mestizos* living inland from the Pacific coast. Coronado explored Costa Rica, treating the Indians he met more humanely than had his predecessors. He decided that the highlands were more suitable for settlement, so he moved the settlers to the Cartago Valley where the climate was pleasant and the soils were rich from the lava deposited by Volcán Irazú. In 1563, Cartago was established as the capital of Costa Rica.

In contrast to the pattern in most Spanish colonies, there was no large exploitable workforce in Costa Rica. The Indian population was decimated early on by war and disease. At one point even the governor was forced to work his own small plot of land to survive.

Costa Rica's Spanish population remained small and their lifestyle humble through the seventeenth century. In 1709, Spanish money became so scarce that settlers used *cacao* beans as currency, just like the Chorotegas. Women wore goat hair skirts; soldiers had no uniforms. Volcán Irazú erupted in 1723, almost destroying Cartago. Nevertheless, they survived, and the area settled by Spaniards actually grew through the 1700's. Three new cities were founded in the Meseta Central: Cubujuquí (Heredia) in 1706, Villanueva de la Boca del Monte (San José) in 1737 and Villa Hermosa (Alajuela) in 1782.

Costa Rica had no riches and was difficult to reach from Guatemala, the seat of Spain's Central American empire, so it was left free from foreign intrusion into its affairs. Forgotten by its "mother country", Costa Rica was almost self-sufficient in its poverty.

INDEPENDENCE

In October 1821, word arrived from Guatemala that on September 15, Spain had granted independence to its American colonies. It had taken the news one month to travel through the mountains and valleys to Costa Rica. After a period of internal strife, Costa Rica declared itself a state in the short-lived Federal Republic of Central America.

The first president of Free Costa Rica, Juan Mora Fernández, built roads, schools, and gave land grants to anyone who would plant coffee. This epoch was one of the most influential in the evolution of Costa Rican democracy, because small farmers were encouraged to grow coffee and sell the beans to wealthier farmers who would prepare the beans for export. Thus rich and poor each had an important place in the coffee-growing process, and mutual respect was developed.

By the mid-1800's, coffee was Costa Rica's principal export, and coffee growers were a powerful and wealthy elite. They built a road to transport coffee from the Meseta Central to Costa Rica's port, Puntarenas. They exported first to Chile, then later to Germany and England. By mid-century, European money was entering the pockets of Costa Rican coffee growers, and Europeans were arriving en masse on this tropical frontier. Costa Rica was becoming cosmopolitan. A university had been founded in 1844 to disseminate European thinking. Costa Rican politicians sported European liberal ideologies.

By 1848 the coffee elite was influential enough to elect its own representative for President. Juan Rafael Mora was a self-made man who had become one of the most powerful coffee growers in the country. He was charismatic, astute, and respected by the coffee elite and the *campesinos* alike. He became a veritable national hero by leading an "army" of Costa Ricans to defend his country when it was invaded by one of the most detested figures in Central American history, the North American William Walker.

THE SAGA OF WILLIAM WALKER

A study of William Walker's early life gives one little indication of how this man came to be the scourge of Central America. Walker was graduated from the University of Nashville at the age of 14, and by the time he was 19, he held both a law and a medical degree from the University of Pennsylvania. He followed this memorable academic record with two years of post-graduate study in Paris and Heidelberg.

His success stopped there, however. Returning from Europe, Walker quickly failed as a doctor, lawyer and journalist. He had an ill-fated courtship with a beautiful deaf-mute New Orleans socialite, then in 1849 turned up as a gold miner in California. He didn't fare well in this occupation either, and soon started working as a hack writer in several California cities.

At this point, something happened in the mind of William Walker, and he launched himself into a career as a soldier of fortune. From then on, he succeeded in creating chaos wherever he took his five-foot, three-inch, one-hundred-pound frame.

In the early 1850's, Walker sailed with several hundred men on a "liberating expedition" to the Baja California peninsula and Mexico. The expedition was financed by the Knights of the Golden Circle, a movement bent on promoting the "benefits" of slavery. Walker spent a year in Mexico during which time he awarded himself the military title of Colonel and proclaimed himself "President of Sonora and Baja California."

Back in the United States after several encounters with the Mexican army, he was arrested for breaking the Neutrality Act of 1818. His acquittal of the charge gained him fame and willing followers. His next expedition was to Nicaragua.

Walker went with two main goals. One was to convert Central America into slave territory and annex it to the southern

La Casona, scene of Walker's defeat

USA, the other was to conquer Nicaragua and ready it for the construction of a trans-isthmic canal. The new riches that were being discovered in California attracted a lot of Easterners, but crossing the United States by land was slow and difficult. Walker had made contacts with a group of economically powerful North Americans who thought that a sea route could be more efficient and profitable. Southern Nicaragua would be a perfect site for the isthmus crossing; ships could sail up the San Juan River that formed the Nicaragua-Costa Rica border, cross Lake Nicaragua, and then pass through a to-be-built 18-mile canal from the lake to the Pacific.

His contacts arranged for an invitation to Walker from the Liberal Party of Nicaragua, which was embattled with the Conservatives. In June, 1855, he landed in Nicaragua with 58 men. After losing his first encounter with the Conservatives, Walker held out until several hundred reinforcements arrived from California, bringing new model carbines and six-shooters. They soon overpowered the Conservatives, and after an "open" election, Walker became "President of the Republic of Nicaragua".

Central Americans from throughout the isthmus rose to fight Walker and his band of *filibusteros*. In February, 1856, President Juan Rafael Mora of Costa Rica declared war on Walker, but not on Nicaragua. Mora raised an army of 9000 in less than a week. This "army", led by the President and his brother-in-law José María Cañas, was composed of *campesinos,* merchants and government bureaucrats ill-dressed for combat, armed with farm tools, *machetes* and old rifles. They marched for two weeks to Guanacaste. Three hundred filibusters were resting at the Santa Rosa hacienda (now a national monument in Santa Rosa National Park), after they had invaded Costa Rica, preparing to conquer San José. The Costa Rican army, by then diminished to 2500 men, attacked the filibusters, who fled back to Nicaragua after 14 minutes of battle.

Two thousand Costa Ricans followed Walker up to Nicaragua and, in a generally masterful campaign, fought him to a standstill. The turning point was in Rivas, Nicaragua. Walker and his band were barricaded in a large wood building from which they could not be dislodged. Juan Santamaría, a drummer boy, volunteered to set fire to the building and succeeded in forcing Walker's retreat. In his action, Juan lost his life, and became Costa Rica's national hero.

Walker's attempt to convert Nicaragua and the rest of Central America into slave territory was backed by US President James Buchanan, and his failure angered the President. When Walker confiscated the trans-isthmic transportation concession that US financier Cornelius Vanderbilt had already started installing, Vanderbilt began to finance some of Walker's enemies. This was the beginning of the end of Walker's career.

After another engagement in late 1856 on Lake Nicaragua where the Costa Rican army brilliantly cut Walker off from his support troops, the rag-tag *filibustero* forces were near defeat. The first of May, 1857, Walker surrendered to a US warship.

The adventurer traveled to Nicaragua again in late 1857, but he was taken prisoner before he could wreak any havoc. When he was released in 1860, he sailed to Honduras, where upon landing he seized the custom house. This brought a British warship to the scene, on board of which Walker, pursued by the Hondurans, eventually took refuge. Offered safe conduct into US hands by the British commander, Walker insisted he was the rightful president of Honduras. The British therefore put him ashore again, and Walker was taken by the Hondurans and promptly shot.

The net result of Walker's Central American marauding was the death of some 20,000 men. The inscription on William Walker's tombstone reads, "Glory to the patriots who freed Central America of such a bloody pirate! Curses to those who brought him and to those who helped him."

Juan Rafael Mora is now acclaimed for having saved Central America from Walker and the interests he represented, but he wasn't so popular when he returned from battle. People accused Mora of having been too ambitious and blamed him for an epidemic of cholera that infected Costa Rican soldiers in Nicaragua and spread to kill almost 10% of the population.

Mora manipulated the 1859 election to win over massive opposition. In August 1859, his enemies overthrew him. A year later, Mora led a coup d'etat against the new president, also a member of the coffee elite. His attempt failed; he was shot by a firing squad in 1860--an inglorious end for a man who is now a national hero. Through the 1860's quarrels among the coffee growers put presidents in power and later deposed them. Nevertheless, most presidents during these years were civilians with liberal and intellectual characters. Despite the political instability of the decade, the country established a well-based educational system. New schools were founded, European professors were brought to design academic programs, and the first bookstores in San José opened their doors.

THE ATLANTIC RAILROAD AND UNITED FRUIT

By the mid-1800's, Costa Rica realized it needed an Atlantic Port to facilitate coffee export to Europe. When Tomás Guardia declared himself Chief of State in 1871, he decided to build a railway to Limón. He contracted Henry Meiggs, a North American who had built railways in Chile and Perú. Meiggs went to England to secure loans for the project. He obtained 3,400,000 sterling pounds, of which only 1,000,000 actually arrived. These loans caused the first foreign debt in Costa Rica's history.

Costa Rica's population wasn't large enough to provide the project with the necessary labor force, so thousands of Jamaican, Italian, and Chinese workers were recruited. After an optimistic start, it soon became evident that it was going to be a slow, dangerous, and costly process. Construction of the railroad claimed some 4000 workers' lives, cost the equivalent of eight million dollars, and lasted 19 years. The jungle proved itself a formidable and deadly barrier.

Meiggs' nephew, Minor C. Keith, became the director a few years after the project started. The railroad he inherited was constantly beleaguered by severe shortages of funds, so he started experimenting with banana production and exportation as a way to help finance the project. When he realized that the banana business could yield very profitable results, Keith made a deal with the new president, Bernardo Soto, in 1884. In return for a grant from the Costa Rican government of 800,000 acres of untilled land along the tracks, tax-free for 20 years, and a

23

99-year lease on the railroad, Keith would renegotiate the project's pending debts to England, and complete construction at his own expense.

By 1886, Keith had settled the financial problems with England. He spent the next four years laying the last 52 miles of track that climbed through the steep, treacherous valley of the Reventazón river. Relations between Keith and the labor force weren't good. In 1888 Italian workers organized the first strike in Costa Rica's history, demanding prompt payments and sanitary working and living conditions.

The railroad was completed in 1890. Until 1970 it was the only route from the Meseta Central to Limón. And, until the line was closed in late 1990, it was still the major means of transportation for many people who lived in the tiny towns it passed. Children took the train to school; it served as an ambulance for the sick and as a hearse for the dead.

After they finished the railway, many Italian workers settled in Costa Rica's highlands. Chinese workers settled in various parts of the country. The Jamaicans stayed on the Atlantic Coast and started working on the banana plantations which Minor Keith established on his 800,000 free acres. The development of banana plantations where there had been jungles forced the Indians to move up into the mountains.

In 1899, Keith and a partner founded the United Fruit Company. *La Yunai,* as it was called, quickly became a legendary social, economic, political and agricultural force in many Latin American countries. Costa Rican author Carlos Luis Fallas describes work conditions on the steamy plantations in his book *Mamita Yunai,* and Gabriel García Márquez tells what it did to the imaginary town of Macondo in *One Hundred Years of Solitude.* Although Costa Rica was the smallest country where United worked, United possessed more land here than in any other country. Costa Rica became the world's leading banana producer.

The year 1907 was United's peak year in Costa Rica, but by 1913 it was facing serious problems. Panamá disease had infected banana trees; United's employees began protesting unfair working conditions. A 1913 strike was broken by the Costa Rican government--two strike leaders were chased into the plantations and killed.

The Company initiated a new policy: it would lease company land to independent growers and buy bananas from them.

Tensions with workers grew; a 1934 strike led by two young San José communists, Manuel Mora and Jaime Cerdas, finally brought better working and living conditions. They maintained the original demands of 1913, and added to the list regular payment of salaries, free housing, medical clinics on plantations and accident insurance. United wouldn't talk with the strikers, but the planters leasing land from United did, and convinced United to sign an agreement.

In the late 30's a new disease, Sigatoka, infected banana trees up and down the coast. In 1938 United started to pick up and move west to the Pacific lowlands.

United lasted as long as it did on the Atlantic Coast only because it possessed so much land. Banana trees deplete soil of its humus and nitrogen. The clay soils of rainforest areas compact easily when the jungle is cut and they are cultivated. Since the soil could last only five to eight years, United used a plot of land until it didn't produce anymore, and then would move on to virgin land.

Minor Keith ended up a very wealthy man who married the daughter of one of the presidents of Costa Rica. Most profits from the banana industry went to the foreign owners of the production, shipping and distribution networks that made export possible.

LIBERALISM ARRIVES IN COSTA RICA

The 1880's saw an increasing split between a traditional, conservative church and a liberalizing state. The bishop of Costa Rica criticized the European ideas that were becoming popular with the elite and the politicians. The bishop was expelled from the country in 1884, and in 1885 there was an official denouncement of an earlier church-state concord that declared Catholicism the state religion. Public outcry at the government's treatment of the church was minimal.

The first truly democratic election characterized by real public participation was in 1889. Liberals saw it as the fruit of their efforts to educate and raise democratic consciousness in the people. In fact, their efforts worked so well that the public gave their overwhelming support to the liberals' opposition. Supporters of the liberals threatened not to recognize the new president, so 10,000 armed opposition members flooded the streets of San José. The liberals then demonstrated their firm commitment to democracy by recognizing the new, rightfully elected president.

Costa Rica's democratic tradition has endured until today with only a few exceptions. One was in 1917, when the Minister of War and the Navy, Federico Tinoco, overthrew an unpopular president. Tinoco's brutal and repressive dictatorship lasted through 30 months of widespread opposition. Finally Tinoco fled the country. A provisional president held office for a year until normality was reached, and Costa Rica resumed its democratic tradition with a fair presidential election.

ROOTS OF THE 1948 CIVIL WAR

Rafael Angel Calderón Guardia was the legally-elected president between 1940-44. A profoundly religious Catholic, Calderón's political ideology was Social Christian. One of his first actions was to reinstate religious education in public schools. Another was to found the University of Costa Rica. He initiated many social reforms which still exist today, including social security, workers' rights to organize, land reform, guaranteed minimum wage and collective bargaining. These reforms earned Calderón the adoration of the poor and the opposition of the upper classes.

Calderón ran a puppet candidate, Teodoro Picado, in the 1944 election. Picado won, but the election was widely criticized as fraudulent. Young, middle-class intellectuals, as well as traditionally anti-communist Costa Ricans distrustful of church-state involvement resented Calderón's grasping for power and criticized the odd alliance he had made with Catholic Archbishop Monseñor Víctor Sanabria and Manuel Mora of the Communist Party.

Farmers, businessmen, *campesinos,* liberal labor unions, and young intellectuals organized against Calderón. Calderón's allies were the government, the Church, the communist labor unions and the army.

In the 1948 election, Calderón ran against Otilio Ulate, who represented the unified opposition. Ulate won the election by a small margin, but the government demanded a recount. Disagreement was complicated by a fire that destroyed half the ballots the day after the election. Government forces refused to yield the power to Ulate. Teodoro Picado remained in power.

Pepe Figueres, a coffee grower and outspoken opponent of Calderón who had been exiled in Mexico, had returned to Costa Rica before the elections. On March 12, 1948, he and his men captured the airport at San Isidro de El General. Foreign arms were airlifted in quickly, due to Figueres' advance planning. Armed groups, trained by Guatemalan military advisors, were formed throughout the country. President Picado declared a state of siege, using borrowed Nicaraguan soldiers and mobilized banana workers from the communist unions. They were unaccustomed to the cool climate of San José, and wore blankets over their shoulders, Mexican style, to keep warm. For this reason, Calderón supporters were called *mariachis*. After 40 days of civil war, during which more than 2000 people died, a negotiated treaty was signed. Picado stepped down and Figueres took over as provisional president.

Figueres governed for 18 months, long enough to draft a new constitution. Prohibition of presidential re-election, banning of communist labor unions and parties, abolition of the army, the right to vote for women and blacks, and the establishment of a neutral body that would oversee elections, were some of the new constitutional laws. Banks and insurance companies were nationalized, and 10 percent of all bank funds were seized for reconstruction. All of Calderón's social reforms were maintained. In 1949, Figueres turned the country over to Ulate, the rightful president.

Costa Rica elected Figueres president twice, in 1954 and 1970. "Don Pepe" died June 8, 1990 and was mourned by people of all political persuasions as the defender of Costa Rican democracy and development.

The 1948 revolutionaries formed the National Liberation Party (PLN). Almost without fail, Costa Ricans have alternated their presidents--one from the PLN, the next from the opposition. There have been only two exceptions to this pattern in the eleven peaceful national elections that have been held since 1948. Voters have a deep distrust of power being concentrated in one party's hands for too long.

The opposition is an odd coalition of wealthy business owners who see the PLN's social democratic direction as harmful to their interests, and poor people who generally side with the party that is out of power. The Partido Unidad Social Cristiana was consolidated during the 1980's under the leadership of Rafael Angel Calderón Fournier, son of Calderón Guardia.

He lost the 1982 and 1986 elections to PLN candidates, but finally won in 1990, and was inaugurated as president 50 years to the day after his father assumed power.

SINCE 1948

Costa Rica fortified its progressive social policies during the three decades following 1948, and enjoyed a gradual upward economic trend. The policy of the sixties and seventies was to try to become more self-sufficient agriculturally and industrially, which led to a heavier dependence on imported pesticides, fertilizers, raw materials, machinery, and oil. Costa Rica and many other third world countries accepted large first-world loans for infrastructure projects like bridges, hydroelectric projects, and roads. When the price of oil rose in the early seventies, the economy could no longer do without it. Then coffee, banana and sugar prices went down on the world market, the loans came due, and Costa Rica found itself entering the eighties with its economy in shambles.

The instability of neighboring countries like Nicaragua and El Salvador impeded cooperation in the Central American Common Market and made Costa Ricans feel insecure. In 1978-9, under President Rodrigo Carazo, northern Costa Rica served as a virtual base for Sandinista operations. Costa Ricans had no sympathy for the Somoza dynasty and were hopeful that the Nicaraguans could make a go of democracy. But after Somoza was deposed, the Sandinista arms build-up and Marxist-Leninist doctrine disillusioned many Costa Ricans, which led them to lend tacit support to the contras while they were operating out of Costa Rica, despite the government's official neutrality policy under PLN President Luis Alberto Monge.

Costa Rica elected a president in February 1986 from the younger generation of the PLN. Oscar Arias is an economist, lawyer and author of several books on the Costa Rican economy and power structure. His main campaign promise was to work for peace in Central America. The first part of his task was to enforce Costa Rica's declared neutrality policy, and to stand up to the United States and the politicians within his own party who were supporting contra activity within Costa Rica, such as the secret airstrip that figured in the Iran-Contra scandal.

As the world knows by now, Arias' untiring efforts to fulfill his promise won him the 1987 Nobel Peace Prize. While the peace process has met with skepticism and even ennui in the first world press, for many Central Americans it signifies a coming of age--a chance to unite and shape their future in a new way. Even though the process has been slower than scheduled, much more communication has taken place between warring factions than ever before. The first democratic elections in Nicaragua's history, held February 25, 1990, in which the Sandinistas were defeated, are largely a result of the peace plan.

The economic and social problems at the root of Central America's conflicts are deep, and require not just talk, but concerted action. Hopefully, as East-West tensions ease, Central Americans who demand social and economic justice in their countries will no longer be labeled as communists, and will be able to enter into the political process without risking their lives.

Costa Rica's economic crisis of the early eighties has been overcome in some ways. With increasing interest in the environment, tourism has become the country's third largest source of income. Non-traditional exports such as ornamental plants and flowers, strawberries and oranges are bringing in as much money now as the traditional exports of bananas, coffee, sugarcane, and meat. Unfortunately, the new agro-industries demand high start-up costs and are not labor-intensive, making them unavailable for small farmers. In addition, it costs less for Costa Rica to import basic grains like corn, beans and rice from the United States than it does to grow them here, because of the high costs of imported fertilizers and pesticides. So government policy has led away from support for the small, independent, subsistence farmer, which has forced *campesinos* off the land, threatening the very basis of Costa Rica's stability and democracy.

The new Unidad government of Rafael Angel Calderón Fournier has promised to address these problems, while at the same time resolving the country's enormous deficit. If he does so, Calderón will undoubtedly run up against the same economic powers which challenged his father's liberal policies during the 1940's. As of this writing, his administration has concentrated on "balancing the budget" by sending through a number of stiff increases in prices of food, gas and utilities causing widespread distress, especially on the part of the many voters who elected him as a champion of the poor.

BIBLIOGRAPHY

American University, Foreign Area Studies. *Costa Rica. A Country Study.* Washington, DC, U.S. Government, 1981.

Casey Gasper, Jeffrey. *Limón 1880-1940.* San José, Editorial Costa Rica, 1979.

Jones, Clarence and Morrison, Paul. "Evolution of the Banana Industry in Costa Rica" in *Economic Geography,* January, 1952.

May, Stacy and Plaza, Galo. *The United Fruit Company in Latin America.* New York, National Planning Association, 1958.

Meléndez Carlos. *Historia de Costa Rica.* San José, Editorial Universidad Estatal a Distancia, 1981.

Rodríguez Vega, Eugenio. *Biografía de Costa Rica.* San José, Editorial Costa Rica, 1980.

THE ECOLOGICAL PICTURE

Costa Rica is part of a land bridge between North and South America. Her geographical and climatic conditions make it possible for flora and fauna characteristic of both continents as well as the Antilles to co-exist, thus creating incredibly diverse ecosystems.

Costa Rica measures only 300 km (185 miles) across at her widest point, but four mountain ranges divide her like a backbone. Mount Chirripó, at 3820 m (12,500 feet), is the highest point in southern Central America. It is part of Costa Rica's oldest and southernmost mountain range, the Cordillera de Talamanca, which extends into Panamá. The Central Volcanic Range is made up of volcanoes Turrialba, Irazú, Barva and Poás. Over half of Costa Rica's three million inhabitants live in the Central Valley, whose fertile soil was created by the activity of these volcanoes over the last two million years. To the northwest is the non-volcanic Tilarán range which reaches 1700 m (5500 feet) at Monteverde. Farthest northwest, towards the Nicaraguan border, is the Guanacaste Range which contains five active volcanoes including Rincón de la Vieja, Miravalles (now being used to generate geothermal energy), and Volcán Arenal. The most ancient rocks in the area, over 100 million years old, occur in the "Nicoya complex", low mountains which outcrop here and there along the Pacific.

31

Climate

Given its location between 8 and 12 degrees north of the Equator, day length and temperature do not change drastically with the seasons. The sun rises around 5 am and sets around 6 pm year-round. One experiences temperature difference by changing altitude. The misty highlands are in the 10-13°C (50-55°F) range, while the Central Valley, at 1200 m (3800 feet), averages 22°C (72°F). Sea level temperature is 26°C (80°F) tempered by sea breezes on the coast. Slight variations occur in December, January and February due to cold winds from the North American winter. These cooler temperatures bring on the dry season or "summer", as Central Americans call it, which lasts from December through April. Temperatures rise as the sun approaches a perpendicular position over Costa Rica. This causes increased evaporation and brings on the rainy season, or "winter", which lasts from May through November, except for a 2-week dry season, the *veranillo,* sometime in July (see p. 43).

Costa Rica's weather pattern is changing. It is not as pre-dictable as it used to be. 1990 had many dry days during the "winter" and a few storms during the "summer". A new rule of thumb is: The more gloriously sun-drenched the morning during the rainy season, the harder it will rain in the afternoon. Con-versely, on a cloudy morning there will be less evaporation, and thus a generally drier day.

The Atlantic coast has always been an exception to the rule. Tradewinds laden with moisture from the Caribbean approach Costa Rica from the northeast. As the moisture rises to the chilly heights of the Cordilleras, it condenses into rain on their eastern slopes. For this reason, there is no definite dry season in the Atlantic zone, but the beaches tend to be sunnier than the mountains. In a similar phenomenon, tradewinds from the southeast discharge their moisture against the mountains that separate the Osa Peninsula from the rest of the country. The Atlantic plains and the Osa both receive 4000-7000 mm (150 to 300") of rain a year, compared to an average of 2500 mm (100") in the Central Valley.

Ecological zones

Costa Rica's 20,000 square-mile territory offers a great diversity of ecological zones, from sub-alpine dwarfed vegetation to rich rain forest, to beautiful tropical beaches. Cloud forests like the one at Monteverde are filled with plants which are specifically adapted to gather water and promote condensation and precipitation. These high, misty forests are responsible for Costa Rica's rich water resources. Augmenting the water-gathering function of the trees themselves are epiphytes, plants which live

bromeliad

on trees in order to have growing space or to better reach the light. Unlike parasites, epiphytes filter their own food from water, dust particles and organic matter accumulated around their roots. They add to the diversity of the forest by adapting themselves to conditions that are impossible for other plants. Costa Rica has 1100 different species of orchids, 95 percent of which are epiphytes. The 200 species of bromeliads, much more commonly seen than orchids, are also epiphytes. Epiphytes, vines and the treetops create a canopy which maintains the humidity inside the forest and provides a home for many small animals which never touch the ground.

The dry tropical forests of Guanacaste like those in Santa Rosa National Park feature huge deciduous trees that burst into bloom at the beginning of the dry season. The scarlet *poró* tree, the orange-red flame-of-the-forest, the purple *jacaranda,* the pink and white meadow oak and the yellow *corteza amarilla* are like huge bouquets on the landscape. Other plants flower during the rainy season, thus keeping active a large number of different pollinating insects and birds.

Six species of mangroves exist in Costa Rica's Pacific salt-water swamps, forming a complex community with marine animals and plants.

The rain forests of the Pacific, like Corcovado National Park on the Osa Península, are some of the most complex ecological systems on the planet. They maintain similar species to those found in the Atlantic rain forests, and because of a short dry season, they also shelter some species common to dry forests.

Diversity and interrelationship

Its 850 bird species, more than there are in the entire North American continent, make this tiny country a birdwatchers' paradise. Keep your eyes open on a walk through any of Costa Rica's wild places, and you'll see the wonderful ways birds, insects, frogs and reptiles have evolved to protect themselves. Some imitate leaves, flowers, and stems of plants; others are indistinguishable from rocks or tree bark. Other animals which are poisonous or taste very bad warn potential predators with their bright coloring (red, blue, metallic green). Some animals hide their brightly colored parts and only display them if attacked. One butterfly's outer wings resemble a dry leaf, but its underwings flash two huge, glinting cat eyes. Several butterflies have a disagreeable taste to birds. Other butterflies which taste good imitate the coloring of the bad-tasting butterflies to gain protection.

Costa Rica abounds in cases of highly specialized interspecies relationships, due to her complex ecosystems. In many cases, both participating species co-evolve by modifying themselves to meet the needs of the other. Many flowers are designed to attract only certain animals which complete their pollination process. Bright colors attract a pollinizing agent with a strong sense of sight, like hummingbirds. If the pollinizing agent has a stronger sense of smell, like flies and some butterflies, the flower will be fragrant. Some of the most fragrant flowers emit their scent only at night. They attract animals with nocturnal habits, like bats. The flower will be shaped to accommodate the part of the body that its pollinizer uses to carry pollen away (beak, wings, feet, etc).

Deforestation

The ecological relationships that are so fascinating to observe in Costa Rica are a lesson for humans in how to live cooperatively with nature, rather than exploiting, exterminating, and controlling, as we are prone to do now. Despite the richness of its forests, Costa Rica takes first place in Latin America for percentage of deforested land. In 1950, 72 percent of Costa Rica was covered in forest. In 1973, it was 49 percent, in 1978, 34 percent, and in 1985, 26 percent. At this rate, Costa Rica's unprotected forests will be destroyed by the year 2000.

One sees evidence of deforestation constantly. Huge trucks piled with massive tree trunks rumble along the highways from Talamanca, Osa, and Sarapiquí, all areas recently opened to roads. A flight to Tortuguero will show you the facts--a thin border of rich tropical forest lines the shore, and inland, where "nobody" sees, the land is naked. Only a few tall trees remain from the forest that is disappearing every day. Part of the Guanacaste region has become a desert due to four centuries of cattle raising and slash-and-burn agriculture.

According to a 1987 study, the reasons for this destruction are the following:

Spontaneous, unplanned expansion of agricultural frontiers, often in response to foreign credit possibilities (in the 1960's millions of dollars in loans were given to Costa Ricans by the US to stimulate beef production); lumbering activity, which often destroys large areas of forest to extract certain profitable (and often endangered) species of trees, leaving the rest to rot; a population that doubled between 1950 and 1970; the concentration of the best agricultural lands into large properties, forcing *campesinos* to clear and work land on hillsides for subsistence; laws which defined clearing of forest for agriculture as proof that the land was being "improved", a requisite for obtaining land titles; and lack of government ability to enforce deforestation laws.

The cattle raising encouraged by banks during the sixties and subsequent conversion of large tracts of forest to erosion-prone pasture have had particularly harmful ecological effects. Raising cattle requires less work and is less labor-intensive than agriculture, but a farmer can make 86 times as much money per acre with coffee, and 284 times as much with bananas. Yet, 23 times the amount of land used to grow coffee and bananas is devoted to cattle. It has been estimated that Costa Rica loses 2.5 tons of topsoil to erosion for every kilo of meat exported. Much of this meat ends up as hamburgers in North American fast-food restaurants.

As a consequence of this deforestation, Costa Rica faces not only erosion, but flooding, long-term hydroelectric shortages, sedimentation in canals and rivers, destruction of beautiful coral reefs from silt, climatic destabilization, loss of forest wildlife and valuable wood resources, loss of genetic reserves of incalculable value, scarcity of drinking water in some areas during the dry season and, of course, loss of natural beauty.

Tripled reforestation efforts, encouraged by government tax incentives, planted about 16,000 acres of trees in 1988. Most reforestation is directed toward planting fast-growing trees that can be sold in a few years for lumber or firewood. Although this form of reforestation is extremely valid and useful, it is important to understand that rain or cloud forest and the habitats they support cannot be reproduced by simple reforestation. Hundreds of years are needed to regenerate an ecologically viable rain forest. Very little effort is being made to replace the precious hardwoods found in natural rain forest, because investors would have to wait generations to reap the profits.

Code of Environmental Ethics for Nature Travel

Tourists can be valuable allies in the fight to conserve natural resources. In fact, one of the ideas behind ecotourism is to prove that the forest is worth more economically in its virgin state than cut down and converted to pasture.

The Audubon Society of Costa Rica has outlined a code of environmental ethics for nature travel. Most responsible ecotourism agencies try to follow the code as closely as possible. If you experience instances where this code is being violated, you can write to Audubon (address below).

1. **Wildlife and natural habitats must not be needlessly disturbed.** Visitors should stay on the trails, avoid using machetes, and not collect plants. Some ecosystems, such as coral reefs, are particularly sensitive, and special care should be taken to avoid damaging them.

Visitors should keep their distance from wildlife so it is not compelled to take flight. Animal courtship, nesting or feeding of young must not be interrupted. Bird nests should be observed from a safe distance through binoculars. Nesting sea turtles should be viewed only with the assistance of a trained guide.

Photographers also should keep their distance; foliage should not be removed from around nests and animals should not be molested for the sake of a picture.

Monkeys and other wild animals should not be fed, because this alters their diet and behavior.

2. **Waste should be disposed of properly**. Tour operators should set a good example for visitors by making sure that all garbage is confined to the proper receptacles. Boats and buses must have trash cans. Special care should be taken with plastic.

No littering of any kind should be tolerated. When possible, tourists and tour groups should use returnable or reusable containers.

3. **Tourism should be a positive influence on local communities.** Tourists and tour operators should make every reasonable effort to allow communities near natural areas to benefit from tourism. By hiring local guides, patronizing locally-owned restaurants and lodges, and buying handicrafts, tourists can help convince residents that wild places are worth saving.

4. **Tourism should be managed and sustainable.** Tour operators should encourage managers of parks and reserves--including the Costa Rican government, to develop and implement long-term management plans. These plans should prevent deterioration of ecosystems, prevent overcrowding, distribute visitors to under-utilized areas, and consider all present and future environmental impacts.

5. **Tourism should be culturally sensitive.** Tour operators should give visitors an opportunity to enjoy and learn from Costa Rica's mix of cultures. Tourism should serve as a bridge between cultures, allowing people to interact and enrich their understanding of how other people live. Tours should be designed to take advantage of and not conflict with local cultural traditions.

6. **There must be no commerce in wildlife, wildlife products, or native plants.** There are strict international laws prohibiting the purchase or transport of endangered or migratory wildlife. Tourists should be discouraged from buying or collecting any wildlife or plants, even if they are legal. Audubon does not tolerate trade in wild birds, feathers, stuffed birds or animals, sea turtle products of any kind, snakes and lizards or their skins, coral, furs or orchids and other plants (except those commercially grown).

7. **Tourists should leave with a greater understanding and appreciation of nature, conservation and the environment.** Visits to parks and refuges should be led by experienced, well-trained and responsible naturalists and guides. Guides should be able to provide proper supervision of the visitors, prevent disturbances to the area, answer questions of the visitors regarding flora and fauna and describe the conservation issues relevant to the area.

8. **Tourism should strengthen the conservation effort and enhance the natural integrity of places visited.** Tour operators

should collaborate with conservation organizations and government agencies in finding ways of putting the economic resources generated by tourism to work improving Costa Rica's environmental programs.

Equally important, tourism's human resources, including visitors, should be harnessed to avid conservation. Visitors should be made aware of Costa Rica's great conservation achievements as well as the problems.

The best tour operators will find ways for interested tourists to voice their support of conservation programs: by contributing money, volunteering to work in a park or in the ecological organizations listed below, writing letters of support, planting a tree, or other creative outlets for concerned activism.

How to help

Despite the bleak ecological picture, many people are working to reverse this situation, and visitors who admire Costa Rica's beauty are important collaborators in these efforts.

One of the most interesting groups is **Arbofilia,** a grassroots organization in which Costa Rican tree-lovers are helping *campesinos* reforest one of the most environmentally degraded areas of the country. Biologists provide high-quality seedlings and voluntary expertise in grafting, planting and greenhouse management. In return for the trees and the technical assistance, the *campesinos* provide voluntary work and make a *"compromiso con la naturaleza"* (commitment to nature), by vowing not to cut trees by water sources, not to burn fields (still a common practice in Costa Rica) and not to hunt endangered birds or animals. The group likes to use the term "ecological regeneration" rather than "reforestation" because they plant only native species and try to observe the patterns in which trees are found in nature. Jungle Trails (55-3486), a nature-tour company, takes visitors on a one-day trip to the Puriscal region, southwest of San José, to see Arbofilia in action. The tour fee includes the cost of a seedling which visitors can plant. You can contact Arbofilia at 40-7145 or 35-5470, (Apdo. 512, 1100 Tibas, CR).

APREFLOFLAS (Asociación Preservacionista de Flora y Fauna Silvestre) organizes volunteers to patrol wilderness areas to report illegal hunting, fishing and logging to the appropriate authorities. They urgently need volunteers, vehicles and funds (31-0792, Apdo. 1192, 1007 San José, CR).

ASCONA, one of Costa Rica's oldest environmental organizations, specializes in research and legal action. Projects have included investigating the environmental effects of coal mining in Talamanca, preventing plans for a coast-to-coast highway through La Amistad Biosphere Reserve and documenting sources of contamination in the Río Tárcoles. ASCONA appreciates donations and help from volunteers, especially if they have technical or scientific backgrounds (22-2296, 22-2288, Apdo. 8-3790, 1000 San José, CR. US tax-deductible donations can be made through World Wildlife Fund; see below).

The **Audubon Society of Costa Rica** lobbies the Legislative Assembly about environmental issues such as illegal logging. It produced the environmental ethics code on p. 36-8. Apdo. 4910, 1000 San José, fax: (506) 56-1533. In the US, write to P.O. Box 025216-700, Miami, Fl, 33102-5216.

CEDARENA (Centro de Derecho Ambiental y de los Recursos Naturales) researches laws pertaining to such areas as urban air pollution, forestry, solid waste management, land tenure and use, and coastal and marine resources, in order to untangle the web of outdated or unenforced legislation emanating from different ministries over the years. It maintains an information bank on environmental law which will be used to help plan an investment and development strategy for the World Bank, other lending agencies, and the Costa Rican government. They willingly accept volunteers interested in environmental law (Apdo. 134, 2050 San Pedro, CR, 24-8239).

Fundación Neotrópica promotes conservation and sustainable development in communities near national parks and other protected areas. Artisanry by people living in those communities is sold at their Nature Stores at Volcán Poás National Park, at the ICT Tourism Office at the Plaza de la Cultura (22-1090) and at Neotrópica's office on c 20, a 3. Their Editorial Heliconia publishes a bilingual photographic guide in paperback to the parks ($12 incl. postage), a larger, beautifully-done coffee-table version (Boza, *Costa Rica National Parks*, 1988, 271pp., hardback, $45 incl. postage) and a map showing park locations with photos ($10 incl. postage). British artist Deirdre Hyde's beautiful posters of the flora and fauna of the parks are published by Heliconia, and are favorite souvenirs ($7 each incl. postage). They also publish postcards and slides. All the above items are cheaper when purchased in CR. A $25 annual fee entitles members to a quarterly newsletter and a 10% discount at the Nature

Stores (Apdo.236, 1002 San José, CR, 55-4254). Tax-deductible contributions can be made through the Nature Conservancy.

The **Fundación de Parques Nacionales** promotes management, protection and development of national parks and reserves. Much of the territory which has been designated as such is still unpaid for, and thus could revert back to private ownership. Donations are matched with endowment funds in Costa Rican government bonds and through debt-for-nature swaps (Apdo. 1008, 1002 San José, CR, (506) 33-0207, 33-0116).

The **Organization for Tropical Studies** (Apdo. 676, 2050 San José, CR, 40-6696, 40-5033), the **Tropical Science Center** (Apdo. 8-3870, 1000 San José, CR, 53-3308), the **Monteverde Conservation League** (Apdo. 10165, 1000 San José, CR, 61-2953), the **Caribbean Conservation Corp.** (P.O.Box 2866, Gainesville, FL 32602, USA, (904) 373-6441, in CR: 24-9215), and **Friends of Lomas Barbudal** (691 Colusa Ave, Berkeley, CA 94707, USA, (415) 526-4115) are active in research, training, environmental education and stewardship of the forest and wildlife reserves they maintain in La Selva, Monteverde, Tortuguero and Lomas Barbudal, respectively. The CCC needs volunteer turtle taggers during the March-September nesting season. If you have a background in biology you can be a research assistant for free room and board. Lay people must pay a minimal fee for lodging.

US tax-deductible donations can be made to support the efforts of some of the above groups through the following organizations:

ASCONA
World Wildlife Fund
1250 24th St NW
Washington, DC 20037, USA

Fundación Neotrópica
The Nature Conservancy
International Program
1815 North Lynn St.
Arlington, VA,22209, USA

Monteverde Cloud Forest
National Audubon Society
950 Third Avenue
New York, NY, 10002, USA

Conservation International
1015 18th St NW
Washington, DC 20036, USA
(202) 429-5660

Rainforest Alliance
270 Lafayette St., Suite 512
New York, NY 10012
(212) 941-1900

Bibliography:

Bonilla, Alexander. *Costa Rica: La Típica Situación Ambiental de un País en Proceso de Desarrollo*. Bogotá, XV Congreso Interamericano de Planificación, 1985.
Ramírez, Alonso and Maldonado, Tirso. *Desarrollo Socioeconómico y el Ambiente Natural de Costa Rica: Situación Actual y Perspectivas*. San José, Fundación Neotrópica, 1988.
Valerio, Carlos E. *Anotaciones sobre la Historia Natural de Costa Rica*. San José, Editorial Universidad Estatal a Distancia, 1980.

PLANNING YOUR TRIP

NOTE: All information in this book is valid as of February 1991.

Weather and Clothing: One of the most surprising things for newcomers to San José is that it's not as warm as they thought it would be. The truly hot months are at the end of the dry season, March and April. December, January, and February are usually rain-free, but the weather can be downright chilly, especially at night or if a wind is blowing. During the rainy season, May to November, the days usually start out warm and sunny and cloud over by noon. The downpour usually starts around 2 or 3 pm and it can get pretty cold then, too. Usually a sweater and long pants are enough to keep you warm (see p. 32). If you go down in altitude from San José's 3800 feet, you'll be able to wear the kind of clothes you hoped you could wear in the tropics.

When it rains, it really *rains,* but afternoon downpours are usually short-lived. In San José during the rainy season, people usually carry umbrellas--brightly colored *sombrillas* for women and black *paraguas* for men. In the mountains, a lightweight rain poncho is usually more convenient. You'll be glad to have high rubber boots if you go hiking in the rain forest, especially in Corcovado or Sarapiquí. You can buy good ones here for under $7 at provincial supply stores, and many places, like Monteverde, rent them to visitors for around $1. Bring boots with you from home only if you wear an especially large size.

Bring at least three changes of lightweight cotton or cotton-mix clothing when you go to the beach or rainforest, protected inside a plastic bag in case of sudden downpours. Even if you are going to the steamy lowlands, you often have to pass through high mountains to get there--Cerro de la Muerte on the way to the Osa, Braulio Carrillo or Vara Blanca on the way to Sarapiquí. You'll be happier if you have a zippered sweatshirt, long pants, and socks that can be peeled off as you get to lower altitudes. The sweatshirt also makes a good pillow for long bus trips.

Many hotels will let you store excess luggage while you adventure off. I can usually fit everything I need for a trip to the country in a day-pack. I start out in a bathing suit, jeans, a cotton overshirt, socks and running shoes. In addition, I bring 2 bathing suits or leotards, 2 pairs of lightweight pants, extra socks, 2 long T-shirts (one to sleep in), flip-flops, the zippered sweatshirt, and a scarf, as well as insect repellent, sulphur powder, a flashlight, a book, an umbrella or rain poncho, a towel and toilet paper. If you are going to Irazú, Poás, Chirripó or other high altitudes, you'll need a jacket on top of a thick sweater and warm socks.

When to come: Tourist season is Christmas through Easter, which corresponds to the dry season. You can almost depend on clear, sunny weather, but there are occasional unseasonal storms from the north, which can last for several days. The rainy season usually takes awhile to get started in May, and often diminishes for a couple of weeks in July, a time called *el veranillo de San Juan,* "the little summer". The rains dwindle down in November.

There are certain advantages to coming during the off-season: The mornings are almost invariably clear and warm. The scenery is fresher and greener. The days are cooled by the rains, which for some people is a blessing, especially at the beach. The clouds usually clear in time for a magnificent sunset. Many hotels offer substantial discounts during the off-season, up to 50%. All places are less crowded, more peaceful. Less harm is done to the ecosystems in the parks when fewer people come trooping through at one time.

Since Costa Rica's tourist infrastructure is struggling to keep up with increased demand, many hotels are completely booked during the dry season, even small backpacker hotels and *pensiones.* This can add a bit of tension and disappointment to a "let's just explore and see what happens" kind of vacation. So be warned--during the dry season, plan way ahead.

What to bring: Things that are not made in Costa Rica are sold with a 100% import tax, and therefore are much more expensive here than elsewhere. Following is a list of items that are imported or impossible to find. Bring them with you. If you plan to stay in low-cost hotels, see also p. 116.

Film and camera equipment
Cassette tapes
Binoculars
Pocket alarm clock or watch
Pocket calculator
Swiss army knife
Good walking shoes
Insect repellent
Sulphur powder (sprinkle on socks to deter chiggers)
Sunscreen
Anti-itch ointment
Water purifying device
Small first aid kit
Contact lens solution
Diaphragms and diaphragm jelly
Vitamins
Earplugs
A universal plug for bathroom sinks
Beach towel and washcloth

Customs: Tourists are permitted to bring two cameras, binoculars, and electrical items that are for personal use only, like a small radio, a hair dryer, etc. Personal computers, electric typewriters and other appliances are sometimes held in customs and taxed. To avoid that, you must prove that what you are bringing is for personal use. The items in question will be noted in your passport and you must have them in your possession when you leave the country. Check with the consulate nearest you for latest regulations.

Traveling expenses: Costa Rica is not as inexpensive for travelers as are México and other Central American countries. Although public transportation is cheap, restaurant and hotel prices are relatively high, but variable. If you are determined to spend as little money as possible, it is good to bring a tent and visit during the dry season, or visit during the rainy season and take advantage of the off-season rates. You can also find clean and decent rooms with shared baths for under $12 almost anywhere. Meals cost between $2 and $6 depending on the "atmosphere". Groceries cost about 2/3 as much as they do in the United States. Two people can travel for about $20/day each, including bus transport, comfortable lodging (double occupancy) and restaurant meals. If you go to the cheapest places, you can get by for $15 each. Camping out is cheaper still, except for the inconvenience of hauling around equipment and making sure your tent is guarded at all times.

Tipping: A 10% service tax is included in your restaurant bill, so it is not customary to tip unless you really feel like it. It is not customary to tip taxi drivers either. In fact, a nice thing about Costa Rica is that people are not standing around with their hands out all the time--partly because tourism is so new, partly because of a tradition of equality and pride. We hope that these qualities survive the influx of massive tourism here. You would be surprised to know how little the staff at most hotels, including luxury hotels, earns (usually less than $150/mo.) so a little gratuity here and there is certainly helpful, especially if you have appreciated the service received.

Airlines serving Costa Rica: Usually the cheapest and most direct flights to Costa Rica are through Miami. **LACSA** is Costa Rica's international airline. It is known for its almost accident-free record, and for jolly Costa Rica-bound flights where everyone gets tipsy on free wine or wired on Costa Rican coffee, and returning Ticos applaud as the plane touches down. LACSA's toll-free number in the US is 1-800-225-2272. In Canada it's 800-663-2344; England: 01499-6731; Japan: 445-48-74; Taiwan: 02-704-94-38.

American Airlines, PanAm, and Continental also have flights to Costa Rica, as well as the Salvadoran airline, TACA, the Honduran airline, SAHSA, and the Nicaraguan airline, Aeronica. The Central American airlines tend to be cheaper than the US-based airlines, but they often make more stops. Try to get a travel agent who is experienced in sending people to Costa Rica, because there are many alternatives, and regular travel agents might not have info about Central American airlines in their computers. See p. 47 for info on charter flights from Canada.

Whatever airline you take, make reservations several months in advance if you are coming during the dry season, and confirm your reservation 72 hours in advance because sometimes schedules change. Get to the gateway airport at least two hours before flight time or allow two hours between connecting flights. Check-in lines are lengthy and documentation checks and payment of airport taxes may take time. You are required to pay a $13 airport tax in Miami.

Following is a list of ports of embarkation, and the stops that different airlines make on their way to Costa Rica:

Dallas: American (via Guatemala)

Denver: Mexicana (via Ciudad Juarez, Mazatlan, Mexico City and Guatemala).

Houston: SAHSA (via Belize, San Pedro Sula, Tegucigalpa), TACA (via Belize and San Salvador), Continental (via Panama).

Los Angeles: LACSA (via Mexico City, Guatemala, and San Pedro Sula), Mexicana (via Mexico City and Guatemala), TACA (via Guatemala and San Salvador).

Miami: Nonstop: LACSA, American, PanAm.

With stops: SAHSA (via Belize, San Pedro Sula, Tegucigalpa), TACA (via Belize and San Salvador).

New Orleans: LACSA (via Cancún and San Pedro Sula), SAHSA (via Belize, San Pedro Sula, Tegucigalpa), TACA (via Belize and San Salvador).

San Francisco: TACA (via Guatemala, San Salvador and Los Angeles).

New York: LACSA (via Guatemala and San Pedro Sula), TACA (via Washington, Miami, Guatemala, San Salvador)

Washington, D.C.: TACA (via Miami, Guatemala and San Salvador).

Mexico City: Aeronica (via Guatemala and Managua), LACSA (via San Salvador or Guatemala), Mexicana (via Guatemala).

Europe: KLM (via Curacao and Aruba), LTU (via San Andres), Iberia (via Puerto Rico and Dominican Republic).

For information on **low-cost flights** to Costa Rica contact the above airlines, or:

González Travel	Americas Tours and Travel
(504) 885-4058	(206) 623-8850, fax: 467-0454
Fax: (504) 443-4737	1-800-553-2513

Charter flights: Canadians have been flocking to Costa Rica because of the availability of charter flights. **Fiesta Wayfarer Holidays** in Toronto (416) 498-5566, and **Fiesta West** in Vancouver (604) 688-1102, charter planes from those cities year-round. The Montreal offices of **Go Travel** (514) 735-4526) charter planes to San José December through April. Tourists have the option of staying one, two, or three weeks.

Senior Citizens: Elderhostel, which sponsors cheap and interesting trips for people over 60 years of age, now includes Costa Rica in their itinerary. Find out more by writing them at 80 Boyleston St., Suite 400, Boston, MA 02116.

Cruises: Many cruise ships stop in Costa Rica. Ask your travel agent about them.

By land: Allow about three weeks from the time you enter Mexico to the time you reach Costa Rica. Avoid the highlands of Guatemala and El Salvador. For a detailed account of one such trip, read the Sept. 21, 1990 tourism edition of *The Tico Times* ($1 incl. postage, Apdo. 4632, 1000 San José, CR).

Entry requirements: When traveling with a passport, citizens of the United States, Canada, and most Latin American and European countries can obtain a 90-day visa from the airline issuing them a ticket. They must enter the country with at least $400 and a departure ticket. Citizens of some Latin American, Asian, African and East European countries must obtain a visa from a Costa Rican consulate and pay a deposit upon entering the country, refundable when they leave. Check with the consulate nearest you for latest information.

Exit and extended visas: All tourists must pay an airport tax of $5 when they leave.

In addition to the airport tax, **if you overstay your 30 or 90-day visa, you will need an exit visa in order to leave the country.** An exit visa is good for 30 days from the date it is issued, so it is an automatic 30-day extension of your visa. If you do not use your exit visa within 30 days, you must buy a new one. Any local travel agent can obtain an exit visa for you, but be sure to request it at least 3 working days before you are scheduled to depart. They charge a small fee for this service, well worth it compared to the hassle of getting the visa yourself. If you leave by air, an exit visa costs about $12. If you leave by land, the exit visa costs $30. Allow at least 48 hours for processing of exit visas. They cannot be processed on weekends or holidays (see p. 60-1).

If you have stayed over 90 days when you apply for your exit visa, you will be charged $4 for each month or part of a month that you were here without a valid tourist card.

You can stay legal by leaving the country for a few days every four months and coming back in with a new tourist card. Longer stays are only granted to those applying for student visas or residency (see p. 249-51).

Children of any nationality who stay in Costa Rica for more than the 30 or 90 days allowed in their visas are automatically subject to Costa Rican laws which require that both parents request permission from the child welfare organization (*Patronato Nacional de la Infancia*) to take the child out of the country. Thus, if a child travels with a guardian or only one parent, written permission to travel from the other parent (notarized by a Costa Rican consul in the country of origin) must be presented to the Patronato in order for the child to leave Costa Rica. They are quite serious about this. Two Costa Rican-sized passport photos of the child must accompany the Patronato exit request form, as well as the child's passport. A travel agent can help you with this also, but you must present him with the proper documents.

After you've gotten your exit visa and are ready to leave, be sure to **confirm your departure flight** 72 hours in advance.

You must get to the airport at least two hours ahead of flight time. Flights are often overbooked. The overflow from an 8am flight might be sent on a 10am flight, causing connection problems.

For further travel information, contact:

Costa Rican Tourist Board
B.I.V. Tower, Suite 801
Miami, FL 33131
Tel: 1-800-327-7033
(305) 358-2150 (within FL)
Fax: (305) 358-7951

Costa Rican Tourist Board
3540 Wilshire Blvd.
Los Angeles, CA 90010
Tel: 1-800-762-5909
1-800-762-5900 (within CA)
Fax: (213) 388-9326

SPECIAL WAYS TO VISIT COSTA RICA

Nature Tours

The following agencies organize tours for nature lovers and birdwatchers. Bilingual naturalists accompany small groups into parks and reserves, and arrange for food, lodging and transportation, which are all included in the trip price. The following Costa Rica-based groups will arrange jaunts for groups of two to ten people, once you are here.

Caribbean Tours and Expeditions
Apdo. 363, San José, CR
23-2125, 33-3992
Fax: 9506) 23-5785
Trekking, biking, surfing, rafting

Costa Rica Expeditions
Apdo. 6941, San José, CR
(506) 22-0333
Fax: (506) 57-1665
Nature tours to all locations, rafting

C. R. Mountain Biking
Apdo. 3979, San José, CR
(506) 22-4380
Fax: 55-4354
Easy cycling to mountain biking

Costa Rican Trails
Apdo. 2907, San José, CR
22-4547, 22-7338
Fax: (506) 21-3011
Hiking, windsurfing, surfing, rafting, cycling

Costa Rica Sun Tours
Apdo.1195, 1250 Escazu,
(506) 55-3518, 55-3418
Fax: (506) 55-4410
All locations, specializing in Pavones and Arenal

Geotur
Apdo. 469 Y Griega
1011 San José, CR
(506) 34-1867
Fax: (506) 53-6338
Wildlife observation in Carara, Santa Rosa, Cahuita, and Braulio Carrillo

Horizontes
Apdo. 1780
1002 San José, CR
(506) 22-2022
Fax: (506) 55-4513
Nature tours to all locations as well as bicycle and hiking tours. Can arrange conventions, seminars.

Interviajes
Apdo. 296
Heredia 3000, CR
Ph/fax: (506) 38-1212
Low-cost tours to many locations.

Jungle Trails
Apdo. 5941
1000 San José, CR
(506) 55-3486
Fax: (506) 55-2782
Camping, hiking, birdwatching and tree-planting trips.

Tikal Tours
Apdo. 6398
1000 San José, CR
(506) 23-2811
Fax: (506) 23-1916
All locations.

US-based nature tour companies: (arranged by state):

Borderland Productions
Tucson, AZ 85710
(602) 882-7650

Wings
Tucson, AZ 85751
(602) 749-1967
Fax: (602) 749-3175

Baja Expeditions
San Diego, CA 92109
(1-800) 843-6967
(619) 581-3311
Fax: (619) 581-6542

Betchart Expeditions
Cupertino, CA 95014
(408) 252-4910
(800) 252-4910
Fax: (408) 252-1444

Costa Rica Connection
San Luis Obispo, CA
(805) 543-8823
(800) 345-7422
Fax: (805) 543-3626

Forum Travel
Pleasant Hill, CA 94523
(415)671-2900
Fax: (415) 946-1500

Geo Expeditions
Sonora, CA
(209) 523-0152
(800) 351-5041

Extraordinary Expeditions
Hailey, ID
(800) 234-1569
Ph/fax: (208) 788-2012

Overseas Adventure Travel
Cambridge, MA 02139
(617) 876-0533
(800) 221-0814
Fax: (617) 876-0455

Voyagers International
Ithaca, NY 14851
(607) 257-3091
Fax: (607) 257-3699

Halintours
Austin, TX 78765
(512) 450-0955
Fax: (512) 450-0958

Wildland Journeys
Seattle, WA
(800) 345-4453
(206) 365-0686

LANGUAGE LEARNING VACATIONS

Many people like the idea of learning Spanish on their Costa Rica vacation. There are many excellent language schools here, offering a variety of experiences. **Conversa** (see below) has a new lodge overlooking the beautiful Santa Ana valley with live-in instructors so that families and individuals can enjoy life in rural Costa Rica while studying. **Centro Lingüístico Latinoamericano** trains participants in international service programs as well as tourists. **Instituto de Lengua Española** is primarily for missionaries, but accepts other students when space is available. It is one of the most intensive and least expensive schools. The **Centro Cultural** teaches Spanish and English (maximum 10 students per class), and sponsors plays and concerts by Costa Rican and US performers. They also have a large, English-language library and a TV room for viewing CNN. Students must pass through security as they enter. **ILISA** guarantees a maximum of 4 students per class and will arrange for students to earn one semester credit for each week of Spanish study (20 hours) evaluated as specified by the Educational Testing Service at Princeton University. See p. 56 for info on their excellent course in Central American History. The **Academia Costarricense de Lenguaje** offers cultural evenings focusing on Latin American customs, foods and musical traditions, as well as optional courses in Spanish guitar and Latin American dancing!

Most schools arrange for students to live with Costa Rican families to immerse themselves in the language. They also set up weekend sightseeing trips for participants. Class size is small. Intensive conversational methods are used for 4 to 6 hours a day in programs lasting one week to several months.

Students are placed according to ability. All language schools assist their students in extending their tourist visas.

Academia Costarricense de
Lenguaje
Apdo. 336
2070 Sabanilla, CR
(506) 21-1624, fax: 25-2610

American Institute for
Language and Culture
Apdo. 200
1001 San José, CR
(506) 25-4313, fax: 24-4244

Centro Cultural Costar-
ricense-Norteamericano
Apdo. 1489, San José, CR
(506) 25-9433, fax: 24-1480

Centro Lingüístico Conversa
Apdo. 17 Centro Colón
San José, CR
(506) 21-7649, fax: 33-2418

Centro Lingüístico
Latinoamericano
Apdo. 151, Alajuela, CR
(506) 41-0261

Forester Instituto
Internacional
Apdo. 6945, 1001 San José
(506) 25-3155, fax: 25-9236

ICAI
Apdo. 10302
San José, CR
(506) 33-8571, fax: 21-5238

ILISA
Apdo. 1001
2050 San Pedro, CR
(506) 25-2495, fax: 25-4665

Instituto Británico
Apdo. 8184
1000 San José, CR
(506) 25-0256, fax: 53-1894

Inst. de Lengua Española
Apdo. 100
2350 San José
(506) 26-9222, fax: 27-0211

Instituto Universal
Apdo. 219
2120 San José, CR
(506) 57-0441, 23-9662

Intensa
Apdo. 8110
1000 San José, CR
(506) 25-6009, 24-6353

STUDY PROGRAMS

Spanish, Latin American Culture, Politics, Economy, Litera-ture, Tropical Biology, Ecology, International Relations, Interna-tional Business--you can study nearly anything in Costa Rica. There are several options for university-level students who want to spend a semester or a year here. All programs require advance planning, so start thinking about it early. Also, since there are two decidedly different seasons, choose your months according to your preferred weather.

Associated Colleges of the Midwest (ACM) is a competitive program run by and primarily for several private midwestern colleges. However, students at any accredited university or college can apply. The fall semester (September-December) offers an intensive course in Spanish and the social sciences (the topic of the course changes each year). Students can do research in an area of their particular interest. The spring semester (February-May) gives students an opportunity to do two months of field research in the social or physical sciences with some excellent professors. Students live with Costa Rican families. For information write:

> Associated Colleges of the Midwest
> 18 S. Michigan Ave, Suite 1010
> Chicago, IL 60603.
> In Costa Rica: 25-0725, fax: (506) 53-5790

Friends World College maintains its Latin American Regional Center in San José. It focuses on understanding world problems through work and study in countries around the globe. Students in San José receive Spanish classes and design their own projects. They work in national ministries, with experimental agricultural projects, in rural communities, etc. Students receive credit based on a journal they maintain during their projects. For information write:

> Friends World College
> Plover Lane
> Huntington, NY 11743.
> In Costa Rica: (506) 25-0289

The **University of Kansas** runs a one, two, and three-semester study program that is open to students who are at least sophomores at any US college or university. Kansas students take full course loads at the University of Costa Rica (UCR) and live with Costa Rican families. The first semester group arrives for an orientation period in February, a month before UCR classes begin. The second semester group arrives in July and doesn't have an orientation. Kansas students like their program for the flexibility it offers them in choosing courses and for the contact they have with Costa Rican students. For more information, write:

> Office of Studies Abroad
> 204 Lippincott Hall
> University of Kansas
> Lawrence, KS 66045.

The **State University of New York** at Albany sponsors one or two semester programs open to college juniors and seniors with at least two years of college-level Spanish. Students live with Costa Rican families selected by program coordinators at the University of Costa Rica and enroll in regular university courses in any discipline at the UCR. Contact:

> Office of International Programs, L1-84
> University at Albany
> State University of New York
> Albany, NY 12222

People who would like to enroll directly in the **University of Costa Rica** do so as "Special Students". All foreigners fall into this category for the first two years of their studies at the UCR. Admission fees are about double those for Costa Rican students, but the price is still quite low compared to US standards. There is also the option of being an *oyente* (auditing a class). The first semester runs March to June, the second July to December. The office is on the west side of campus, near the Oficina del Registro.

During the December-March break there is a series of *cursos libres* on many subjects. They are open to the public for a nominal registration fee. For more information contact:

> Oficina de Asuntos Internacionales
> Ciudad Universitaria Rodrigo Facio
> San José, Costa Rica
> 24-3660

The **University for Peace** is located on a beautiful tract of forested farmland in Villa Colón, southwest of San José. The goal of the University is to create pilot projects for peace studies programs in universities around the world. By exploring different aspects of peace education and the most effective methods of teaching them to cross-cultural groups, the University hopes to foment fundamental change in the orientation of university programs and to establish peace education in unions, churches and other community groups. Presently the University for Peace is offering two-year masters degree programs in Communications for Peace, Human Rights, and Ecology and Natural Resources. To request the University's bulletin write Apdo. 199, Escazú. To arrange a visit, call 49-1072.

The **Monteverde Institute** gives courses in Tropical Biology and Ecology. Students do research in a private reserve near Monteverde. Spanish language study is included.

> Monteverde Institute
> Apdo. 10165
> San José, CR
> (506) 61-2550

The **Organization for Tropical Studies** is a consortium of universities and research institutions dedicated to education, investigation, and conservation in the tropics. They offer Tropical Biology: An Ecological Approach, a 2-month lecture/field experience course twice a year at their research stations in La Selva, Palo Verde, and Wilson Gardens, as well as several other courses. They also provide logistical support for dissertation research.

> OTS
> PO Box DM, Duke Station
> Durham, NC 27706
> (919) 684-5774
> In San José: 40-6696

The **Institute for Central American Development Studies** aims to stimulate critical evaluation of current development strategies, identifying and overcoming inherent "first-world" biases, and to search for alternative policies. They offer structured internships, in Costa Rica or Nicaragua, which help integrate theory with real-world experiences, and allow students to give something back to the host society through the projects on which they work. Courses include Spanish Grammar, Conversation and Culture, Women in Central America, Agriculture and Hunger in Central America, Ecological and Environmental Issues, and Multinationals and Foreign Investment.

> ICADS
> P. O. Box 145450
> Coral Gables, FL 33114
> In CR: (506) 25-0508

The **Central American Institute for International Affairs** (ICAI) offers a course on Central American Issues and Perspectives, including lectures on history, politics, the impact of "perestroika" in the region, environmental issues, and Costa Rica as a model for development. Students have the possibility of meeting the Presidents of Nicaragua, Costa Rica and Panamá, as well as opposition leaders. Contact:

> Consortium for International Education
> P.O.Box 18882
> Irvine, CA 92713
> (714) 955-1700, fax: (714) 955-2945
> In CR: (506) 33-8751, fax: (506) 21-5238

ILISA offers an excellent 2-week course, in English, in Central American history and culture. Starting with a lecture on the complex historical issues affecting the area, students visit coffee and banana plantations, museums, an agricultural co-operative, as well as the Central Bank, where foreign debt and structural adjustment issues affecting third world countries are explained. The course ends with a weekend in Manuel Antonio National Park.

> ILISA
> Apdo. 1001, San Pedro 2050
> San José, CR
> (506) 25-2495, fax: (506) 25-9090
> In US: (818) 843-1226

Mesoamerica (The Institute for Central American Studies) runs study tours to Nicaragua to promote a better understanding between U.S. citizens and the people of Central America. The 12-day tours include five days of orientation seminars in San José and seven days in Nicaragua. Participants meet with high-level government officials, opposition parties, journalists, religious leaders, academicians, etc. There are visits to an agricultural cooperative, historic sites, and local artisan markets.

For those interested in Central American politics, Mesoamerica is a great place to work as an intern. People who are willing to volunteer for at least 20 hours a week for six months can read newspapers and journals, help maintain Mesoamerica's extensive clipping file, do research, and write articles for the monthly newsletter. Internships must be confirmed in advance. College credit can be arranged. Write:

> Mesoamerica
> The Institute for Central American Studies
> Apartado 300-1002
> San José, Costa Rica.
> (506) 27-9928

ECO-SEMINARS

In this small country, one can encounter some of the most positive--and some of the most negative--environmental developments on earth. Mesoamerica's new environmental seminar topics include deforestation, reforestation, commercial agriculture and pesticide use, the future of the oceans, and the impact of US policy on international environmental issues. Field trips include visits to a rain forest, a coastal national park, and a sustainable agriculture project, as well as a river rafting trip to a proposed hydroelectric dam site. ICAS will plan special study seminars for interested groups on request. Total cost is $750, not including airfare to Costa Rica. Write to Mesoamerica (address above) for more information.

RETIREMENT SEMINARS

ICAI (see p. 56) offers a twelve-day "pre-retirement" seminar including legal aspects of *pensionado* status, medical and insurance systems, real estate, rentals, and investments. In Costa Rica call: (506) 33-8751 or fax: (506) 21-5238. In US, contact:

Ecotours
3325 Wilshire Blvd., Suite 504
Los Angeles, CA 90010
(213) 385-1215, fax: (213) 385-4405

Lifestyle Explorations offers a 13-day tour for those interested in living here with trips to the Atlantic and Pacific coasts as well as San José residential areas. Long-time residents share their experiences.

P.O. Box 57-6487
Modesto, CA 95355
(209) 577-4081

Invaluable for potential retirees is the Tourism Issue of *The Tico Times,* the local English-language weekly newspaper. The Tourism Issue is published each fall: 100 information-packed pages for $.25 (that's 25 cents) plus postage. A year's subscription is $45 to the US (Apdo. 4632, 1000 San José, CR, fax: (506) 33-6378, tel: (506) 22-8952).

PHOTOGRAPHY TOURS

ICAI also offers an eight-day tour to La Selva and Puerto Viejo de Talamanca for amateur and professional photographers. Call 33-8571 (fax: (596) 21-5238) in CR or contact:

Photo Adventure
P.O.Box 5095
Anaheim, CA 92814
(714) 527-2918, fax: (714) 826-8752

Photo Safaris offers two 7-day workshops: one, based at Chalet Tirol in the mountains near San José, combines lectures, technical demonstrations and field work; the other, for experienced photographers, uses Dundee Ranch Hotel near Orotina as a base for forays into Carara Biological Reserve. Another 10-day photo-safari takes you all over Costa Rica. Call 39-7070, 39-7104, fax: (506) 39-7050, or write Apdo. 7812, 1000 San José, CR.

GENERAL INFORMATION

Reservations: Costa Rica is becoming so popular that you should make reservations several months in advance for the dry season. We have mentioned fax numbers whenever possible to facilitate this, but most hotels also require a deposit to secure reservations.

Arrival: You can change money at the airport until 5 pm. Taxi service into San José is about $8 per taxi. A bus ($.25) goes into San José, but you can't take much baggage on it.

You might prefer to skip the noise and pollution of San José altogether and stay at the inexpensive **Hotel Alajuela** (41-1241), or the lovely country hotels, some of which offer airport pickup, like **Posada Pegasus** and **Pico Blanco** near Escazú (see p. 118, 121), **La Posada de la Montaña, Chalet Tirol, La Rosa Blanca, El Pórtico,** or **Las Ardillas** above Heredia (see p. 136-8), or **Chatelle** and **Tranquilidad** near Alajuela (p. 130).

Currency: The currency unit is the *colón (¢)*. Bills come in denominations of ¢5 to ¢1000, and coins from 10 *céntimos* to ¢20. The current exchange rate is around ¢120 per US$1. After the *colón* was devaluated, the government shrank the size of the coins, so you may be given change with both the older, larger and the newer, smaller coins.

It is illegal to exchange dollars for *colones* anywhere but in the national banks and in some hotels. If anyone offers to buy dollars from you on the street, be aware that you and he could be prosecuted for it. Costa Rica needs all the dollars it can get to pay off its external debt, so it is important for your dollars to go into national rather than private hands. Unless you are changing huge amounts of money, there is really very little economic advantage to exchanging on the black market. When you leave Costa Rica you will be able to change only a certain amount of *colones* back into dollars. Presently you can receive only up to $50 in cash. This amount may be subject to change.

Changing money: This is often a time-consuming process. Banks are open 9-3. There is always a special window for changing dollars. A branch of the Banco de Costa Rica (a 1, c 7) is open 8am to 6pm M-F. You can use a Visa or Mastercharge card to buy *colones* at the banks, otherwise travelers checks are acceptable.

It is best to change money in San José before going to the provinces, and to carry small bills with you (not just 1000's) because everyone has a problem stocking enough change. The larger hotels are authorized to change money and travelers checks for their guests, and many smaller hotels in the provinces do too, but sometimes you get fewer colones than you do at the bank.

Holidays: Costa Rica has 17 official holidays (*feriados*) per year, and they are taken quite seriously. Do not expect to find government offices, banks, professional offices and many stores open on *feriados*. Two times during the year, the whole country shuts down completely. These are Semana Santa (the week before Easter) and the week between Christmas and New Year's. Transportation stops totally Holy Thursday and Good Friday, making Wednesday's buses very crowded. Good Friday is the most important day of Holy Week in Costa Rica and is a day of mourning throughout the country.

Easter week is the time to see picturesque religious processions in the countryside. There are also large non-religious parades in San José on Labor Day, Independence Day and during Christmas week. The Tico Times will tell you where the most interesting events are. It's best to avoid visiting the beach during Easter week because it's the last holiday young *ticos* have before their school starts and they're all at the beach with their radios.

Following is a list of Costa Rica's *feriados*:
January 1: New Year's Day
March 19: Feast of Saint Joseph (San José's patron saint)
April 11: Anniversary of the Battle of Rivas
Holy Thursday through Easter Sunday
May 1: Labor Day
Corpus Christi

June 29: Saint Peter and Saint Paul
July 25: Annexation of Guanacaste Province
August 2: Our Lady of the Angels
August 15: Assumption, Mother's Day
September 15: Independence Day
October 12: Día de la Raza (Columbus Day, Carnaval in
           Limón)
December 8: Immaculate Conception
December 24, 25: Christmas Eve and Christmas Day

Buses: Since most Costa Ricans don't have cars, buses go almost everywhere. Most buses that travel between San José and the provinces are quite comfortable, and fares rarely run more than $2-6 to go anywhere in the country. Some provincial buses are a bit rickety, but all buses are fairly punctual. Buses from San José to the provinces are crowded on Fridays and Saturdays and the day preceding holidays or 3-day weekends. Likewise it is difficult to get buses back to San José on Sundays, Mondays and the days following a holiday. This is especially true of trying to make connections in Liberia, Puntarenas, Quepos and Limón.

Some buses don't have buzzers or bells to tell the driver when you want to get off. When the bus gets close to your stop, shout *"La parada!"* or whistle loudly. If you are traveling cheaply by bus, it is good to leave most of your luggage at a San José hotel and travel lightly. Big suitcases are very inconvenient for bus travel.

The second half of this book gives detailed information on transportation including locations of bus stops and numbers to call to check schedules. English is usually not spoken.

San José and suburban buses: The Sabana-Cementerio bus will take you through the area between downtown and the Sabana. Downtown, it stops at Parque Central, at c 7, a ctl and at the Post Office. The San Pedro buses (a 2, c 5/7) cover the eastern side of the city, through Los Yoses to San Pedro. The northern and southern boundaries of downtown are only an 8-or 9-block walk from Avenida Central. Most urban buses cost about $.10. Suburban buses cost $.15-20 and run from 5 am to 10 or 11 at night.

If you are returning to San José by bus from the north or west, and want to get all the way downtown, get off early on

Paseo Colón and hop on the Sabana-Cementerio. That way you avoid going to the Coca Cola or some other bad neighborhood terminal. (The Coca Cola is a large bus terminal on c 16 between a 1/3. See map at back of book.) Following is a list of *paradas* (bus stops) for buses to the suburbs:

Coronado: a 3, c 3/5
Curridabat: c 3, a 2/4
Escazú: a 6 c 12/14 (minibus), a 1, c 16/18 (big bus)
Guadalupe: a 3, c 1/3
La Uruca: c 6, a 3/5
Moravia: a 3, c 3/5
Pavas: a 1, c 16/18
Sabanilla: c 7, a 2/4
San Ramón de Tres Ríos: c 7, a 2
Santa Ana: Coca Cola
Villa Colón: Coca Cola

Buses to Panamá and Nicaragua: Since both countries are somewhat unstable, it is essential to talk to people who have been there recently before going. Be sure to get an exit visa if you have been in Costa Rica over 90 days (see p. 47-8).

People who have only read about **Nicaragua** in the headlines are usually surprised by the friendliness of the Nicaraguan people, and their willingness to talk about their lives. You do have to watch out for contaminated water carrying amoebas or hepatitis. Because of the desperate economic situation there, it is good to bring simple things that people might need like toilet paper, pens, toothpaste, clothes, canned or dried food. US citizens don't need a visa to enter, Canadians do. Check latest rules with the Nicaraguan consulate, 33-8747. Most car rental agencies will not allow you to rent a car to go to Nicaragua. Airfare costs $105 one way.

The SIRCA bus leaves San José for Managua at 5am Weds, Fri, Sun (c 11, a 2, 22-5541, $26 round trip). Tica Bus also goes to Managua daily at 7 am, arriving around 5 pm (c 9, a 4, 21-9229, 21-8954, $25 round trip, better buses than SIRCA, buses every other day during rainy season).

People used to go to **Panamá** to change dollars and buy film before continuing to South America, but the economic situation is very precarious there now. Between the police and the robbers, personal safety is not assured. Check with the Panamanian consulate about visa requirements (25-0667, open

8am to noon). Presently US citizens and Canadians must present their passport, tickets in and out of the country and $10 to get a visa, which takes 24 hours. Tica Bus leaves for Panama City daily at 8pm, arriving at 5pm (c 9, a 4, 21-9229, 21-8954, $48 round trip, buses every other day during rainy season). A Tica Bus was attacked in October 1990 by pro-Noriega guerrillas and the passengers were robbed. A TRACOPA bus leaves San José daily at 7:30am, and arrives in David, Panamá at 4:30pm (a 18, c 4, $7.50, 21-4214, 23-7685). From David you can get hourly buses to Panama City (7 hours), or an express bus at noon and midnight (5.5 hrs). You can avoid at least 7 hours on the bus by flying with SANSA to Coto 47 (Mon thru Sat, 10am, $20, see below) and taking a taxi to Paso Canoas on the border, then catching a bus from there. The border closes for lunch from 12 to 2pm. It's very hot and muggy in Paso Canoas. Airfare from San José to Panamá is $124 one way.

Train service to Limón, the famed "Jungle Train" has been discontinued. A large landslide and an even larger operational deficit caused the demise of the old railroad, which would have completed its hundredth year of service on December 7, 1990. Tourists can still take the ride on Thursdays and Saturdays. Swiss Travel Service drives you to Turrialba where you board a refurbished train car to Siquirres. The tour winds up with a visit to banana plantations and a drive through Braulio Carrillo National Park back to San José ($69, 31-4055).

The **Puntarenas** train station is at c 2, a 20. Trains leave at 6:30am and 1pm on weekends and at 1pm weekdays. They return from Puntarenas at 6am and 4pm weekends and at 6am during the week ($.80, 26-0011). The train lurches back and forth, makes a lot of stops, and takes twice as long as the trip by car or bus. Local people come on at each stop selling roasted cashews, hard-boiled eggs, water apples and whatever other fruit is in season in that agriculturally abundant region.

Planes: Because of Costa Rica's mountainous terrain, small aircraft transport is frequently used. A 20-minute flight can get you to Quepos and Manuel Antonio on the Pacific coast, instead of 4 hours by bus. SANSA, the local airline, flies to all corners of the country. Here is their schedule:
Barra del Colorado: Airstrip under repair; call for info.
Coto 47: Daily except Sun, 10am, returns at 11am ($20).

Golfito (near Corcovado N.P.): Daily except Sun, 8am, returns at 9am; via Palmar Sur on Mon, Th, and Fri, 12:30pm, returns at 1:55 ($20).

Nosara: Tu, Th, Sat, 6am, returns at 6:50 ($20)

Quepos (Manuel Antonio) : Daily except Sun at 7am and 3pm, returns 35 min later ($10).

Samara: Mon, Weds, Fri, 6am, returns at 6:50am ($20).

Tamarindo: Mon, Wed, Fri, Sat, 8am, returns at 8:50am ($20).

Check current timetables before making plans. Make reservations at least 2 weeks in advance during the dry season (33-0397, 33-3258, fax: (506) 55-2176), but note that **your SANSA reservation means nothing until you have bought your ticket**. A microbus will take you to the Juan Santamaría Airport from the SANSA office on calle 24, north of Paseo Colón. SANSA planes leave from the smaller terminal west of the main air terminal. In some places, like Quepos, SANSA buses will pick you up at your hotel for the return trip. SANSA also offers some of the cheapest tour packages around to the areas they serve (23-4179, 33-2714, fax: 55-2176).

Small 5-passenger planes can be rented for about $220 an hour from VEASA (32-1010) or SAETA, (32-1474) at the Tobías Bolaños smallcraft airport near Pavas ($3 by taxi from San José). They go places inaccessible by larger aircraft.

The only drawback to air travel is that sometimes flights are delayed by climatic conditions, and passengers must wait at either end. With luck this won't happen to you, and you'll have the thrill of seeing Costa Rica's symphony of mountains, sea and sky as you fly next to the clouds.

Taxis are relatively inexpensive by northern standards. Drivers have just begun to use computerized meters, called *marías*. If your taxi does not have one, or if you are going more than 12 kilometers, agree on a rate with the driver before you get into a taxi. Ask at your hotel how much it should cost to get to where you're going. Official rates are ¢60 for the first kilometer and ¢25 for each additional km, with a 20% increase after 11pm. Each hour that a *taxista* waits for you costs ¢400.

Taxis can come in handy if you want to visit hard-to-get-to places but do not want the expense of renting a car. You can take an inexpensive bus trip to the town nearest your destination and hire a jeep-taxi to take you the rest of the way. Usually taxis hang out around the main square of any small town. It's best to ask several drivers how much they charge to make sure you are getting the going rate.

Hitching: Since there is bus service almost everywhere, most people prefer to take buses. Hitch-hiking is rare but possible on the major highways. In the country, where bus service is infrequent or nonexistent, cars often stop to pick up pedestrians.

Car rental costs $52/day including insurance and mileage (4-wheel-drives cost $80/day). You can usually get a 10% discount during the off-season. Valid foreign drivers licenses are good in Costa Rica for 3 months. If you don't have an Amex, Visa or Mastercharge card, you must leave a US$700 deposit. All repairs must be okayed first with the main office, or you will not be reimbursed. Some agencies will rent tents, coolers, portable tables, trailers and even surfboards by the day. It is best to reserve a car a few days in advance, or even to fax before your arrival. All major rent-a-car agencies have branches in Costa Rica (under "*alquiler de automobiles*" in phonebook).

Renting a car, of course, makes exploring easier and is less time-consuming than taking the bus. However, renting a car just to get around San José is more hassle than it's worth. The cars must be left in parking lots at all times. Traffic is crazy. Left turns from right lanes are not uncommon. Taxis or buses are much cheaper and easier for city travel. If you do rent a car for trips, do not leave anything in it, even for a minute, unless it is in a well-guarded place. Rent-a-car plates are an open invitation to thieves.

Gas: Fill up before leaving San José going west--there are no gas stations on the highway between San José and the airport. There are several gas stations on Avenida Central going east from downtown. Gas costs about $2/gallon. There are no self-service stations in Costa Rica.

Accidents: 27-7150 and 27-8030 are the numbers to call for a traffic official if one doesn't appear. Do not move vehicles until you are authorized to do so by an official. Offer paper and pencils to witnesses to write their names and *cédula* numbers (legal identification).

Do not remove badly injured people from the scene. Wait for the Red Cross ambulance (21-5818). Make no statements on the cause of the accident except to the official or a representative of the National Insurance Institute (INS).

Make a sketch of the area and the positions of the vehicles before and after the accident. Make note of the principal characteristics of the other vehicles involved, as well as the damage to your car and others. Avoid further damage by staying with your car. You must report the accident to the local municipality or Tribunal de Tránsito within 8 days. A copy of this report must be presented to the INS, along with your drivers' license, insurance policy, police report and information about injuries and witnesses (23-5800, 23-3446, a 7, c 9/11).

Foreign **insurance** policies are not effective in court and only the INS can provide local service for defense or adjustment of claims. Insurance is included in car rental fees.

Road trouble: If you have a rented car, call the rental agency first in all cases, and they will tell you what to do.

If you are driving your own car, by law you should have fluorescent triangles to place on the road in case of road trouble as a warning to other vehicles. Probably the best service to call in case of trouble with your own car is Coopetaxi Garage (35-9966). Some operators understand English.

Do not abandon your car, if you can possibly avoid it. If you don't speak Spanish well, have someone explain your location in Spanish when you make the telephone call. If a wrecker is needed, it can be called by Coopetaxi radios.

Telephones: Pay telephones are frustrating to use. They take ¢5, ¢10, and ¢20 coins, so bring a stack of them. Put a coin in the groove at the top of the box. Pick up the receiver and dial. The phone starts to beep. When the person answers, the call is sometimes cut off. Go to another phone. This one probably has a long line of people waiting in front of it. They already know that the phone you tried to use is *malo*. When you finally get through, be prepared for a second series of beeps after a few minutes. These mean that you are about to be cut off. Drop in another coin if you still want to talk. It's wise to tell the person you're calling the number of your pay phone so they can call you back and you can talk uninterruptedly. The number is often above the phone on a yellow sign. Good luck.

In rural areas, like Puerto Viejo or Monteverde, hotels and *pulperías* have phones to call out on. They do the dialing and charge you for the length of time you speak.

International calls: There are three public phones on which you can make collect or credit card calls directly to North America: at Juan Santamaría Airport, in the Hotel Aurola lobby (c 5, a 5), and at Radiográfica (c 1, a 5). No coins are needed. Just pick up the phone and give the operator the number.

If you have access to a private phone, direct dialing is easy from Costa Rica. The telephone directory has a list of codes for various countries. To dial the US or Canada directly, for example, dial 001 first, then the area code and number. To call person-to-person or collect, dial 09 first, then the country code, area code, and number. For international information, dial 124. If you don't have access to a phone, go to Radiográfica, c 1, a 5, open 7 am to 10 pm.

Radiográfica also offers **telex** and **fax** services. You can send or have faxes sent to you at their number: (506) 23-1609. Call them at 87-0513 or 87-0511 to check if you have received a fax, or have your correspondent include the number of your hotel, and Radiográfica will notify you.

Mail: The main Post Office (Correo Central) is located on c 2, a 1/3. Mail letters from a post office. There are hardly any mailboxes on the streets, and they are seldom used.

Beware of having anything other than letters and magazines sent to you in Costa Rica. A high duty is charged on all items arriving by mail, in an attempt to keep foreign merchandise from entering illegally. Receiving packages can mean two trips to the Aduana in Zapote, a suburb of San José. The first trip is to unwrap and declare what you have received. The second one, 3 to 5 days later, is to pay a customs charge on every item in the package before you can take it home. Photographs can be received duty-free if just a few are sent at a time. Individually-sent cassette tapes can also make it through. Usually anything that fits in a regular-sized or magazine-sized envelope will arrive duty-free. But you will have to pay outrageous fees for a box of blank checkbooks, or the cookies Grandma sends to remind you she cares--in short, beg your loved ones not to send you anything. If you don't pay, the package will be sent back, but you wouldn't want to hurt Grandma's feelings, would you?

You can send most things from Costa Rica to North America or Europe with no problem, although postal rates for packages are pretty expensive. Mail packages from the entrance to the far left of the main entrance as you face the Post Office. Surface mail *(marítimo)* is somewhat cheaper than *correo aéreo* (airmail), and takes 4 to 6 weeks to arrive.

There is a General Delivery service *(Lista de Correos)*. If you are planning to stay in Costa Rica for awhile, rent a post office box *(apartado)* or have your mail sent to a friend's box. It is much more common for people to have post office boxes here than elsewhere, because delivery to an *apartado* is quicker and more secure than home delivery.

Carry your passport: Never, never go anywhere (not even to the post office) without your passport or tourist card. The huge influx of foreigners makes it necessary for immigration officials to perform routine identification checks. They can walk up to you anywhere (they might even knock on your hotel room door) or at anytime (they might greet you walking down the street at 11pm). They will courteously ask you to present your identification, including tourist card or visa. Not having it with you could mean unnecessary trouble.

Bombetas: If you hear two very loud explosions in rapid succession, don't run for cover--that's just the Tico way of celebrating momentous occasions. Usually the fireworks are from the neighborhood church which is celebrating a Saint's Day, or are to announce events at a town fiesta *(turno)*. In the case of a turno, the bombetas usually begin at dawn and are fired off at regular intervals during the day, usually ending around 9 or 10pm. Sounding all the sirens in town is another way of expressing joy, as when the Pope or Tico astronaut Franklin Chang Diaz arrived in San José.

Avoid theft: So far, San José is much safer than most other cities, except for theft. The zippered compartments of backpacks are excellent targets in the area around the Coca Cola. It's best not to wear them on your back downtown. Don't carry a lot of packages at once. Purses should be zippered and have short shoulder straps so that you can protect them with your upper arm. Wallets and passports should not be carried in your back pocket, and expensive watches, chains and jewelry should not be worn. If on a bus or in a crowd you feel yourself being jostled or pinched between several people at once, don't just be polite. Protect your purse or wallet and elbow your way out of the situation immediately. Don't leave tents or cars unguarded anywhere. Don't leave cameras or binoculars in sight of an open window, even a louvered one. A pole can be stuck in and they can be fished out. If you follow these precautions, you probably won't have any trouble.

Notes for women: Even if you consider yourself a little on the chunky side in other cultures, you'll have plenty of admirers here. Ticos like to *piropear* (make flirtatious compliments to) women, especially unaccompanied ones. As you walk down the street, they will direct little comments at you, like *guapa* (pretty), *machita* (if you are blond), *mi amor* (my love) or will just lean toward you with a meaningful *adiós*. If they are farther away from you, they hiss as you pass. This can be quite tiresome, but they mean no harm and there's not much you can do about it. Complete obliviousness is the best policy.

Ticos can be very compelling in their professions of eternal devotion. Whether they're married or not doesn't seem to have much to do with it. Real romantic relationships and friendships usually take a long time to develop in Costa Rica, so take anything that is too rash with a large grain of salt. Foreign women are regarded as loose and easy game *(conquistas)* by Latin men, but their hearts belong to *la Virgen Purísima*. Don't become another notch on another *gringa*-chaser's gun. If you act like a lady, most Tico men will respect you.

Notes for men: Costa Rican women are sought out by foreign men because of their loveliness and their reputation for being *chineadoras,* i.e., able and willing to take care of men as if they were babies. Many men, frustrated from trying to "deal with" more assertive women back home, dream of a pretty Tica wife who won't give them any problems. These dreams may come true for awhile, until deeply ingrained cultural differences arise, causing major communication problems which can lead to *gringos* being taken to the cleaners in divorce courts. Of course there are many successful inter-cultural marriages as well. This is just a warning that, as in any aspect of life, you cannot leave an unresolved problem behind and expect it not to resurface in another form elsewhere.

Prostitution is legal in Costa Rica, and the women are given medical tests on a regular basis. Some prostitutes however have been found to be carrying AIDS. Others have been known to gang up on men in the street and rob them. Recently, there have been various cases of men being drugged and robbed after having invited women to their apartment or room. Be careful, guys.

Student Travel: OTEC is Costa Rica's student travel agency, affiliated with the International Youth Hostel Federation. If you are under 26 years old or have a student or teacher ID card, you can become a member for ¢1000 and a photo. Affiliated youth hostels exist in San José, Rincón de la Vieja National Park and Guayabo National Monument. An OTEC membership can get you discounts on international flights, and at stores, restaurants and hotels in Costa Rica. OTEC is on a 3, c 3/5, 22-0866. The Toruma youth hostel coordinates low-cost trips to other hostels in the country (a ctl, c 29/31, 24-4085).

You can get a 40% discount on PanAm flights to Costa Rica with an International Student Card (all those under 26 are eligible for an International Youth Card, and teachers can apply for a Teacher Card which qualifies them for discounts as well). To apply for a card ($14) in North America, request a free Student Travel Catalog from the Council on International Educational Exchange (CIEE, 205 E. 42nd St., New York, NY 10017, (212) 661-1414). The catalog has an application form. With card in hand, one can purchase the discounted PanAm ticket only through a student travel agency. Council Travel is a chain of US student travel agencies affiliated with CIEE: a list of locations can be requested at the above address. Travel Cuts is a Canadian student travel agency. Their headquarters are at 187 College St., Toronto, Ontario, (416) 979-2406. Student/Teacher/Youth ID Cards are also available at student travel agencies.

Water: Water is safe to drink in San José. Bottled water is recommended in the suburbs of Escazú and Santa Ana, in Puntarenas and Limón. *Soda blanca* is the term to use when asking for soda water. Orvian has recently started producing non-carbonated mineral water here, but it is not well-distributed yet. Call Aguas Minerales de Costa Rica (42-1539) for more information.

Laundry: Laundromats are uncommon in Costa Rica because most people have maids or relatives who do their laundry for them. Many hotels have laundry services. Most cheaper hotels have large sinks *(pilas)* where you can wash your own clothes, or they can connect you with a lady who will wash for you for about $1 an hour. There are many *lavanderías* (non-self-service laundries) in San José, but they are quite expensive. Recently some self-service laundromats have opened up--**Lava Más** in Los Yoses, next to Spoon (25-1645), and **Betamatic** behind Burger King (34-0993) where it costs about $3.50 to wash and dry one load of clothes.

Health Care: The following hospitals have emergency medical, X-ray, laboratory and pharmacy services available to foreigners: Clínica Bíblica (a 14, c ctl/1, 23-6422), Clínica Católica (Guadalupe, 25-9095), Clínica Santa Rita (specializes in maternity care, a 8, c 15/17, 21-6433).

According to a United Nations study, Costa Rica holds first place in Latin America for development of preventive and curative medicine. It is ranked near the United States and Canada among the 20 best health systems in the world. Many Costa Rican doctors have been trained in Europe and the United States, and the University of Costa Rica Medical School is considered one of the best in Latin America.

The Social Security system makes low-cost medical care available to those who need it, but doctors also have their private practices in the afternoons. A gynecological exam including papsmear costs around $15; a sonogram costs about $25; a complete cardiac stress exam runs about $45. Dental care is also considerably less expensive here than elsewhere. All the above services are available to foreigners.

Facelifts and other plastic surgery cost a fraction of what they do elsewhere, and post-operative care is also a lot cheaper.

Countdown to Recovery has a Costa Rican branch for outpatient treatment of alcohol or addiction (Apdo. 5043, 1000 San José, (506) 31-0618) as does the Florida-based **Polestar,** 29-1094, (305) 669-1888, fax: (305) 669-1777, see p. 140.

The low cost of health care and labor make full-service custodial care of the elderly less expensive. **Golden Valley Hacienda** offers specialized care for Alzheimer's patients, and **Villa Confort Geriatric Hotel** provides a comfortable atmosphere for the elderly who just need help in everyday living.

Both are in converted homes near Alajuela, about 20 minutes from San José. Monthly cost ($1500) includes round-the-clock care, meals, two visits a week from a geriatrician, laundry and basic medicines (43-8191, 43-8575, fax: (506) 24-3821).

Amoebas, etc.: Even though Costa Rica's water is good in most places, visitors traveling in the provinces sometimes get intestinal problems. If they are persistent, they might be due to *amibas* or *giardia*. If you get a strong attack of diarrhea, it's wise to take a stool sample to a local lab to have it analyzed. Put it in a clean glass jar, and deliver it immediately. Amoebas can't be found in samples that are a few hours old. The Clínica Bíblica lab is open weekends and holidays (23-6422). Clínica Americana, 22-1010, has a good lab, and Dr. Gil Grunhaus, across from Hospital San Juan de Dios, 22-9516, gives the most complete reports. Your results will be ready the same day, especially if you bring your sample before noon ($4 in advance). If results are negative, take up to three samples. Sometimes the offending organisms are not found the first time. The most dangerous one is *entamoeba histolytica*. This can migrate to your liver and cause damage later.

It is not necessary to go to a doctor unless you want to. A pharmacist can give you the needed drug based on your lab results. We have not found that natural methods cure amoebas. Even if you get over your diarrhea, the organisms can still be doing damage to your system unless you've taken medicine. This often shows up in a tendency towards constipation and a feeling of depression and low energy. It's best to take the chemicals and be done with the bugs. Be sure and ask for the literature that goes with the medicine so you'll know about possible side effects. To avoid bugs when traveling outside San Jose, avoid drinks made with local water or ice, and avoid fruits and vegetables which cannot be peeled.

Insects: Mosquitos can be a problem even in breezy San José at night during the dry season. Anti-mosquito spirals can be bought at supermarkets and *pulperías* for about $.40 a box. Smaller stores will often sell you just a pair for about $.12. Be sure to ask for the little metal stand *(soporte)* that goes with them. Light up the spiral and circle it several times over your bed, then put it as far away from your bed as possible, or even outside the window or door. They usually work pretty well.

If you have been on the Atlantic coast, beware of sandfly bites that seem to become infected and grow instead of disappearing. This could be a sign of *papalomoyo,* (Leishmaniasis) a disease that can be life-threatening if untreated. See a tropical disease specialist immediately.

Purrujas are perhaps the most aggravating of Costa Rican insects. They bite you without your even seeing or feeling them, then they itch for days. They seem to hang out at the edge of the beach where the sand meets the trees. They also seem to be more active at dusk. Bring sulphur powder from home to sprinkle on your socks to discourage them. That means you should wear shoes and socks on the beach for your sunset walk. Dusk is generally the time when you have to apply insect repellent too.

Africanized **bees** have been working their way north from Brazil, and can attack humans with fatal results if their nests are disturbed. It is wise to be aware of this when exploring hot, dry areas, where bee colonies are ten times denser than in rainforests. If attacked, run as fast as you can in a zigzag direction, or jump into water. Bees don't see well over distances. Never try to take cover; don't crawl or climb into a precarious position from which you cannot make a quick exit. Throw something light-colored over your head to protect your eyes and nose; keep your mouth closed. If you know you are allergic to bee stings, talk with your doctor before you come and carry the proper medication with you. For more detailed information, contact the OTS, 40-6696.

Some people have serious allergic reactions to **ant** bites. They might begin to itch all over, then turn red and swell up. Get them to a hospital as soon as possible. To avoid getting ant bites, wear closed shoes whenever you're in the jungle or on the beach.

Snakes: If you want to be able to recognize a poisonous snake if you run across it in the wilds, visit the **Serpentorium** on a 1, c 9/11 (2nd floor, open 10am-7pm daily, $1 entrance fee). Live native poisonous and non-poisonous frogs, snakes and reptiles are on exhibit there, as well as foreign snakes, such as the black cobra and a 19-foot python. At first we thought that the reptiles were very realistic plastic replicas, because they move so little, but after awhile we'd see that their positions had changed slightly, so they must be alive.

BEACH SAFETY--HOW TO HANDLE RIP CURRENTS

Each year, hundreds of ocean bathers suffer serious near-drownings or death due to their ignorance about rip currents, a phenomenon found on wave-swept beaches all over the world--including Costa Rica. Ironically, they can be fun if properly understood--yet they are responsible for 80 percent of ocean drownings, or four out of five.

A rip current is a surplus of water put ashore by waves, that finds a channel to drain and reach equilibrium. All rip currents have three parts: the feeder current, the neck, and the head. The feeder current is water moving parallel to the beach. You know you're in one when you notice, after a few minutes, that your friends on the beach have moved down 30 to 50 yards, yet you thought you were standing still.

At a depression in the ocean floor, the water turns out to sea. This can occur in knee- to waist-deep water, where the "neck" begins. The neck, which is very swift, can carry a swimmer out to sea at three to six miles per hour, faster than a strong swimmer's rate of two to four miles per hour. It's like being in a river, and can move a person 100 yards in just a moment. It is typical to experience panic when caught in the neck, and it is here that most drownings occur.

The rip current loses its strength just beyond the breakers, dissipating its energy and eventually delivering the swimmer to relatively calm waters. This area, known as the "head", may appear to have a mushroom shape from the air, as debris picked up by the current is dissipated.

Here, the water is deep, but calm. The swimmer can get back to shore by moving parallel to the beach in the direction of the bend of the current, and then back to shore at a 45-degree angle rather than straight in, to avoid getting caught in the feeder current again. (See diagram, next page).

As a safety precaution, before you enter the ocean, throw a buoyant object like a coconut or a stick into the water and watch where the current carries it, for this is the direction you will have to go in before you can get back to shore. There is definitely one direction that is better than the other.

The weak swimmer should call for help as soon as he notices that a current is moving him and making it difficult for him to walk in towards land. Most drowning victims are caught in water just above waist level.

BIRDSEYE VIEW OF A RIP CURRENT

When a person realizes he can't walk directly in, he should turn and walk sideways, leaping towards the beach with every wave, to let the water "push" him towards shore.

Once a person is no longer touching bottom and in a rip, he should not fight against the current in a vain effort to get back to shore, for this is like "swimming up a river" and will sap his strength.

Floating conserves energy. The human body is buoyant, even more so in salt water. Everyone should learn to float, because every minute that you can salvage gives someone the opportunity to make a rescue.

There is a crashing surf that can throw you off balance. One of the signals of someone who's in danger is one who turns his back to the crashing surf. Once off balance, a swimmer is unable to get traction on the ocean floor and can be dragged out four or five feet into deeper water with each swell. After a few swells he may be in over his head, and it becomes even more important to float--arching his back, head back, nose pointing in the air.

If water gets into the lungs of the person in trouble, he sinks out of sight, feeding the myth of a fearsome "whirlpool" that pulls one down.

There are four different types of rip currents: permanent, fixed, flash, and traveling.

75

Permanent rips occur at river mouths, estuaries, or by small streams, and can be quite wide. They also occur at finger jetties designed to prevent beach erosion, where the water's lateral drift is forced to turn seaward. Fixed, flash, and traveling rips are caused by wind-generated waves.

Fixed currents, which appear only on long, sandy, surf-swept beaches, can move up or down the beach depending on shifts in the ocean floor, but they are generally stable in one spot, staying there for hours to a day.

Flash or temporary rips are created when an increased volume of water is brought to shore from sudden wave build-ups. These currents can occur on a warm, sunny day, generated by storms whose waves do not lose their energy until they crash on a distant shore. The excess water build-up has no opportunity to drain and reach equilibrium while the unusually large and fast waves are coming in; a flash rip current therefore forms during a lull in wave action.

A traveling rip current is just what the name implies. You'll see it in front of you, and in five minutes it may move 15 yards up or down the beach. They can move 30 yards in a minute. They occur on long, sandy beaches where there are no fixed depressions on the ocean floor.

Some beaches, such as Espadilla at Manuel Antonio, or Jacó, are known to have rip currents and must be approached with caution at all times. The currents can be spotted by the trained eye as a brownish discoloration on the surface caused by sand and debris, or there can be a flattening effect as the water rushes out to sea, making it appear deceptively smooth.

Rip currents are not dangerous to people who understand them. The more you know about the ocean, the more fun they can be. Surfers use the rip currents as an energy saver since they provide "a free ride out" to sea just beyond the breakers.

Good swimmers are encouraged to seek out rip currents under controlled conditions and with experienced trainers. As long as you swim in the ocean, you might be caught in one, and it's critical that you know how to get out.

Following are some rip current rules of thumb:
° Weak swimmers should avoid surf-swept beaches and swim instead at safer beaches like the 3rd beach at Manuel Antonio.
° Inexperienced swimmers should not swim alone.
° Always be prepared to signal for help at the earliest sign of trouble.

For more information, contact the Costa Rican Lifesaving Association at 77-0345 in Quepos.

FISHING
By Jerry Ruhlow

With two oceans, beautiful freshwater lakes and endless miles of magnificent rivers--all only a few hours' drive or minutes by air from the capital city of San José--Costa Rica offers fishermen some of the most fantastic and diverse sportfishing in the world.

For the freshwater angler, Lake Arenal and many of the rivers provide outstanding action on rainbow bass *(guapote)*, beautiful, fine-eating fish that may run eight pounds or more and are fished just as you would largemouth bass. See p. 175-7 for a description of places to stay in the Arenal area.

There are rainbow trout in the mountain rivers, and a range of such exotic species as the *machaca, bobo, mojarra* and *vieja* to be found in lower elevation waters.

But Costa Rica's greatest claim to fame is the incredible deepsea fishing for billfish and other gamesters on the Pacific Coast, and what is without doubt the world's finest tarpon and snook angling on the Caribbean.

Interest in Costa Rica sportfishing has increased dramatically in recent years, resulting in a tremendous expansion of the sportfishing industry, with new areas opening, improved and expanded facilities, and the introduction of world-class boats and equipment.

Pacific Coast anglers routinely catch and release 500 or more marlin during the peak season from January through August. The Costa Rican Amateur Fishing Club's annual International Sailfish Tournament posts the highest catch-per-angler record of any billfish competition in the world. Raising 10 to 20 sails a day is considered pretty ho-hum fishing in Costa Rica, and 20 to 30 a day isn't at all unusual. While both marlin and sails are around all year, heavy winds in Guanacaste hamper fishermen in January and February, and sometimes well into April. During the windy months, the action centers farther south, where the shoreline configuration offers protection. That's when boats out of Quepos post their best scores.

Billfish are certainly the major attraction on the Pacific Coast, but there is also world-class angling for wahoo, jack

77

crevalle, mackerel, roosterfish, *corvina*, Pacific dogtooth snapper, rainbow and blue runners and a host of other species. It's a rare day when fishermen on the Pacific side don't tie into dorado in the 30-pound-and-up class, and tuna are nearly always abundant.

Quepos-based **Sportfishing Costa Rica** offers year round trips out of all three primary west coast fishing areas: Flamingo in Guanacaste, Quepos on the central coast, Drake Bay and Caño Island to the south. **Costa Rican Dreams** fishes out of the latter two ports, while **Tom Bradwell** operates out of Flamingo and Quepos. The major center of west coast fishing, however, is still the northern province of Guanacaste where **Bahía Pez Vela, Flamingo Bay Pacific Charters, Ocotal** and **Papagayo Excursions** all have added new, modern boats to their fleets. **Pesca Bahia Garza** and **Guanamar** are based at luxury hotels on the isolated Pacific side of the Nicoya Peninsula, where they enjoy better fishing during the winter months because they are protected from the fierce winds on the Bahía Papagayo. Additional boats operate at **Tango Mar**, just inside the gulf of Nicoya, and **Oasis del Pacífico** further north near the Puntarenas ferry landing.

For information, reservations, or free brochures, contact the following operators on the Pacific Coast:

Sportfishing Costa Rica: At Quepos, 37-8312, fax: (506) 38-4434.

Costa Rican Dreams: 39-3387, 77-0593, fax: (506) 39-3383. Out of Quepos.

Oasis del Pacífico: Across the Gulf of Nicoya via ferry from Puntarenas, Apdo. 200, Puntarenas, CR, (506) 61-1555.

Hotel Flor de Itabo: Near Playa del Coco, 67-0111, 67-0292, fax: (506) 67-0003.

Hotel Ocotal: Near Playa del Coco. Apdo. 1013, San José 1002, CR, (506) 22-4259, 67-0230.

Bahía Pez Vela: Near Ocotal, 21-3594, 21-1586, 67-0129.

Flamingo Bay Pacific Charters: At Flamingo Beach. (305) 765-1995, 467-0532. Outside FL (800) 654-8006. In CR, (506) 34-0906.

Flamingo Beach Resort: (506) 68-0976.

Tom Bradwell: Based at Flamingo Beach and Quepos. Apdo. 109, Santa Cruz, Guanacaste, CR, (506) 68-0942.

Papagayo Excursions: At Tamarindo Beach, ph/fax (506) 68-0859, 68-0652, 32-6854.

Pesca Bahía Garza: At Punta Guiones de Garza, near Nosara, 68-0784.

Guanamar: 39-4433, 39-4544, fax: (506) 39-2405

Tango Mar: Near Tambor on the Nicoya Peninsula, 61-2798, 23-1864, fax: (506) 55-2697.

Diving Safaris: c/o Hotel Ocotal, Apdo. 1013, San José 1002, (506) 67-0230. Offers dive trips, rentals and instruction at Hotel Ocotal.

Caribbean Coast: If you have never battled a tarpon, you have a surprise and perhaps a shock in store. When those silver rockets, weighing an average of 80 pounds each, take to the air, jumping and twisting and turning and tumbling, and then running halfway to hell and back, only to start jumping again... well, all I can say is, "try it."

You fish the tarpon from 16-foot outboards, and much of the action is in quiet jungle rivers and lagoons where you're likely to see bands of monkeys in the trees overhead, alligators basking along the shoreline and a host of brilliantly-plumed birds flitting through orchid-draped tropical growth.

While I have caught tarpon every month of the year in Costa Rica, the peak season is considered to be from January through May. However, June through October frequently produces outstanding action as well, and it just doesn't get much better than it was last August and September.

Like tarpon, snook can be taken year around, with 17 to 25 pounders common and a generous share of big fish (including the IGFA all-tackle world record) coming from the area. Peak season for big fish is usually late August into November. From late November through January, the area enjoys a run of smaller snook (known locally as *calba),* that average about five pounds and pour into the river in huge numbers. Catches of 20 or 30 a day are not unusual.

In addition to the tarpon and snook, Caribbean coastal waters abound in mackerel, jack crevalle, saltwater catfish, sharks, grouper, snapper and more, while exotic freshwater species provide great light tackle action up river and in the lagoons.

Five lodges provide accommodations, boats and guides for visiting anglers. For information and free brochures, contact:

Casamar: (506) 43-8834, fax: (506) 43-9287.

Río Colorado: (506) 32-8610, fax: 31-5987. In USA call 1-800-243-9777, fax: (813) 933-3280.

Parismina Tarpon Rancho: Ph/fax: (506) 35-7766.
Tortuga Lodge: (506) 57-0766, fax: (506) 57-1665
Isla de Pesca: (506) 23-4560, fax: (506) 21-5148.

Fresh water fishing permits can be obtained from the Information Dept. at the Banco Nacional de Costa Rica, located behind the Central Post Office (a 1, c 2/4, open 9am-3pm weekdays). Permits cost about $10 and must be presented with your passport if you encounter wildlife rangers at your fishing site. The same permits are good for fishing from the beach or at river mouths. Deepsea fishing permits will be taken care of by your fishing guide.

Fishing equipment and tide tables are sold at La Casa del Pescador (c 2, a 18/20) and Deportes Keko (c 20, a 4/6). They can also give you good advice on which lures to use.

SPORTS

Soccer: Costa Ricans are very sports-minded. There isn't a district, town or city where *fútbol* (soccer) isn't played. It's said that Costa Ricans learn to kick a ball before they learn to walk! There are teams all over the country in every imaginable category including all ages and both sexes, although only men play on the major teams. In June, 1990, a Costa Rican team competed in the World Cup for the first time. All government employees were given time off to watch the games, and the streets of San José became a huge fiesta when they won.

Tennis: Among the most important international tennis matches here is the World Friendship Tournament at the Cariari Country Club in March and April. The Costa Rica Country Club hosts the Coffee Cup Tournament. Los Reyes Country Club (La Guácima), the Costa Rica Tennis Club (Sabana Sur), Cariari and La Sabana courts offer programs for learning and practicing tennis. Most beach and mountain hotels have tennis courts.

Golf: The Costa Rica Country Club in Escazú and the Los Reyes Country Club in La Guácima, Alajuela each have nine holes and professionals to teach the game. The only 18-hole golf course in the country is at the Cariari Country Club. Cariari hosts the Friendship Golf Tourney and the American Professional Golf Tourney which attract PGA professionals. Cariari rents equipment and provides pros for golf lessons. Tango Mar

Surf and Saddle Club, on the Gulf of Nicoya near Tambor, also has a 9-hole golf course.

Gyms: There are plenty of gymnasiums in the San Jose area, which you can use for $12 to $25 per month. Look for them in the telephone directory under "Gimnasios". The deluxe hotels in San José all have gyms.

Running: There are many marathons throughout the year, including the one sponsored by the University for Peace each April. The Hash House Harriers, a world-wide organization devoted to running and beer-drinking, also meets here once a week. Call Bill Barbee at 28-0769 for info.

Horses: The **Portón del Tajo** at Hotel Cariari offers riding and jumping lessons, dressage and trail riding (39-2248). International horse riding competitions are held each year at **Club Hípico La Caraña** in Río Oro de Santa Ana, west of San José (28-6106, 28-6754). **Club Paso Fino** in Santa Ana specializes in purebred Paso Fino horses and gives instruction in the techniques needed to ride this special breed. Horse lovers can also stay at the Club, which is decorated with riding memorabilia and offers creative gourmet meals (49-1466).

Most beach and mountain resorts rent horses.

Whitewater sports: Rafters, canoers and kayakers are beginning to flock to Costa Rica because of its exciting rivers. The Río Pacuare, considered world-class by sportspeople, is threatened with being dammed for a huge hydroelectric project. **Ríos Tropicales** (33-6455), **Costa Rica Expeditions** (22-0333), and **Aventuras Naturales** (25-3939) will take you on one- to three-day rafting trips, with challenges graded to your level of skill and experience. The one-day trip is $69 including transportation, lunch and expert guides. Ríos Tropicales also offers sea-kayaking trips. **Rancho Leona** takes beginners on river kayaking trips down the Río Puerto Viejo in Sarapiquí (71-6312).

Surfing: Costa Rica has become famous for its great waves. The Pacific, with its long point breaks, river mouths and beach breaks keeps surfers busy from late March to late November. If they want to get serious, they go to the Atlantic from December through March, where waves from deep water break over the shallow reef, creating the perfect imitation of Hawaiian surf.

The nearest surfing beach to San José is **Boca Barranca**, between Puntarenas and Puerto Caldera, known for long waves. About a half hour to the south are **Playa Jacó** (good for beginners) and **Playa Hermosa** (not to be confused with Playa Hermosa in Guanacaste), where an international surfing contest is held each year. The whole area between Jacó and **Playa Dominical** to the south has many excellent surfing spots. **Playa Pavones,** south of Golfito on the Golfo Dulce is said to have a left wave "so long you can take a nap on it". **Playas Nosara, Junquillal** and **Tamarindo** in Guanacaste have areas for surfing as well as swimming and snorkeling spots. **Playa Naranjo,** in Santa Rosa National Park, is known for **Witch Rock,** which creates tubular waves. If you don't have 4-wheel-drive you have to hike 13km with your surfboard on your back, and camp out. On the Atlantic coast, **Playa Bonita,** just north of Limón, offers waves which are very thick, powerful and dangerous. There is an international competition there each year. **Puerto Viejo,** south of Limon, is famous for "La Salsa", a challenging ride responsible for many a broken surfboard. See the Index for more information about the above beaches. Most surfers say they can't decide which coast they like best.

The **Mango Surf Shop,** 25 mts. west of the Banco Popular in San Pedro, buys and sells surfboards and accessories, as does **Tsunami** in Los Yoses. Marco Pacheco, of **Keola Surf and Ding Shop** makes and repairs surfboards, guides surfing tours, and has up-to-date wave information (25-6041, 100m. E, 100m. S Banco Popular, San Pedro, Apdo. 6280, San José, CR). There are surfboard rental shops in Puntarenas, Jacó, Manuel Antonio, Limón and Cahuita. Many car rental agencies and hotels give discounts to surfers, especially May through November.

NATIONAL PARKS, RESERVES AND WILDLIFE REFUGES

Costa Rica's 46 national parks, reserves and wildlife refuges protect jewels of the country's rich but diminishing wilderness. They occupy approximately 27% of national territory, when added to Indian reserves and forest buffer zones. Most national parks have camping facilities. Most reserves and wildlife refuges do not. Nominal fees are charged for entering the parks, as well as for camping and anchorage.

All national parks, reserves and refuges are indicated on the map of Costa Rica in the back of this book, and are described in the sections on the various regions (see index). If you need more information, call Parques Nacionales, 33-4070, 33-4246,

33-4118, fax: (506) 23-6369. If you need specialized information on scientific aspects of the parks, call the Conservation Data Center at the **Instituto Nacional de Biodiversidad**, in Santo Domingo de Heredia, just outside San José (36-4269). Ask for Rita Alfaro.

The Association of Volunteers for Service to Protected Areas helps visitors donate support services to the severely understaffed parks and reserves. Volunteers receive free transportation and lodging, but sometimes have to chip in on food. They should understand basic Spanish, and provide two letters of reference from organizations abroad or individuals in Costa Rica. Contact Stanley Arguedas at Parques Nacionales (numbers above).

Warning: Although Costa Rica has been described as a "Disneyland" of ecological wonders, you must be aware that here you are dealing with Mother Nature in all her harsh reality. Five foreigners were reported missing in 1989, and only three were found.

Three German hikers were lost in unseasonal fog and rain for 11 days on Barva Volcano on the west side of Braulio Carrillo National Park. Their goal was a simple day-hike around the crater lake, but landslides blocking the trails threw them off course. Costa Rica's famous parks are victims of the country's budget deficit, and trails are not maintained with the same rigor foreigners are used to. Tropical weather itself makes trail maintenance a full-time job. The three hikers could keep each other warm and encouraged, and survived their ordeal well, but two older tourists disappeared without a trace, one on Coco Island National Park, the other in Cahuita National Park. Both were hiking or swimming alone when they disappeared. See beach safety information, pp. 74-7.

Maps: The ICT has put out a new road map which includes the locations of most national parks, reserves and wildlife refuges. Order it through the ICT offices listed on page 48, or pick one up at the ICT office under the Plaza de la Cultura. ITMB Publishing also puts out an excellent map (736A Granville St., Vancouver, BC, V6Z 1G3 Canada, fax: (604) 687-5925).

Even with a map, it's best to call a hotel at or near your destination and ask about current road conditions and travel times. Hotels will also have current bus schedules.

Topographical maps can be purchased at Librería Lehmann (c 3, a ctl/1), Librería Universal (a ctl, c ctl/1), or the Instituto Geográfico Nacional (a 20, c 5/7). Ask for *mapas cartográficos.* You'll be shown a little map of Costa Rica divided up into 20 x 30 km. sections. Indicate which one you want. Maps show roads, trails, water sources including rapids, and contours at every 20 meters. They cost ¢125 a section.

Small yellow posts mark the distance in kilometers from San José on Costa Rica's highways.

You can buy **camping, snorkeling and kayaking equipment** at several stores. Probably the best equipped is the Centro de Aventuras on Paseo Colón between c 22/24. They also buy and sell used camping, rafting and kayaking gear. Other camping stores are Aro (a 8, c 11/13), and El Palacio del Deporte (c 2, a 2/4).

FRUITS AND VEGETABLES

The abundance of fresh, delicious fruits and vegetables in Costa Rica is amazing. You can get an idea of it by elbowing your way through the **Mercado Borbón** (c 8, a 3/5), a two-level circus of fruit and vegetable vendors in a rough-and-tumble part of town. Or you can go to any of the Saturday morning *ferias del agricultor,* where streets are shut off and truck farmers bring their fresh produce to the neighborhoods. In San José the Saturday morning market is west of Plaza Víquez (c 7/9, a 16/20). There you will find fresh homemade wholewheat bread and pastries, eggs, chickens, fish, cheese, and honey, as well as every imaginable fruit and vegetable. Bring your own shopping bags.

Unfortunately, pesticide use is still unregulated in Costa Rica, and most farmers are not aware of organic gardening. However, a small group of farmers from the Cartago area is experimenting with organic methods. You can buy their beautiful, fresh organic produce at **Club Vida Natural**, 100 m south of Restaurant La Nueva China in San Pedro. Call 24-8713 or 73-6079 for more info.

Here are some tips on how to identify and choose the best produce:

A ripe **papaya** will always be slightly soft, but a too-soft papaya is to be avoided. It is customary for papaya vendors to cut a triangular piece out of the papaya to show you its color. Some people are fans of the rounder *amarilla* or yellow-orange papaya. Others will swear that only the more elongated and red-orange *cacho* papaya is worthy of the name. You don't have to buy a papaya just because the vendor cut a piece out of it for you. At least Ticos don't. Just make sure you feel it first.

Mangos should be slightly soft and red and yellow in color, without any brown or mushy spots. By far the most delicious are the large *mangas,* given feminine gender because of their voluptuous size. The neatest way to eat mangas is to slice them close around the flat oval seed to get two meaty halves. With the skin-side down, score each piece into one inch divisions without cutting through the skin. Now gently turn each half inside out, and you will have a bunch of delicious bite-sized pieces offering themselves to you (see diagram).

Ticos love to eat green mangoes sliced and sprinkled with lemon and salt. Some people get a rash or irritation around their lips from eating mangos. This can be avoided by cutting off the part of the fruit nearest the stem, as the irritation is caused by the sap.

Ticos judge the ripeness of a pineapple by giving it a slap. A good **piña** should sound firm and compact. The yellow pineapple is best for eating. The white pineapple is more acid and is used in cooking and to tenderize meats. It produces a hollow sound. A green color on the outside does not necessarily reflect unripeness. You should be able to easily pluck a leaf from the top of a ripe piña.

Watermelons are also considered sweeter if they produce a firm rather than a hollow sound. The best watermelons come from the hot coastal zones. One of the nicest parts of driving to Puntarenas is stopping at the fruit stands in Esparza for a delicious **sandía**.

Don't make the mistake of a friend of ours who, on a hot San José afternoon, came home with what he thought was a delicious, red, juicy watermelon. "And what a bargain!" he said as he thirstily cut into the **chiverre**, only to find a mass of whitish spaghetti-like pulp. Chiverre looks just like a watermelon from the outside. You'll see them sold on the roadsides during Semana Santa. Their pulp is candied with *tapa dulce* to make special Easter treats.

Cantaloupe, **melón** in Costa Rica, is also judged for sweetness by its firm sound, but a fragrant smell is the best indication of a fully ripe melón.

Blackberries are called **mora** and are used mainly in *refrescos* and ice cream. You have to liquefy moras in a blender and then strain and add sugar and water to the sour juice.

Four types of **limones** (lemons) grow here. The seedless *verdelio* is rare. The *criollo* is small, juicy and greener. The *bencino* is more the size of a North American lemon but is green and has much less juice than the criollo. The *limón mandarina* looks like a bumpy tangerine, and is very sour and juicy. It's good for making lemonade.

Guayabas (guavas) are plentiful in Costa Rica from September through November. Their pink fruit is used for jam or guava paste.

Cas is a little round fruit similar to the guayaba whose tart tropical flavor is popular in *refrescos* and sherbets. Try the *nieve de cas* at Pop's.

Tamarindo is a tart and sweet *refresco* made from the seed pod of the tamarind tree. You will see the orange-sized balls of brown tamarindo seeds and pulp at the markets. The seeds are put in hot water so the sticky tamarindo washes off. Then sugar and cold water are added. The resulting light brown *refresco* is somewhat similar in flavor to apple juice.

Granadillas (passion fruit) are yellowish-red and slightly larger than an egg. They have a crisp but easily-broken shell.

Inside are little edible seeds surrounded by a delicious, delicately-flavored fruit which is first slurped and then chewed.

Mamones are little green spheres which you can break open with your fingers or teeth, to expose a large seed covered with a layer of fruit which tastes like a peeled grape.

Mamón chino is the mamon's exotic cousin, sporting a red shell with soft spines growing all over it. It resembles a fat, round, red caterpillar and has an even larger delicious grapelike fruit inside its outrageous shell.

When you slice a yellow **carambola**, the pieces look like five-pointed stars. It makes a delicious *refresco*.

Mamón chino and carambola

Marañón is an unusual fruit. Its seed, the cashew nut, grows on top of it in a thick, rubbery shell. Don't try to bite open the shell; it's very bitter. Cashews must be roasted before they can be eaten; they are poisonous when raw. If you take the train to Puntarenas, people will try to sell you home-roasted cashews. The ripe fruit can be eaten or made into a *refresco* or fermented into wine. The dried fruit is like a cross between a prune and a fig and is sold in supermarkets. You can make a quick and elegant dessert with half a dried marañón topped with a dollop of cream cheese and a cashew.

Avocados are called **aguacates.** They are usually a little less buttery and flavorful than their North American counterparts. They are soft when ripe, but if bought green can be left inside a paper bag to ripen.

Zapotes look like big brown avocadoes, and their texture is avocado-like, but their pulp is bright red-orange and sweet. Some places make zapote ice cream.

87

Fresh coconut meat (**coco**) can be found at fruit stands downtown. *Pipas* or green coconuts are popular with Ticos on hot days at the beach. They are sold whole, with a straw stuck through a hole in the outer shell so that the coconut water can be drunk.

The best way to get coconut meat out of its shell is to hack it open with a machete or a hammer and then heat the shells on top of the stove in a pan. This makes the meat shrink a little bit so that it is easier to remove.

Pejibaye, a relative of the coconut, is one of Costa Rica's most unusual treats. Pejibayes grow in clusters on palm trees, like miniature coconuts. The part that you eat would correspond to the fibrous husk, while the hard pejibaye seed, when cracked open, reveals a thin layer of bitter white meat around a hollow core. The bright orange or red pejibayes are delicious boiled in salted water, then peeled, halved and pitted and eaten alone or with mayonnaise. You'll see them sold on San José streets year-round. Their flavor is difficult to describe. They are not sweet, but more a combination of chestnut and pumpkin with a thick, fibrous texture. You can buy a *racimo* (bunch) of raw pejibayes at the Mercado Borbón and boil them up for parties, or you can buy them in the supermarkets peeled and canned to take home as souvenirs.

Pejibaye

Palmito (palm heart) is another delicacy worth trying. It is sold raw in the supermarkets or tenderly pickled in jars or bags. It is the succulent inner core of small palm trees. Even though whole trees must be cut so that you can savor palmito, the trees are cultivated as a crop, so are replaced.

As human nature would have it, the most highly prized fruits in Costa Rica are imported apples, grapes, and pears. They signify the advent of the Christmas season, and Ticos pay big prices for them.

COMIDA TIPICA (NATIVE FOOD)

Sodas are small restaurants where you can get inexpensive snacks and light meals. They line the streets of San José and fill the Mercado Central. These are some of the foods you'll run across at sodas or at the Fiesta de Maíz in La Garita (see p. 130).

arreglados: sandwiches, usually made of meat, on a tasty but greasy bun.

arroz con pollo: rice with chicken and vegetables.

cajeta de coco: delicious fudge made of coconut, *tapa dulce* and orange peel.

casado: a plate of rice, black beans, cabbage and tomato salad, meat or egg, *picadillo,* and sometimes fried plantains.

ceviche: raw seabass cured in lemon juice with *culantro* (chinese parsley) and onions. Delicious.

chorreados: corn pancakes, sometimes served with *natilla.*

cono capuchino: an ice cream cone dipped in chocolate. A Pop's delicacy.

dulce de leche: a thick syrup made of milk and sugar.

elote asado: roasted corn on the cob.

elote cocinado: boiled corn on the cob.

empanadas: corn turnovers filled with beans, cheese, or potatoes and meat.

gallos: meat, beans or cheese stuck between two tortillas.

gallo pinto: the national breakfast dish of rice and beans fried together.

guiso de maíz: fresh corn stew.

horchata: a sweet drink made of corn and cinnamon.

masamorra: corn pudding.

melcochas: candies made from raw sugar.

milanes and *tapitas:* small, foil-wrapped, pure chocolate candies, available in corner stores and restaurants all over the country. Beware: these delicious little things are addictive.

natilla: sour cream, often more liquid than northern sour cream.

olla de carne: literally "pot of meat", but actually a meat soup featuring large pieces of *chayote* (a green, pear-shaped vegetable that grows on vines), *ayote* (a pumpkin-like squash), *yuca, plátano,* etc.

palomitas de maíz: "little doves". Popcorn.

pan de maíz: a thick, sweet bread made with fresh corn.

pan bon: a dark, sweet bread with batter designs on top. A Limón specialty.

patacones: fried, mashed green plantains, served like french fries with meals on the Atlantic coast.

patí: flour-based *empanadas* filled with fruit or spicy meat, sold on the Atlantic coast.

picadillo: a side dish of fried vegetables, which often contains meat.

plátanos: plantains. They look like large bananas, but cannot be eaten raw. Sweet and delicious when fried or baked. Also sold like potato chips. A Central American staple.

queque seco: pound cake.

refrescos: cold fruit drinks. Most refrescos are made with a lot of sugar. If you order a refresco that is not made in advance, like *papaya en agua, papaya en leche,* or *jugo de zanahoria* (carrot juice), you can ask for it *sin azúcar* (without sugar) and add your own to taste. Similarly an *ensalada de frutas* (fruit salad) might come smothered in jello and ice cream. You can ask for it *sin gelatina, sin helados.*

sopa de mondongo: tripe soup.

sopa negra: soup made from bean gravy, with hard-boiled egg and vegetables added.

tacos: a bit of meat topped with cabbage and tomato salad.

tamales: cornmeal usually stuffed with pork or chicken, wrapped in banana leaves and boiled. A Christmas tradition.

tamal asado: a sweet cornmeal cake.

tamal de elote: sweet corn tamales, wrapped in corn-husks.

tapa dulce: native brown sugar, sold in a solid form that looks like an inverted flower pot. It's grated with a knife or boiled to make syrup from which is made *agua dulce,* a popular campesino drink.

torta chilena: a many-layered cake filled with *dulce de leche.*

tortas: sandwiches on a bread roll.

tortilla de queso: a large, thick tortilla with cheese mixed into the dough.

tortilla: may mean the Costa Rican thin, small, corn tortilla, but also another name for an omelette.

yuca: manioc, a thick tuber, another staple of the Central American diet. *Enyucados* are *empanadas* made from a yuca-based dough.

TIQUISMOS--HAVING FUN WITH COSTA RICAN SPANISH

Ticos are amused and delighted when foreigners try to speak Spanish, especially when they include *tiquismos*, expressions that are peculiar to Costa Rican or Central American culture.

Not only the vocabulary, but the way of using words is important. Spanish speakers use a lot of *muletillas* (fillers, literally "crutches") in their speech. They "address" the person with whom they are speaking more often than is done in English, and they do it in a way that English speakers might consider slightly offensive. It is common that women will be called *mamita, madre, mi hijita,* (little mother, mother, my little daughter, all roughly corresponding to "honey"). Latins love to use salient physical characteristics as nicknames. Common ones are *gordo* (fatty), *flaco* (skinny), *macho* or *macha* (Costa Rican for fair-skinned or fair haired), *negro* (dark-skinned), *chino* (it doesn't matter if you're Asian or just have slightly slanting eyes, your name is Chino), *gato* (blue or green eyes). You just have to be slightly *gordo* or *flaco* to merit those names. If you're really *gordo* or *flaco,* and people really like you, you get a special name like *repollito* (little cabbage) or *palito* (little stick). *Gordo* and *negro* are commonly used as terms of endearment, regardless of appearance.

Any male under thirty is usually called *maje* by his friends. This is a special Costa Rican measure of friendship, which literally means "dummy" but figuratively is more like pal or buddy. It is used widely as a *muletilla*. *Majes* have various expressions of approval such as the famous *pura vida* (great, terrific), or *tuanis* (cool), *buena nota* (groovy). *Mala nota* is ungroovy, *furris* is uncool and *salado* means "too bad for you".

91

Expressions of extreme approval are *qué bruto, qué bárbaro,* and disapproval, *qué horror,* or *fatal, maje.*

The above are the slang expressions of urban youth. However, all Ticos are aware of polite, courteous and respectful forms of speech. They make their world more pleasant by using little expressions of appreciation. For example, if someone helps you in a store or on the street, you say *"Muchas gracias, muy amable"* (Thank you very much, you are very kind), and they will say *"Con mucho gusto"* (With much pleasure).

It is customary in the morning to ask *"Como amaneció?"* (How did you wake up?) *"Muy bién, por dicha, y usted?"* (Very well, luckily, and you?) *"Muy bién, gracias a Dios."* (Very well, thank God.)

When talking about a future event or plan, Ticos will often include *si Dios quiere* (if God wants, God willing): *"Nos vemos el martes, si Dios quiere."* (We'll see each other Tuesday, God willing.)

If you are in the city and see someone on the other side of the street that you know, you call *"Adios!"* In the countryside, when you pass someone on the road, it is customary to say *adios* even if you don't know them. In these situations, *adios* means hello. It is only used to mean goodbye when you're going away for good. Everyday goodbyes are *hasta luego* (until then, until later), and the other person might add *"Que Dios le acompañe"* (May God accompany you).

Giving a coin to a beggar in the street often earns you a special blessing: he or she will say *"Dios se lo pague"* (May God repay you).

Vos is a form of second person singular address used throughout Central America instead of *tu.* Small children, however, are usually addressed as *usted,* probably in order to teach them to use this more respectful form with their elders, until they know how to make the differentiation themselves. The fact that the archaic *vos* is used even now in Costa Rica shows how isolated it was during colonial times. The verb form used with *vos* is made by changing the *r* on the end of an infinitive to *s* and accenting the last syllable. Thus with the verb poder, *"tu puedes"* becomes *"vos podés",* and with sentirse, *"tú te sientes"* becomes *"vos te sentís".*

Other fillers that are used commonly in Spanish are terms like *fijate, imaginate,* and *vieras que,* for which there are no real equivalents in English. Roughly, they could be translated as "would you believe" or "just think!" These expressions are used to give emphasis to what the speaker is saying. For example:

"Fíjate vos que no me dejaron entrar!" (Would you believe it--they wouldn't let me in!)

"Imagínese cómo me dió pena verla así" (Imagine how bad I felt to see her like that.)

Vieras is often used to give the equivalent of the way we use *"sure"* in English: *"Vieras qué susto me dió!"* (I sure was scared, or, you should have seen how it scared me.)

Achará is another particularly *tico* expression which indicates regret at a loss: *"Fíjese que el perro comió mis begonias. Achará mis florecitas."* (Would you believe it--the dog ate my begonias. My poor little flowers!)

When you come to someone's house, especially in the country, it is customary to stand on the ground near the porch and say *"Upe!"* as a way of letting them know you're there. When they ask you to come in, as you enter the house you say *"Con permiso"* (with your permission). If they offer you something to eat, it is much more polite to accept than not to accept. Giving makes people happy, and if you don't let them give to you, it hurts them. People will ask you about your family, whether you're married, how many children you have. Most can't quite grasp the idea of people not being married or not having children. When you're sitting and talking and finally no one can think of anything else to say, you say, *"Pues, sí"* (Well, yes).

Learn some of these expressions and practice them until you don't make any *metidas de pata* (literally, "putting your foot in it", or mistakes). Ticos will be glad to help you. If you do make a mistake, there is a word which is instant absolution: just say, *"Diay?"* That means, "Well, what can you expect?" or "What can be done about it?" As you get to know the Ticos, you'll find out that this little word comes in very handy.

GETTING TO KNOW SAN JOSE

As you can see from the map, San José's streets are laid out in a very logical system: odd-numbered streets *(calles)* are east of Calle Central, even-numbered streets are west. Odd-numbered *avenidas* are north of Avenida Central and even-numbered avenues are south. So if an address is on c 17, a 5/7, it is in the northeastern part of the city.

Perhaps because Costa Rica is a small country in transition from rural to urban, most Ticos completely ignore the street numbering system. *Calles* and *avenidas* appear in the phone book, and that's about it. The accepted way to give directions is from *puntos cardinales* or landmarks. If you call for a taxi you have to give the name of a church or a *pulpería* (corner store) or a well-known business (like Pollos Kentucky). Then you state how many *metros* you are from there and in what direction. *Cien (100) metros* roughly corresponds to one city block. These are some examples of typical ways of giving directions: *"De la pulpería La Luz, cien metros al norte y cincuenta al oeste."* (From the La Luz grocery store one block north and half a block west.) *"De la Iglesia La Soledad, doscientos al sur y trescientos al este."* (From the Soledad Church, two blocks south and three blocks east).

The area bordered by *Calle 4* on the west, *Avenida 9* on the north, *Calle 23* on the east and *Avenida 2* on the south is the heart of downtown culture and nightlife, and is usually quite safe (always follow precautions on p. 69-70, however).

If you have come to Costa Rica to get close to nature, you will probably want to get out of San José as fast as possible. It

94

is crowded, noisy, and polluted with black diesel fumes. But you might have to spend some time there, so here are some tips:

1. When crossing streets in downtown San José, always look over your shoulder at the cars coming from behind you. In practice, the pedestrian does not have the right of way. Drivers love to whip around corners whether or not people are trying to cross.

2. When a traffic light for oncoming cars changes from green to yellow or red, do not take it to mean that the cars will stop. Look at the cars, not the light. When you see that the cars have stopped, run across real quick. This habit is easily developed because another loveable characteristic of San José is that traffic lights are hung so that pedestrians cannot see them. *Buena suerte.*

3. Street numbers are attached to the sides of buildings near intersections. Not all corners have them, but keep looking and you're bound to find one.

4. To orient yourself in cities and villages, remember that most Catholic churches have their entrances on the west so that the altar faces east.

WALKING TOUR

The following tour can take several hours to one day, depending on how involved you get. The route is traced on the small map on the opposite page.

We will start out at the **Central Post Office** *(Correo Central)* on calle 2 between avenidas 1 and 3. The entrance is in the middle of the block. The stamp windows are directly in front of you as you enter. Slots for mailing letters abroad are directly to your left. Philatelists will be interested in the commemorative stamp department on the second floor. The Correo is open from 8 am-midnight M-F and 8 am-12 noon Saturdays.

Walk two blocks west on avenida 1 and you're at the **Mercado Central**, entering through the flower section. The market is a crowded, bustling maze of shops, restaurants, and produce stands covering the whole block between avenida central and 1 and calle 6 and 8. Although there are quite a few more sedate places to buy souvenirs, at the Central Market you can get a glimpse of the lives of everyday Costa Ricans. Everything from leather. goods to hammocks and fresh fish to mangoes is sold there. Of special interest are the stands where herbs are labeled with their medicinal uses. It's easy to get quite disoriented in the market, but try to come out at the southeast entrance on avenida central and start walking east again. If you don't like crowds, skip the market.

Between calles 6 and 4, you'll pass **La Gloria,** Costa Rica's largest department store. Across from that is the huge black marble **Banco de Costa Rica.** You can take an elevator there to the eighth floor to get a bird's eye view of the city. Turn left at calle 4 and you'll pass a branch of **Pop's,** Costa Rica's excellent chain of ice cream stores. At calle 4, avenida 1, turn right, heading for the Post Office again. You'll pass the **Banco Nacional** on your left. It often has art exhibits. Continuing on avenida 1, a block and a half past the Post Office, you'll pass the **Librería Universal** where you can buy almost anything. They sell large-scale maps which are helpful for hiking.

Look to your left at the intersection of calle 1 and avenida 1. Two blocks north is **Radiográfica,** where you can make long-distance phone calls, send telegrams, or send and receive faxes. **LACSA** airline ticket offices face Radiográfica.

But you are still on avenida 1. In the next block after calle 1 is **The Bookshop,** which sells newspapers, cards and books in English. Continue east to calle 5. Turn left. You'll pass three excellent crafts stores: **Atmósfera**, on the corner to your right, **Magia,** on your right in the middle of the block, and **Suraja** on your left at the corner of avenida 3. All merit a browse.

Now **Parque Morazán** is on your right, with its music temple patterned after Le Trianon in Paris. On the northwest corner of the park is the **Hotel Aurola Holiday Inn,** with its mirrored panels that reflect San José's changing skies. The third floor features a swimming pool and gym. One block south of the **Music Temple** is the popular **Hotel Amstel,** with its quiet bar and excellent, reasonably-priced restaurant. Across from the Amstel (a 1, c 7) is a smaller branch of the **Banco de Costa Rica** where you can cash traveler's checks. It's open until 6 pm weekdays. Three blocks north of the Music Temple is the entrance to **Parque Bolívar, San José's** zoo. If you are idealistic about Costa Rica's commitment to wildlife, you will be disappointed in the zoo, which has received widespread criticism for it inadequate facilities. Open 8-4 Tues-Fri, 9-5 weekends, $.20.

East of the Music Temple is the green **Escuela Metálica,** which was bolted together from parts shipped from France.

Next comes **Parque España** with its venerable and beautiful trees. Continue to avenida 7 and the tall **National Insurance Institute** (INS) which houses a fine exhibit of jade, ceramics and art in the **Jade Museum** (11th floor, open 9am-3pm, M-F).

Continuing east on avenida 7, you will pass the **Casa Amarilla** with its wide stairways. It houses the country's Department of Foreign Relations. This building and the park in front of it were donated by Andrew Carnegie.

On the east side of the park is the **National Liquor Factory**, founded by President Juan Rafael Mora in 1856. Guided tours of the building, including generous samplings of their products, are available after 4pm during the week. Call 23-6244.

Now we're going east again on avenida 7, up a gentle hill, passing the Mexican Embassy on the north and arriving at the intersection of avenida 7 and calle 15. Turn right towards the **National Library** (Biblioteca Nacional). On its western side is the **Galería Nacional de Arte Contemporáneo**, which often has good exhibits (open 10am-1pm, 2pm-5pm, Mon-Sat). Entrance to the library is on avenida 3.

The library faces **Parque Nacional**. To the east of the Park are the bus stations for the scenic trip to Limón. In the center of the Park is the massive **Monumento Nacional**, depicting the spirits of the Central American nations driving out the despicable William Walker. The statue was made in the Rodin studios in France and shipped to Costa Rica. Across the street from the park you will see a statue of **Juan Santamaría**, holding aloft his torch in front of the **Legislative Assembly** building, the Costa Rican Congress. Inside is a small library and an exhibit recounting the momentous decisions in Costa Rica's legal history.

Two blocks south of the Parque Nacional, on calle 17, is the **Museo Nacional,** housed in the former Buenavista Fortress. There are bullet holes in the turrets from the 1948 civil war. Inside are exhibits of indigenous gold and ceramics, colonial religious objects and furniture, political history and art. Open Tues-Sun, 8:30am-5pm, admission $.45).

The western entrance to the Museum is on the **Plaza de la Democrácia**, built by the Arias Administration to receive visiting presidents during the historic Hemispheric Summit in October 1989. Return to Avenida Central, which borders the northern side of the Plaza. Heading west, you'll pass the popular **Mas x Menos** supermarket. One and a half blocks to the left from the corner of calle 11 is the **Mercado Nacional de Artesanía,** a good and inexpensive place to shop for souvenirs. One block to the right from the same corner is **CANAPI,** another souvenir cooperative.

Continue west on avenida central. You might be ready for a bite to eat at the **Balcon de Europa** or **Finisterre** (a ctl, c 7), or coffee and cake at **Spoon** (a ctl, c 5/7). **ANDA** (a ctl, c 5/7) features crafts made by Costa Rican Indians.

Now you're coming to the **Plaza de la Cultura** on avenida ctl, calle 5/3. Down the grassy steps on calle 5 is the **Tourism Institute's Information Center** to the left. There too is the entrance to the excellent exhibition rooms and **Gold Museum** below the Plaza (open Fri, Sat, Sun).

Cross the Plaza to the famous **National Theatre.** In 1890 the world renowned prima donna, Adelina Patti, appeared with a traveling opera company in Guatemala. She could not perform in Costa Rica because there was no appropriate theater. Newly-rich coffee merchants offered to finance the construction of a theater with a tax on every bag of coffee exported from the country. Belgian architects were called in to design and supervise the building, and metal structure was ordered from Belgian mills. Painters and decorators were brought from Italy, along with that country's famous marble. The Teatro Nacional was inaugurated in 1894 with Gounod's *Faust*. The opening night cast included singers from the Paris Opera. A source of cultural pride for many years, the Theater was made into a national monument in 1965. Extensive restoration work has recently renewed its beautiful ceiling paintings and sumptuous decor, but tropical weather and recent earth tremors have taken their toll on the old building, so its auditorium is closed until at least mid-1992. Tourists can make donations to help with its preservation in the lobby. The **Café del Teatro Nacional,** to the left as you enter the building, has changing art exhibits. They specialize in exotic coffee combinations and desserts. Sit down there--you deserve a rest.

CREATIVE ARTS

Costa Ricans are well known for their interest in culture and the arts. The Ministry of Culture stimulates activity by sponsoring theater, choral music, opera, dance, literature, poetry, art, sculpture and film.

Music: Since 1972, Costa Rica has had the only National Youth Symphony in Latin America. It was inaugurated by ex-President Figueres' famous quote: "We need to concern ourselves not only with the standard of living but the quality of life as well. Why have tractors without violins?" Many of the young musicians trained in the Youth Symphony have graduated to participate in the **National Symphony,** which performs Thursday and Friday nights at 8 and Sundays at 10:30am in the Teatro Melico Salazar across from Parque Central (a 2, c ctl). Call 22-2653 to check showtimes. Internationally-famed guest directors and soloists are often featured in their programs. Entrance fees are kept low so that people of all economic levels may enjoy the concerts. The least expensive seats are in the *galería* section which is up three flights of stairs through an entrance on the east side of the theater. The *butacas* are in the first tier of boxes above the *luneta* (orchestra) section. The *palcos* are on the second tier. The symphony season starts in April and ends in December.

Retired musicians, amateurs and some symphony members play together for fun on Monday nights in Heredia. Foreigners are welcome to join. Call German Alvarado at 21-1185 for information.

Since economic difficulties have limited the Ministry of Culture in recent years, the **Ars Musica Foundation** has been formed to generate international and local funding for valuable projects like the Youth Symphony (Ars Musica, Apdo. 1035, San José, 33-9890).

Radio Universidad at 870 AM and 96.7 and 101.9 FM plays classical music all day, interspersed with educational programs. **FM96** also has classical music. **Radio Estereo Azul,** 99 FM, plays a lot of new age music and jazz.

Peñas and **La Nueva Canción:** The *peña,* literally "circle or group of friends", is a tradition brought to Costa Rica by Chilean and Argentinean exiles. People of all nationalities come together at a favorite cafe and sing the moving and inspiring songs that have become the themes of today's Latin America: *La Nueva Canción.* **Luis Angel Castro, Rubén Pagura** and **Juan Carlos Ureña** are some of the favorite leaders of *peñas* these days. **El Tablado** (next to Toruma Youth Hostel in Los Yoses) and **Baleares** (25 m east of La Nueva China in San

Pedro) often have peñas. Also keep your ears open for concerts by **Adrián Goizueta** and his Grupo Experimental, **Cantares** and **Canto America.**

Theater: Ticos are great actors. It is said that Costa Rica has more theatre companies per capita than any other country in the world. Even if you don't understand Spanish, it might be worth it to go, just to see the creativity that these people bring to the stage. The English-speaking community also puts a lot of energy into their **Little Theater Group**, which presents musicals and comedies several times a year. Call 31-0813 for info.

The *Tico Times* and the *Viva* section of *La Nación* will tell you what is playing. Admission is about $1.50. Theater addresses are listed below:

Teatro de la Aduana, c 25, a 3/5
Teatro del Angel, a ctl, c 13/15, 22-8258
Teatro Bellas Artes, east side of University of Costa Rica campus.
Teatro Carpa, a ctl, c 29, 34-2866
Sala de la Calle 15, a 2, c 15
Teatro Laurence Olivier, a 2, c 28, 23-1960, 22-1034
Teatro La Mascara, c 13, a 2/4
Teatro Melico Salazar, a 2, c ctl/2, 21-4952
Teatro Tiempo, c 13, a ctl/2, 22-0792
Teatro Vargas Calvo, c 3/5, a 2, 22-1875

Films: North American movies dominate the film scene here, and are usually shown 3-6 months after they appear in the States, with Spanish subtitles. The **Sala Garbo** (a 2, c 28) features excellent international films with Spanish subtitles. Next door, the **Teatro Laurence Olivier** offers films, plays and concerts as well as a gallery and coffee house. Recently local jazz groups have been playing in their Shakespeare Gallery. Take the Sabana-Cementerio bus (c 7, a ctl/2) and get off at the Pizza Hut on Paseo Colón. The two theaters are one block to the left (south). You can walk there in 25 minutes from downtown. All movie theaters charge about $1.50. Check schedules in the *Tico Times* or *La Nación*.

Art: The Ticos converted their former air terminal into the **Museum of Costa Rican Art.** Located in the Sabana at the end of Paseo Colón, this tastefully done museum displays the works of the country's finest painters and sculptors as well as international exhibits. Open 10am-5:45pm. Admission $.30. Free Sundays, closed Mondays.

The **Center for Creative Arts,** in Santa Ana to the west of San José, combines art classes with yoga and relaxation in order to release creative energy (82-6556, 82-8769).

Check *La Nación* and the *Tico Times* for exhibits at the many galleries downtown. The Centro Cultural has monthly art exhibits. Their openings are a good place to meet people.

MISCELLANEOUS INFORMATION

Embassies and consulates:
> Austrian Consulate: a 4, c 36/38, 55-3007
> British Embassy: Centro Colón, 21-5566
> Canadian Embassy: c 3, a 1, 55-3522
> Dutch Embassy: Los Yoses, 34-0949
> German Embassy: Rohrmoser, 32-5533
> Guatemalan Consulate: Guadalupe, 33-5283
> Japanese Embassy: Rohrmoser, 32-1255
> Mexican Consulate: c 5, a 5, 33-8874
> Nicaraguan Consulate: La California, 33-8747
> Norwegian Embassy: Centro Colón, 57-1414
> Panamanian Consulate: San Pedro, 25-0667
> Swedish Consulate: La Uruca, 32-8549
> Swiss Embassy: Centro Colón, 33-0052
> United States: Pavas, 20-3939

Newspapers and magazines: English-language newspapers and magazines are sold at the Candy Shop of the Gran Hotel Costa Rica (c 3, a ctl/2), The Bookshop (a 1, c 1/3), the Automercado (c 3, a 3/5), the Hotel Aurola (c 5, a 5), Yaohan's (across from the Hotel Corobicí), the Hotel Amstel Shop (c 7, a 1), the Hotel Bougainvillea, and Librería Lehmann (a ctl, c 1/3). Most of them carry the *New York Times*, the *Wall St. Journal* and the *Miami Herald*, as well as *Time* and *Newsweek*. You can also have the above periodicals delivered to your home by calling Publiserisa, 55-3883, 55-3996, or Periódicos Internacionales, 55-4567.

The best source of local news in English is the *Tico Times*, available for $.25 at the above places and at many hotels.

Winner of the 1981 Interamerican Press Association award for distinguished service to the community, the *Tico Times* offers a well-researched synthesis of weekly events in Costa Rica and Central America as a whole. They are without comparison in their coverage of local environmental and political issues, and also give an excellent rundown of cultural activities. Published Fridays, Apdo. 4632, San José. Tel: 22-8952 or 22-0040.

Casey's (c ctl, a 7/9), and **Book Traders** (in the Omni Building, a 1, c 3/5) sell and trade used books in English.

Meeting places: The **Friends' Peace Center** in San José is a network for the various groups working for peace in Central America. It provides meeting space, coordination of activities, a library and educational programs as well as a weekly meditation time in which peace workers can renew their spirits. The staff of the center is made up of both Central and North Americans, most of them volunteers. They welcome donations of time or funding from interested people. The Peace Center is located on c 15, a 6 bis. Tel: 33-6168.

The Women's Club, Bridge Club, Newcomer's Club, Republicans Abroad, Democrats Abroad, American Legion, Disabled American Veterans, Retired Officers Association, Masonic Lodge, Amnesty International, La Leche League, Lions, Rotary, Women's Aglow Fellowship, Christian Women's Club, Amateur Fishing Club, Canada Club, Cricket Club, Coffee Pickin' Square Dancers, the Canoeing/Kayaking Club and the US Citizens Concerned for Peace all meet regularly in San José. Current hours and numbers are often listed in the *Tico Times*.

Supermarkets: Name-brand products from the U.S. are flooding Costa Rican supermarkets. Because they are imported, they are very expensive. Right next to them on the shelf will be a comparable locally-made product for a quarter of the price.

Stores are often closed between 12 and 2 during the week. The **Mas x Menos** supermarkets are open 8 am to 8 pm and do not close for lunch or on Sundays. Ask at your hotel for the nearest one. The **Automercado**, less crowded, cleaner and more expensive than the Mas x Menos, is also open all day, but is closed Sundays. **Yaohan's**, a large Japanese-owned supermarket across from the Hotel Corobicí, Sabana East, is open on Sundays. It has a good produce section. On the east side, **Munoz y Nanne** in San Pedro is famous for good produce.

Orchids and butterflies: Orchid lovers should plan to visit during March or September when the **National Orchid Shows** are held. Butterfly enthusiasts will enjoy the **Museum of Entomology** at the University's *Facultad de Agronomía,* UCR campus, San Pedro. Open Weds and Thurs, 1-6 pm, admission free. See p. 130 re The Butterfly Farm in La Guácima.

RELIGIOUS SERVICES

Baha'i: Prayer breakfast every Saturday at 8am, 800mts. S of the first entrance to Bello Horizonte, Escazu. Info center on c 22, a 4, 22-5335.

Baptist: English services Sundays at 9am, followed by fellowship and Sunday school, 150m N of Banco Anglo in San Pedro, 25-4885.

Catholic: Saint Mary's Chapel. English mass Sundays at 4pm. Adjacent to Sheraton Herradura Hotel, 39-0033. Mass in English Saturdays at 5pm at San Rafael de Escazú Church.

Christian Science: Sundays at 11am, a 8 c 21, 21-0840.

Episcopal: Services in English Sundays at 8:30am at the Church of the Good Shepherd, a 4, c 3-5, 22-1560.

Escazú Christian Fellowship: Church and Sunday School, Sundays 6-7pm, annex to Country Day School, 28-2754.

Hare Krishna: Finca Nueva Goloka Vrindavana, Cartago-Paraíso Road, 51-6752.

Jewish: Reform: Bilingual services Fridays at 8pm at Congregation B'Nei Israel, 600m W of Pop's La Sabana, Hebrew school, pre-school, teen study and social programs. Call 31-5243 (1-5pm) or 57-1785 for info.
Conservative: Synagogue Shaare Zion, Fridays at 5:30pm, c 22B, a 1, 22-5449

Methodist: El Redentor. Sundays at 10:30, Sunday school 9:30. Women's Aglow Fellowship meets on Wednesdays, a ctl, c 9/11, 22-0360.

103

Mormon: Sacrament meetings 9am, English adult Sunday school, 9:30am Sundays, 100m S, 100m E of Pulpería La Luz, Barrio Los Yoses, 25-0208.

Quaker: Bilingual worship service at 11am Sundays at the Friends Peace Center, a 6 Bis, c 15, 33-6168, 24-4376.

Theosophical Society: nightly lodges, a 1, c 11-15, 21-7246.

Union Church: Free bus service, nursery and Children's Church, neighborhood Bible Study Groups. Sunday school at 9am, fellowship at 10, services at 10:25; Moravia, 26-3670.

Victory Christian Center: Sundays at 10am, 125m W of Tennis Club in Sabana Sur, 82-7720, 28-9934.

Yoga: Gran Fraternidad Universal, a 7 (B), c 15, 57-0928.

PLACES TO JOG OR WALK IN SAN JOSE

La Sabana: We know of no other city which has converted its outgrown international airport into a metropolitan park with sports facilities. The National Gymnasium was built on the southeast corner of the former airfield; the National Stadium on the northwest corner. A small lake, which had been filled in, has been restored and residential districts have been built on three sides of La Sabana (the flatland). The Air Terminal Building is now the National Art Museum.

With an Olympic swimming pool, jogging and walking paths, tennis, volleyball, basketball courts, soccer and baseball fields, La Sabana has become a favorite recreation area on weekends and a training ground for joggers during lunch hours (showers provided). There's a hill for kite-flying. People fly-cast in the lake. There are lots of trees for relaxing in the shade. Take the Sabana-Cementerio bus (c 7, a ctl; or c 2, a 3).

Behind the Zoo: Walk through Parque Morazán and Parque de España to the Casa Amarilla. Go north on calle 11, which becomes a winding, quiet, tree-lined street along the upper border of Parque Bolívar. Keep winding around until you come to the railroad tracks and a rural guard station. Climb the steps and you're in Barrio Aranjuez, a nice, older neighborhood.

You'll be walking east on avenida 11. Go to your left two blocks after the tracks and soon you'll be at the edge of a cliff with cement stairs going down it. You'll see basketball courts, a soccer field, and a track, free from San José's diesel fumes.

The back way to San Pedro: Walk through Parque Nacional to the Limón train station. Follow the tracks going east, across calle 23 and on past some graceful old houses with lovely flower gardens. Follow the tracks one block past the *pulpería* Ambos Mares till you see a sign that says *"Final del Patio"*. After this point there is no sidewalk, so keep jogging to your left and head east at the next block. You'll only have to zigzag once; then, after the Colegium Fidelitas (notice the Centro Cultural Costarricense-Norteamericano to your right), it's a short zigzag and you're heading east again. This street ends across from one entrance to the University of Costa Rica campus. A circular drive one mile long goes around the campus and is pleasantly shaded by beautiful trees. If you go early in the morning you'll see joggers, walkers, and a lot of birds.

Parque del Este: This rather deteriorated park above San Pedro in San Rafael de Montes de Oca is a great place to escape from pollution for a few hours. It's an expansive green area cleared out of a lush canyon. There's a Vita Course jogging and exercise trail with little signs that tell you to do all sorts of strenuous things along the way. There's also a pool, basketball courts, a soccer field, picnic tables, playgrounds, a lookout point with a sign that identifies the mountains on the horizon, and a zigzagging nature trail. Get there on the San Ramón de Tres Rios bus that leaves from c 7, a 2, and passes through San Pedro. The park is open until 4 pm, closed Mondays, and pretty crowded on weekends and holidays.

RESTAURANTS

Coffee shops: Below are some of the best places we've found to eat a quick meal or have a cup of coffee. The traditional Tico way to serve coffee is in two separate pitchers, one filled with strong black coffee and the other with steaming hot milk. You can mix them to suit your taste. Many establishments have stopped this practice for economic reasons, but Manolo's, Spoon, and Giacomín have retained the tradition. Unfortunately, decaffeinated coffee is unavailable in Cosa Rica, and most places do not offer herbal teas, although some excellent ones are manufactured here. You can always bring your own and ask for a pot of hot water at restaurants. Incidentally, the concept of smoking and non-smoking areas in restaurants is unheard of. If it matters to you, stick to vegetarian restaurants.

Elegant Coffee Shops

Abacus: Crepes, salads, yummy desserts. Moderate. Next to Tega on the road to Escazú; 28-5350.

Azafrán: Delicious sandwiches and desserts, can be made to go. Excellent catering service. Their *torta Azafrán* has to be one of the classic best cakes of all time. Los Yoses, next to Dr. Starke. Open every day 11am-10pm, Sundays 11-9pm, 25-5230.

Giacomín: Their upstairs tea room is a nice place to enjoy coffee and pastries or homemade candy. Next to Los Yoses Automercado. Open 8am-12, 2pm-7pm, Mon-Sat.

Café Ruiseñor: A lovely place with delicious pastries and light meals made with pure, healthful ingredients. Some outdoor tables. Los Yoses, 150m E of Automercado. Open 11:30am to 7pm, Mon-Fri. A 20-minute walk from downtown towards San Pedro, 25-2562.

Spoon: Outrageous desserts and light meals. Three locations: downtown, a ctl, c 5/7; Los Yoses, 100m W, 100m S of Cancún, before the three fountains; Pavas across from the US Embassy.

INEXPENSIVE EATERIES: The Mercado Central is filled with inexpensive places to eat--many of them, like the Marisquería Ribera, recommended for good food. By the way, if you must, Pizza Hut, Burger King, McDonald's, Kentucky Fried Chicken and Taco Bell all have branches here. The best thing about them is that they usually have clean, easy-to-find bathrooms, a boon in downtown San José.

El Escorial: Lunch for $1, good buffet for $3. Open Mon-Sat 11 am-2pm, 5 pm-11 pm; a 1, c 5/7.

Finisterre: A good place to go for a quick lunch. Italian specialties. Next door to the Balcón de Europa, a central, c 7, open every day, noon to 9pm, 21-4841.

Soda La Casita: Small, clean, homey. Good for a quick breakfast or lunch; a 1, c ctl/1. Open weekdays.

Soda Central: Specializes in thick chicken empanadas; a 1, c 3/5.

VEGETARIAN RESTAURANTS

Don Sol: Pleasant, inexpensive vegetarian restaurant. Try their *energético,* a delicious natural fruit salad; their *plato fuerte* (lunch of the day) is very filling, a 7B, c 15, northeast of the Casa Amarilla.

La Mazorca: Macrobiotic fare. Wholewheat pastries and natural food products. 100 m. north, 200 m. east of the San Pedro Church. Open 9am-8pm Mon-Fri, 9am-2pm Sat, 24-8069.

Mordisco: Elegant vegetarian meals, as well as fish and chicken. A bit more expensive than the others, but worth it. Paseo Colón, next to Mercedes Benz. Open 9am-9pm. Closed Sundays, 55-2448.

La Nutrisoda: Pure vegetarian food; homemade natural ice cream. Open 11-6; 55-3959; Edificio Las Arcadas, next to Gran Hotel Costa Rica.

Shakti: Vegetarian goodies, open 7am-4pm M-F, c 13, a 8.

Vishnu: Inexpensive, generous servings; two locations: 3, a ctl/1 and c 14, a ctl/2. Crowded at lunch--get there early.

DINING OUT
All restaurant bills include a 10 percent tip and a 13 percent tax. Tipping is not customary, but is certainly appreciated, especially when service is good (see p. 45).

Ambrosia: A quiet, cozy place for lunch, tea or dinner. Vegetarian and non-vegetarian fare, all specialties named after

Greek deities. Open Tues-Sat 11:30am to 10:30pm, Sun and Mon 11:30am to 4:30pm, 53-8012, Centro Comercial de la Calle Real, San Pedro.

Hotel Amstel: Well known for its reasonably-priced, excellent meals and service. On c 7, a 1/3, 22-4622.

Arirang: Korean specialties, Edificio Colón, 23-2838.

Ave Fénix: Authentic Chinese cuisine, Szechuan specials. Moderate. 200 m. west of the San Pedro church, 25-3362.

Balcón de Europa: Homemade fettucine, delicious cheeses. Chef Franco Piatti does his best to make you feel at home; a ctl, c 7/9, 21-4841.

Beirut: Middle Eastern specialties. Open Tues-Sat 11:30 am-11 pm, Sun 11:30-6; a 1, c 32, 1 block north of Pollos Kentucky on Paseo Colón. Moderate prices. 57-1808.

Le Bistrot: One of our favorite places, very small, with a relaxed French *savoir faire*. 100 m. east, 20 m. north from San Pedro Church, 53-8062.

Hotel Bougainvillea: The Barrio Tournón and new Santo Domingo Bougainvilleas, well-known as fine hotels, have excellent restaurants as well. Tournón: 33-6622, Santo Domingo: 36-5310.

Chalet Suizo: A San José landmark with a traditional European menu. Crowded at lunch; c 5/7, a 1, 22-3118.

Chalet Tirol: Near the cloud forest above Heredia, a truly elegant restaurant with two French chefs specializing in *nouvelle cuisine*. Open 8am to 11pm every day, closes around 8pm on Sunday. Call for reservations, 39-7070, 39-7050.

Le Chandelier: Fancy French cuisine. Paseo Colón west of Banco Anglo, 21-7947.

Cronopios is a cozy gathering-place in the mountains above San Isidro de Coronado. They serve soups, salads, mini-pizzas and main dishes, and make desserts from the strawberries that grow in the area. There's a fireplace and a good collection of Latin American and North American music. Open Friday nights, Saturday from noon to 11pm, Sunday noon to 6, 29-0517.

Flor del Loto: Delicious Hunan and Szechuan Chinese specialties. Open every day for lunch and dinner. East side of ICE building, Sabana Norte, 32-4652. Moderate.

Restaurant La Galería: Excellent European cuisine. One of the best. Call ahead for reservations. Los Yoses, 34-0850.

L'Ile de France: Excellent French cuisine, superb service. Expensive, but you don't have to order a whole meal there; c 7, a ctl/2, 22-4241.

Machu Pichu: Authentic Peruvian *ceviche*, pizco sour, *anticuchos*, c 32, a 1, 125m N of Paseo Colón, 22-7384.

Kudamm: German specialties. Open 11:30-2:30 and 6-11. Curridabat, 53-7601.

Lai Yuin: Specializes in Chinese seafoods. Curridabat, across from Indoor Club. Moderate, 53-5055.

La Masía de Triquell: Spanish cuisine in a lovely colonial atmosphere. Expensive, elegant; c 40, a 2, 21-5073.

Mirador Ram Luna: This large, family-style restaurant in the mountains 15km S of San José is famous for tender steaks and fantastic views of the central valley. Jukebox, dancefloor, playground equipment for kids. Go through Desamparados to Aserrí and follow a lovely winding road 5 km up from there, or take an Acosta (c 8, a 12/14) or San Gabriel (c 10, a 12/14) bus to the Mirador. Tel: 30-3060 (see map, p. 128).

La Nueva China: One of San José's best Chinese restaurants. San Pedro, across from the Banco Popular, 24-4478.

Paprika: Delicious soups, salads, omelettes, main dishes and desserts. Very rich. Quiet, comfortable atmosphere. Open for lunch and dinner; a ctl, c 29/33, 25-8971.

Sakura: Costa Rica's only authentic Japanese restaurant. Expensive. At the Herradura Hotel near the airport, 39-0033, ext. 258. Open 11:30am-3pm, 6-10pm, closed Mon.

Valerio's: Delicious pizza and lasagne, great desserts, reasonable prices. Los Yoses, in the shopping center next to Cancún, 25-0838.

Vía Veneto: Excellent Italian food, elegant atmosphere, delicious pastries. Curridabat, across from Indoor Club, tel: 34-2898.

Zermatt: Swiss specialties, including fondue. 100 m. north, 25 e. Santa Teresita Church, 22-0604.

NIGHTLIFE

These are some of our favorite nightspots. Most of them serve the traditional *bocas,* little plates of food that accompany each drink. *Ceviche* (raw fish "cooked" in lemon juice), fried fish, pork and beans and *mondongo* (tripe) are common bocas. Usually they are free. As for national beers, we recommend Bavaria, Imperial, or the more expensive Heineken.

Amstel Hotel Bar: Simple, elegant, *quiet,* c 7, a 1/3.

Antojitos: Good Mexican food, great mariachis. Paseo Colón near Pizza Hut, and in Los Yoses.

Chelles: As far as atmosphere goes, there's not much, but if you're a people-watcher, you'll enjoy hanging out at Chelles. Probably because it remains open 24 hours a day, seven days a week, Chelles has become a landmark. You'll see actors, musicians and dancers from the National Theater there having a midnight snack. You'll see middle-aged Costa Rican men amusing each other with toothpick tricks. You'll be asked to buy wilted roses from intriguing old ladies and persistent young boys. There are free *bocas* with every drink. For those who tire of the glare of Chelles' bare lightbulbs, there is **Chelles Taberna** around the corner, where you can hide in booths. The Taberna has better *bocas* too. Chelles Lite, a ctl, c 9, Chelles Dark, c 9 a ctl/2. Overpriced.

Charleston: Nice 1920's decor, often have good vintage jazz tapes, c 9, a 2/4, 55-3993. Open 5pm-4am, Closed Sun.

Crocodile Club: Friendly bar featuring gringo-style hamburgers. Huge video screen, dance floor; San Pedro, across from Banco Anglo.

El Cuartel de la Boca del Monte: By day a quiet, artistically-decorated restaurant featuring Costa Rican dishes. By night, the bar in the back becomes one of the most popular in San José. The *bocas* aren't free, but they're good. Most fun are their fantastic cocktails, extravagantly decorated with tropical fruit and sometimes even sparklers. Reasonably priced; a 1, c 21/23.

Dennie's: Quiet bar and restaurant, featuring live music and Caribbean food. Excellent curry, generous *bocas*; a ctl, c 19/21.

La Esmeralda is lots of fun. It's the home of the Mariachi Union. Groups of musicians stroll between the tables while their vans wait outside to transport them to emergency serenade sites. I'll never forget the best party I ever went to in Costa Rica--my landlady's 80th birthday. After eating, drinking and dancing till 1:00, I was ready to retire, but that's not the way Ticos celebrate birthdays. At 2 am the mariachis arrived to serenade her with guitars, harps, trumpets and violins. But I digress. La Esmeralda offers good, reasonably-priced food as well as fun; a 2, c 5/7. Open round the clock every day but Sunday.

Los Lechones: You have to buy the bocas here, but the atmosphere is great when a calypso band plays weekends; a 6, c 11/13.

Bar México: One of San José's most revered traditional nightspots where *boca*-making has been elevated to an art. Live mariachi bands. To get there from downtown you have to walk through a bad neighborhood, so it's better to take the Barrio México bus at c 7, a ctl. A cab will take you there for about $1. It's kitty-corner from the Barrio México church.

El Pueblo is a huge maze of Spanish colonial-style alleyways and tiled roofs. You can spend hours wandering around there, getting lost and spending money. **Amaretto's, Chaveta's** and **Me-K** (pronounced in Spanish like "mecca") feature live music from calypso to jazz. There is a small bar where you can hear authentic Argentinean tango. **Lety's** has a variety show with Costa Rican native dancers, comics and singers.

A skating rink and three discotheques also await you at El Pueblo. **Lukas** is a popular place to go for a late dinner or snack; **Rias Bajas,** one of San José's most elegant seafood restaurants, is also there. At the **Cocina de Leña** you can eat Costa Rican native dishes in authentic *campesino* atmosphere, for twice the price of the Mercado Central. The rest of El Pueblo is full of more restaurants, nightclubs, boutiques, galleries and offices. Most nightspots have a cover charge, especially on weekends or holidays, but it's fun to go and wander there anyway. It's across the river north of downtown, next to the Hotel Bougainvillea. Walk, or take a Calle Blancos bus from c 1, a 5.

Soda La Perla, Soda Palace: Like Chelles, these two restaurants are not special in themselves. They are mentioned as places where budding novelists can go to polish their powers of character description. Apparently the 1948 insurrection was planned over fried fish bocas and beer at the Soda Palace. It's open all night. Roving calypso bands come in, take a table, and play for everyone just for the joy of it. The restaurants are on either side of the Teatro Melico Salazar, a huge auditorium run by the Ministry of Culture as a forum for local artists. Be careful in the Soda Palace neighborhood. Parque Central can be dangerous at night (a 2, c ctl/2).

SOUVENIRS

Moderately-priced souvenirs can be found at the government crafts cooperatives: **CANAPI** (c 11, a 1) and the **Mercado Nacional de Artesanía** (c 11, a 2b, behind the Soledad Church), as well as in the **Mercado Central** (a ctl/1, c 6/8), and **La Casona** (c ctl, a ctl/1). One of the most charming, complete, and inexpensive souvenir shops is in the converted home of one of Costa Rica's ex-presidents, now the **Hotel Don Carlos** (c 9, a 9). **Arterica**, a small shop next to the entrance of the Teatro Melico Salazar (a 2, c ctl/2) is a showcase for crafts-people who are revitalizing Costa Rican native artisanry, such as weaving, basketmaking, ceramics and woodcarving.

They also offer free courses in native crafts through the University of Costa Rica, and give workshops in the countryside to people wishing to develop their skills. You can also see indigenous crafts at **ANDA** (a ctl, c 5/7).

Be sure to stop by the **Tiendas de la Naturaleza** in the ICT information office underneath the Plaza de la Cultura and at Volcán Poás. They sell delightful handicrafts made by people living near the national parks, helping the benefits of tourism to filter down to local *campesinos*.

If you have a little more money to spend, visit **Atmósfera**, **Magia** (c 5, a 1/3), **Suraska** (c 5, a 3), or **La Galería** (c 1, a ctl/1) where more artistic items are sold, including the innovative woodwork of two North Americans, Barry Biesanz and Jay Morrison. Biesanz specializes in exquisitely-crafted bowls and boxes, as well as furniture, which can be seen at his workshop in Bello Horizonte, above Escazú (28-1811). Morrison's creative hardwood furniture is also displayed at his showroom, Tierra Extraña, in Santa Ana (82-6697).

Another extraordinary woodworker is Paul Smith, one of the early settlers in Monteverde. His lovingly-crafted stringed instruments are made of European wood aged for ten years. You can find Paul at his Grecia workshop (44-6990).

The capital of Costa Rican woodcraft is **Sarchí**, about an hour northwest of San José (see p. 132). Everything from salad bowls to rocking chairs to miniature oxcarts can be purchased there. The capital of Costa Rican leathercraft is Moravia, a suburb of San José, where there are a couple of blocks filled with souvenir shops near the main square. Moravia buses leave frequently from a 3, c 3/5.

Tiny *huacas*, copies of precolumbian jewelry representing frogs, lizards, turtles and humanesque deities, are relatively inexpensive and make lovely necklaces, earrings and tiepins. Some nice copies of precolumbian jadework and ocarinas are sold around the National Theater. Authentic precolumbian artefacts are not allowed to be taken out of the country, so don't believe anyone who tells you something is original. If it is original, the item has been stolen from an archaeological site.

If you need lightweight souvenirs, there are plenty of T-shirts, woven hemp shoulder bags, and jewelry made of wood and metal. Colorful scarves, hats, blouses, bags and sun visors made by Go Bandannas are unusual souvenirs, with motifs of native flora and fauna. Their creative coloring and activity book, *Let's Discover Costa Rica*, is the answer for the kids on your souvenir list. They are sold almost everywhere, but if you go to the **Bandanna Republic Jungle Shop** in Villa Colón between December 1 and April 1, you can enjoy a free swim at their spectacular 75-foot waterfall. Call for arrangements and directions, 49-1179.

If you're staying for awhile, take advantage of the low prices and excellent work of local tailors and seamstresses. They make fine formal clothes, or can copy your favorite designs. Ask a well-dressed Tico whom he or she would recommend.

You can buy freshly ground coffee or coffee beans at the Central Market, or in souvenir shops. It is usually ground finer than percolator coffee, for use in the *chorreador,* a filter bag that hangs from a wooden stand. There are percolator grinds available in supermarkets, where you'll also find **Caferica**, a delicious coffee liqueur, as well as dried bananas, coconut twirls, macadamia nuts, cashews, and yummy El Angel jams, fruit leathers and pastes. A *tapa dulce,* the native hard brown sugar, can be grated to add a rich flavor to baked goods or used in cereals or coffee. We've heard of tourists who take home cases of **Salsa Lizano**, a tasty bottled sauce that Ticos love to sprinkle on their *gallo pinto.*

If you are going to Monteverde, save some of your souvenir budget for **CASEM**, the women's craft cooperative there, which specializes in embroidered and hand-painted clothing depicting cloud forest wildlife. You'll see it on the right as you enter Monteverde. There is also a crafts cooperative on the main square in Ciudad Quesada.

The beautiful handicrafts of Guatemala and El Salvador can be found at **Sol Maya** on Paseo Colon across from Hospital San Juan de Dios. Guatemalan textiles are also sold on Calle 3, a 3/5, next to the Automercado (closed weekends).

Wicker, raffia and woven palm leaf items should be spray varnished when you get home. Don't be tempted to buy tortoise shell or alligator skin goods--they are made from endangered animals which are internationally protected. Customs officials will confiscate these items at your home country airport.

HOTELS

Our hotel rate categories, based on *double* occupancy, and including the 16% tax, are as follows:

XL $80-150	A $40-50	D $12-20
LL $60-80	B $30-40	E $7-12
L $50-60	C $20-30	F under $7

Please keep in mind that prices change, and although we try to be as accurate as possible, don't take it on faith that a hotel still charges what we said it charges--always ask. Also remember that our categories are based on double occupancy. Rates will vary if you are alone, or in a group, or if meals are included. The Tourism Institute (ICT) will give you a computer print-out of "current" hotel rates if you ask. Unfortunately, their listings bear little relation to reality.

Costa Rica is racing to build hotels to keep up with tourism demands, and existing hotels are often booked far in advance. Make reservations at least two months ahead for the dry season, and three months at Christmas or Easter. Most hotels have fax numbers, some demand a deposit. Travel agents have told us that even if you have confirmed your reservation, you can still get bumped if you haven't sent a deposit.

The following codes are used to describe hotel facilities in the rest of the book, especially when referring to low-cost places. You can assume that any room in the D category or above will have a private bath except at bed-and-breakfasts, but only the most expensive places at the beach have hot water.

pb: private bath   cb: communal bath
hw: hot water, either referring to an electric device which warms the shower water, or hot water from regular water tanks.
cw: cold water
a/c: air conditioning
tf: table fans
cf: ceiling fans
nf: no fans

You can find clean, fairly comfortable rooms almost any-where for under $15 for two. Atmosphere costs more. If you can afford it, there are plenty of places with great atmosphere, equipment and service. If you are traveling cheaply, you will find the following items handy:

Your own cup
A universal plug for the sink
A cotton sheet or two (some hotels have nylon or polyester covers which are uncomfortable in the humid heat at the beach)
String and clothespins for hanging up wash
Towel, washcloth and soap
Toilet paper
Flashlight
Earplugs

Of course, most places, even cheap ones, supply towels and soap, but there is an occasional one that doesn't. Our main complaint about many hotels, even some expensive ones, is that you're often subject to noise pollution from somebody's high-powered sound system, usually a nearby dance hall, or neighbors with a loud radio. A place can seem perfectly *tranquilo* when you arrive during the day; the thumping disco across the river only comes on at night. The best solution is to get up and dance. Places that are owned by foreigners are generally quieter than places owned by Ticos, who regard loud music as *alegre*.

We should clarify the meaning of various terms which you'll see throughout the book referring to lodging. *Hotels* usually have more than one story, but not always. *Cabinas* are the most common form of lodging at the beach or in the mountains. They can be either separated, or connected in rows or duplexes. They roughly correspond to what a North American would call a "motel". However, here, *motel* refers to a small number of establishments, mostly on the southeastern side of San José, which couples use for clandestine romantic trysts. The couples are often married, but not to each other. The motels rent by the hour. *Villas* and *chalets* are fancy cabinas, usually separated. *Pensiones* and *hospedajes* are usually converted houses which often serve family-style meals. A *posada* is an inn.

Beach and mountain hotels often give discounts in the rainy season. Weekly and monthly rates are common as well. If you are staying in one place for awhile, consider renting a house. See *The Tico Times* for listings, or ask at a local *pulpería*.

116

LARGE DELUXE HOTELS: All are convention centers and are in category XL ($80-150 double occupancy).

Aurola Holiday Inn: Downtown, indoor pool, sauna, gym, cable TV, casino, non-smoking floor, firesafe, earthquake-proof, 33-7233, 33-7036, fax: (506) 55-1036.

Cariari: Resort hotel (golf, tennis, pools, exercise classes, horses, cable TV, bus service to downtown). Located on airport highway 20 min. from San José; 39-0022, fax: (506) 39-2803.

Corobicí: Tennis, sauna, pool, cable TV. Northeast corner of La Sabana; 32-8122, fax: (506) 31-5834.

Herradura: Cable TV, health spa, golf, tennis. Airport highway 20 min. from San José. 39-0033, fax: (506) 39-2292.

San José Palacio: Very luxurious, Spanish-owned hotel (pool, cable TV, gym, sauna and steam room), 20-2034, fax: 20-2036. We decry their over-use of native endangered hardwoods such as *cristobal* to make ceilings, walls and doors.

SMALL DELUXE HOTELS

L'Ambiance: Small, exclusive hotel in an old Spanish style home with courtyard and fountain, very quiet, filled with antiques, gourmet restaurant, cable TV, complete *concierge* service, 22-6702, 23-1598, c 13, a 9/ll, Apdo. 1040, 2050 San Pedro, SJ, CR. XL.

Tara Resort: In an elegant ante-bellum-style mansion high in the hills above Escazú, a western suburb of San José. Pool, restaurant; breakfast and airport pick-up incl., 28-6992, fax: (506) 28-9651, XL.

FIRST CLASS HOTELS. Most are downtown, so look for the quieter rooms off the street.

Ambassador: Staying here gets you a 10% discount at discos, jewelry stores and boutiques. A 20-minute walk from downtown. No extra charge for kids under 12. Paseo Colón, c 26/28; 21-8155, fax: (506) 55-3396, L.

Amstel: Best known for its excellent restaurant, central, quieter rooms on east side of building, 22-4622, fax: (506) 33-3329, c 7, a 1/3, A.

Balmoral: Central, cable TV, sauna; 21-1919, 21-5022, fax: (506) 21-7826, a ctl, c 7/9, LL.

Bougainvillea: Quiet, well-appointed rooms, excellent restaurant and service. Make reservations far in advance. Two locations: Barrio Tournon, north of downtown (33-6622, fax: 22-5211) and Santo Domingo de Heredia, 9km from San Jose (36-8822, fax: 36-8484), L.

Don Carlos: Charming decor, pleasant historical neighborhood. Cable TV, gym, tour videos, great souvenir shop. Very strict reservation and deposit policy, 21-6707, fax: (506) 55-0828, c 9, a 9 No. 779; A and L.

Europa: Distinctive European style, light and airy, indoor pool, cable TV, central, streetside rooms discounted because of noise and fumes, 22-1222, fax: (506) 21-3976; c ctl, a 3/5, L.

Gran Hotel Costa Rica: Across from National Theater, cable TV; 21-4000, fax: (506) 21-3501, a ctl/2, c 3, LL.

La Gran Vía: Streetside rooms with balconies, back rooms quieter. Central, clean; 22-7737, fax: 22-7205, a ctl, c 1/3; A.

Irazú: Large hotel, convention center, attractive rooms, casino, pool, cable TV, tennis, sauna, bus service; 15 min from downtown on airport highway, 32-4811, fax: (506) 32-3159, LL.

Royal Gardens: Casino, authentic Chinese food, central, 57-0022, 57-0023, Apdo. 3493, 1000 SJ; A.

Pico Blanco: Very lovely small mountain hotel with a great view. Clean, charming rooms, restaurant, friendly atmosphere, recommended. San Antonio de Escazú, 8 km west of San José, 28-3197, 28-5189, Apdo. 900, Escazu, CR; A.

Presidente: Casino, discotheque, glitzy decor, good service, cable TV, central, 22-3022, fax: (506) 21-1205, a ctl, c 7/9, LL.

Tennis Club: Pool, tennis, gym, sauna, skating rink, southwest side of La Sabana Park, 32-1266, fax: 32-3867, L.

Torremolinos: Quiet, pool, sauna, cable TV, near Sabana, shuttle bus to downtown, 22-5266, 22-9129, fax: (506) 55-3167; c 40, a 5 bis, LL.

BED-AND-BREAKFASTS

Casa María: Pool, cable TV, kitchen privileges, some shared baths. One km east of Escazú church, in residential neighborhood, 28-2270, fax: 28-0015, A.

Dunn Inn: Clean, cable TV, phones, pb, hw, fans, all rooms on second floor, corner building in old neighborhood. 22-3232, 22-3426, fax: 21-4596, A.

Hotel Santo Tomás: Beautifully remodeled old home with many nice touches. It's in the middle of the block, so rooms are back off the street, a real boon in noisy downtown San José, secure; pb, hw, group and off-season rates, 55-0448, 22-3946, fax: (506) 22-3950, L.

Pensión de la Cuesta: Run by artists--the rooms are filled with paintings and creative touches. Four rather dark rooms in an interesting old building. The fun will be in hanging around with other guests in the light-filled living-diningroom. Shared baths, fridge, near museum and galleries, 55-2896, B.

Park Place: 1.5 km above Escazú, views, on bus line, 28-9200, Apdo. 1010, 1250 Escazú, CR.

Tres Arcos: A 20-minute stroll from downtown. Ph/fax: (506) 25-0271, 3773 a 10, Los Yoses. A, pb; B, cb.

See p. 130-8 for B-and-B's in the mountains near San Jose.

HOMESTAYS

Bell's Home Hospitality sends you a description of the neighborhood and the interests of people who are offering rooms for rent to tourists. They ask you to describe yourself and your interests so they can match you up with the most compatible home. Rates are $35-40 per person, incl. breakfast, dinner $5 extra, airport pick-up, $10. Free information service, 25-4752, fax: (506) 24-5884. Write Apdo. 185, 1000 San José.

Costa Rica Homestays Bed and Breakfast, 40-6829

APARTHOTELS: As the word implies, these are a cross between an apartment and a hotel. All have kitchens, phones and TV. Discounts for weekly or monthly rental. They tend to lack atmosphere, although the Lamm, D'Galah, Don Carlos, Maria Alexandra and Villas Cariari are exceptions.

Castilla: c 24, a 2/4, 22-2113, near Paseo Colon, 21-2080, Apdo. 4699, SJ, CR; A.

D'Galah: Across from the University of Costa Rica campus in San Pedro. Quiet, friendly, music room, sauna, rooms with or w/o kitchens, 34-1743, 53-7539, Apdo. 208, 2350 San José, CR; C. Good value.

Don Carlos: Cable color TV, views, c 29, a ctl/8, 21-6707, fax: (506) 55-0828, B, weekly rates only.

El Conquistador: Los Yoses, near shopping, pool, quiet, 25-3022, Apdo. 303, 2050 San Pedro, CR; C.

Lamm: c 15, a 1, 21-4920, near parks and museums, attractive older apartments, traffic noise, Apdo. 2729, SJ, CR; B.

La Perla: La Uruca, friendly staff, close to shopping, 15 minutes by bus from downtown, color TV, 32-6153, B.

Los Yoses: Very clean, pool, parking, breakfast incl., 25-0033, fax: (506) 25-5595, Apdo. 1597, 1000 SJ, CR; A.

María Alexandra: Escazu, west of San Jose. Cable TV, washing machines, a/c, pool, sauna, excellent restaurant, quiet, very clean, 28-1507, fax: 28-5192, A.

Napoleón: c 40, a 5, near shopping and Sabana Park, pool, kind of stuffy, 23-3252, Apdo. 86340, SJ, CR; A.

Ramgo: Near Sabana, 200m W, 100m S of Tennis Club, 32-3823, Apdo. 1441, SJ, CR; B.

San José: a 2, c 17/19, 21-6684, fax: (506) 21-2443; A.

Villas de Cariari: In Cariari Hotel complex near airport; pool, golf course, 39-1003, fax: (506) 39-2083, XL.

MID-RANGE HOTELS, $20-40 double occupancy

Alameda: Near Coca Cola and other bus stops, simple, friendly; a ctl, c 12/14, 21-3045, 21-6333, B.

Cacts: In a neighborhood west of the Coca Cola, quiet, very friendly, helpful with travel arrangements, breakfast incl., airport pickup, 50% deposit requested when making reservations, 21-2928, fax: (506) 21-8616; a 3 bis #2845, c 28-30, C.

Capital: Clean, private baths, phones, hw, central; c 4, a 3/5, 21-8497, C.

Costa Rica Inn: Central, small rooms, some with windows that open onto a corridor, 22-5203, fax: 23-8385, c 9, a 1/3, C.

Diplomat: Clean, well-run, central, a favorite with foreigners, good restaurant, 21-8133, fax: 33-7474, c 6, a ctl/2, B.

Fortuna: Clean, borderline neighborhood, 23-5344, fax: (506) 23-2743, a 6 c 2/4, C.

Galilea: Light, airy rooms, especially on 3rd floor, clean; English-speaking staff, near Plaza de la Democracia and Museum; 33-6925, fax: (506) 21-1505, a ctl, c 11/13, C.

Plaza: Small rooms, clean, central, well-run, restaurant open 6 am-10 pm, 22-5533, fax: (506) 22-2641, a ctl, c 2/4, B.

Posada Pegasus: "Dedicated to serenity, individuality, natural beauty." Views, light meals served. Jacuzzi. San Antonio de Escazú, next to Pico Blanco, 28-4196, B, lower weekly rates. Apdo 370, Escazú, CR.

Ritz: Small rooms, convivial atmosphere, hw, not the best neighborhood; 22-4103, fax: (506) 22-8849, c ctl, a 8-10, C.

San José Garden Court: New 70-room hotel with pool, sauna, exercise room, parking, a/c, pb, hw, full breakfast incl. In a central but lousy neighborhood. Taxis wait outside to whisk you away, a 7, c 6/8, 22-3674, fax: (506) 32-4152, B.

Talamanca: Adequate 52 rooms, restaurant, parking, casino, 33-5033, a 2, c 8/10, C.

INEXPENSIVE HOTELS ($7-19, double)

Astoria: Quiet, funky religious decor, small dark rooms, a 7, c 7/9, 21-2174, E, pb, less with cb, lower weekly rates.

Bellavista: Has chintzy charm but not a lot of fresh air. Most windows open onto a corridor. Friendly owners run Dennie's Restaurant next door, famous for Caribbean cooking; 23-0095, a ctl, c 19/21, near Limón bus stop and Museum, D.

Boruca: Clean, quiet, family-run, secure though neighborhood not good, near buses, very cheap, shared baths, recommended; c 14, a 1/3, 23-0016, F.

Central: Clean, pb, central; a 3, c 4/6, 21-2767, F.

Centro Continental: c ctl, a 8/10, cb, hw, E, 33-1731, fax: (506) 22-8849. Next to Ritz, Swiss-owned.

Cocorí: Private baths, hw, close to Guanacaste bus stops, noisy; c 16, a 3, 33-0081, E.

Gran Hotel Centroamericano: Good for wheelchairs, inexpensive cafeteria, private baths, a 2, c 6/8, 21-3362, D.

Marlyn: Borderline neighborhood near old penitentiary. Central, fairly clean--an old house with elegant tiled floors chopped up into rooms, pb, hw and cw, c 4, a 7/9, 33-3212, F.

Morazán: Older building, big bare rooms; near Parque Morazán, Parque Nacional; a 3, c 11/15, 21-9083, E.

Musoc: Peace Corps hangout, next to Coca Cola bus station, bad neighborhood, clean, well-run, noisy; c 16, a 1/3, 22-9437, D, cheaper with shared bath, hw.

Otoya: Dark and dingy but cheap and friendly. Central location, c ctl, a 5/7, 21-3925, E, pb; F, cb, hw.

Petit: Near Sabana Park, good neighborhood yet close to buses, kitchen privileges; c 24, a ctl/2, 33-0766, D, pb; E, cb.

Príncipe: Rooms have big windows, pb, phones, secure but borderline neighborhood, a 6, c ctl/2, 22-7983, E.

Roma: Near buses, noisy, cheap; c 14, a 1, 23-2179, F, cw.

HOSTELS

Toruma: Headquarters of the Costa Rica Youth Hostel Network. Dormitory-style rooms, washing machine, kitchen, inexpensive soda open 7:15 am-9 pm, a ctl, c 31/33, 24-4085, F per person, less with IYHF card.

Casa Ridgway: A small *pensión* next to the Quaker Peace Center on a 6 bis, c 15, especially for people concerned with peace and environmental issues (cb, hw, kitchen privileges, 33-6168, Apdo. 1507, 1000 San José, CR), E per person in private rooms; F, dormitory-style bunks.

Renting a room with a Tico family is a good way to get to know the people and practice your Spanish. The going rate for room, board and laundry service is $180-200 per person per month, less with fewer meals. Call the language schools, look for signs at the University, or contact Sra. Soledad Zamora (24-7937) or her sister Virginia (25-7344) who specialize in connecting renters with rooms (Spanish only). Be prepared for a lot of hospitality. If noise bothers you, check first to see if your family leaves the TV or radio on all the time.

DO-IT-YOURSELF TOUR PLANNING

The following chart will help you plan your own tour based on your interests and the time you have available. Travel time to and from San José plus time to relax and explore are calculated into the "Days Required for Trip" column, but should be regarded as the *minimum* relaxed travel time possible. Tours, when available as marked, can be arranged through the travel agencies listed on p. 49-50, or with agencies recommended by the ICT in their information office on Calle 5, under the Plaza de la Cultura. Places and transportation are described on the pages indicated. "Good for Children" means either that there are activities designed for children, or that, in the case of beaches, there are gentle waves.

Have a great time exploring Costa Rica!

THE CENTRAL VALLEY	Birdwatching	Botany	Crafts	Fishing	Hiking	Churches	Volcanoes	Water sports	Wildlife	Good for children	Camping	Days required for trip	Tours available	Page number
Ojo de Agua								x		x		1/2		129
La Guácima								x		x		1/2	x	130
Zarcero			x									1	x	131
Grecia			x					x		x		1/2		132
Sarchí			x									1/2	x	132
Poás N.P.	x	x	x		x		x			x		1/2	x	133
Heredia					x						x	1/2	x	136
Braulio Carrillo N.P.	x	x			x							1/2	x	140
Rancho Redondo					x							1/2		140
Cartago						x				x		1/2	x	141
Irazú N.P., Prusia					x		x			x		1/2	x	141
Orosi				x	x	x		x		x		1/2	x	142
Tapantí	x	x		x	x				x	x		1/2		142
Turrialba, Guayabo N.M.	x	x			x	x		x		x		1	x	143

THE ATLANTIC COAST	Birdwatching	Botany	Crafts	Fishing	Hiking	History, archaeology	Volcanoes	Water sports	Wildlife	Good for children	Camping	Days required for trip	Tours available	Page number
Cahuita N.P.	x	x	x	x				x	x		x	3	x	150
Hitoy Cerere B.R.	x	x		x					x			3		154
Puerto Viejo	x	x		x	x			x	x		x	3	x	154
Tortuguero N.P.	x	x		x				x	x	x		3	x	161

THE NORTHERN ZONE

	Birdwatching	Botany	Crafts	Fishing	Hiking	History, archaeology	Volcanoes	Water sports	Wildlife	Good for children	Camping	Days required for trip	Tours available	Page number
Puerto Viejo de Sarapiquí	x	x		x	x			x				2	x	168
Rara Avis	x	x			x					x		3	x	171
Arenal Volcano and Lake Arenal				x	x		x	x		x	x	2	x	173

GUANACASTE

	Birdwatching	Botany	Crafts	Fishing	Hiking	History, archaeology	Volcanoes	Water sports	Wildlife	Good for children	Camping	Days required for trip	Tours available	Page number
Cañas, Lomas Barbudal	x	x			x			x	x	x		3	x	179
Palo Verde N.P.	x								x		x	3	x	179
Rincón de la Vieja N.P.	x	x			x		x		x		x	3	x	181
Santa Rosa N.P.	x	x			x			x	x		x	3	x	183
Guanacaste N.P.	x	x			x				x			3		185
Beaches near Liberia				x				x		x	x	3	x	187
Beaches near Santa Cruz				x				x	x	x	x	3	x	189
Nicoya, Guaitil			x			x						3		194
Nosara	x	x		x	x			x	x	x	x	4	x	195
Ostional W.R.									x			4		196
Sámara, Carrillo				x				x		x	x	4	x	197
Barra Honda N.P.					x				x		x	3	x	198

THE CENTRAL PACIFIC	Birdwatching	Botany	Crafts	Fishing	Hiking	Churches and archaeology	Volcanoes	Water sports	Wildlife	Good for children	Camping	Days required for trip	Tours available	Page number
Gulf of Nicoya	x			x				x				1	x	202
Curú W.R.	x				x			x	x		x	3		204
Tambor				x	x			x	x	x	x	3	x	204
Montezuma, Cabo Blanco	x	x			x			x	x		x	4	x	205
Monteverde	x	x	x		x				x	x	x	3	x	208
Carara B.R.	x	x			x				x	x		1	x	214
Herradura, Jacó				x				x			x	1	x	215
Manuel Antonio N.P.	x	x		x	x			x	x			3	x	217
THE SOUTHERN ZONE														
Copey de Dota	x			x	x							1		224
San Gerardo	x			x	x							1	x	225
Chirripó N.P.	x	x			x						x	4	x	226
Dominical	x							x		x	x	3		230
Boruca			x		x							3		230
Pavones								x	x		x	4	x	235
Zancudo				x				x				4		236
Corcovado N.P.	x	x			x				x		x	5	x	238
Marenco	x	x			x				x			3	x	243
Drake Bay	x			x	x			x	x		x	4	x	244
Wilson Gardens	x	x			x				x			3	x	245
La Amistad N.P.	x	x		x	x				x		x	4	x	246
Isla del Coco N.P	x	x		x	x			x				4	x	247

Rapids in the Río Reventazón

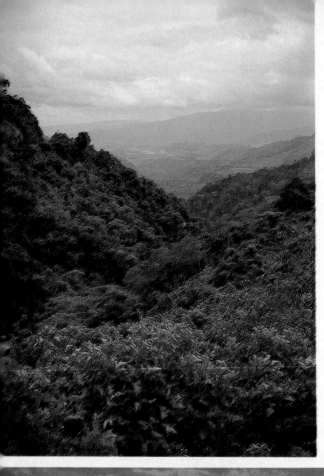

Caribbean kaleidoscope: Costa Rica is full of green vistas, like this one near the old road to Limón through Turrialba (left). Below, a beach in coastal Talamanca. Right, a hibiscus, some homemade music, and a typical Atlantic Coast village. The low structure in the center is a dryer for *cacao* beans.

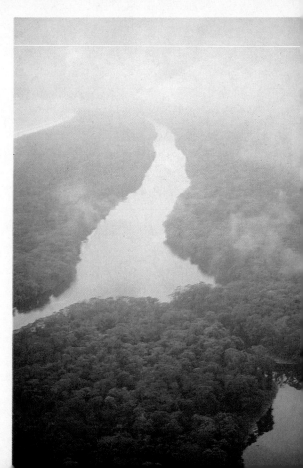

Flying to Tortuguero, one sees the rich rain forest of Braulio Carrillo National Park giving way to deforestation inland from the famous canals. Right: paddling through the smaller canals in a *cayuca*.

Sunset from Monteverde, Arenal blows, Montezuma's rocky coastline, one of Montezuma's waterfalls

View from the hills of Manuel Antonio, horses bathing in a cove near Manuel Antonio

Cacho de venado

THE CENTRAL VALLEY AND SURROUNDINGS

Volcanoes, cloud forests, lakes, and a good deal of Costa Rican history and culture lie within a 30- to 90-minute radius of San José by car. In this chapter we will mention places in or near the Central Valley, going clockwise from Alajuela, west of San José, and ending up in Turrialba to the east (see map on page 128).

Although only 20 km from San José, **Alajuela** is 200 meters lower, and so considerably warmer. It is full of shady parks. On Sundays, oldtimers sit in the Parque Central and entertain each other by thinking up nicknames for passersby. The **Juan Santamaría Museum,** housed in the former jail one block north of Parque Central, features relics of the 1856 rout of William Walker, including his incursion order and defense plea in English. It is open Tuesday through Sunday from 2 pm to 9 pm. Admission is free. In San José, buses leave continuously for Alajuela from a 2, c 12/14.

Hotels: The Juan Santamaría International Airport is about 5 minutes from Alajuela, and the elegant resort hotels, **Cariari** and **Herradura** are just before the airport (see p. 117). **Hotel Alajuela,** 25 meters south from the SW corner of Alajuela's Parque Central, is an alternative for folks who want to avoid San José's bustle and pollution and still be close to the airport and buses. It's a friendly hotel with clean, pleasant rooms (D and E) and some very reasonable apartments in the older part of the building (D, hw, pb, 41-1241).

Ojo de Agua is a recreational complex about half an hour outside of San José. Cold, clear water gushes up from an *ojo*

129

de agua (spring) and is pumped down an artificial waterfall into large swimming pools. There's a man-made lake where you can rent rowboats, grassy fields for soccer, volleyball, sunbathing and picnics, and a big *soda*. It is very crowded on weekends, but not so bad during the week. The lowering of the water table due to deforestation is starting to affect Ojo de Agua at the end of the dry season.

Buses leave at least once an hour for Ojo de Agua from c 18/20, a 1, a half block west of Coca Cola.

Southwest of the airport, in **La Guácima**, is **The Butterfly Farm**, featuring a variety of covered garden habitats where you can observe up to three dozen species of butterflies. A one-hour tour of the grounds shows you the different stages through which caterpillars grow, butterflies' territorial practices, and defense mechanisms such as mimicry, with which they ward off predators. Early morning visitors can see the metamorphosed butterflies emerging from their chrysalises. Open every day, 7am to 4pm, adm. $7, discounts for students and kids. Call 48-0115 for directions by either car or bus.

La Garita is the home of **La Fiesta del Maíz,** a restaurant where you can sample the wide variety of foods that Costa Ricans make from corn. Everything is delicious and homemade. The waitress will offer you little samples of the dishes if you ask (open Fri-Sun). If you have kids, they might like to go to **Bosque Encantado**, a rather dilapidated amusement park with swimming pools, horses and motorized swans that you can ride around in on a lake. Open weekends and holidays only (48-7050), about 2km to the left at the Fiesta del Maíz.

Chatelle is a bed-and-breakfast located about 1km to the left at the Fiesta del Maíz. Most of it's spacious, hexagonal cabinas have kitchenettes (LL incl. continental breakfast, pool, restaurant, weekly, monthly and off-season rates, phones, hw, airport pickup and shuttle into San José, 48-7781, 48-7095).

Villa Tranquilidad is a bed-and-breakfast on a secluded organic coffee farm in Atenas, 15 minutes west of La Garita. The large rooms are part of the main house (C incl. full breakfast, other meals available, pb, hw, small pool, weekly, monthly and off-season discounts, owners can arrange private sight-seeing tours). Write Frans and Kwin Lamers, Apdo.28, 4013 Alajuela, CR, or call (506) 46-5460.

To get to the above places, take the Atenas turnoff about half an hour from San José on the highway to Puntarenas. The Fiesta del Maíz is 2.5km to the left. The Atenas bus leaves hourly from the Coca Cola in San José.

The **Zoo-Ave**, a collection of exotic birds, is 3.5km to the right at the Atenas exit, on a back road to Alajuela. There you'll see scarlet macaws, parrots, rosy-cheeked cockatoos, peacocks, pheasants, toucans, tanagers, orioles, swans, ostriches, falcons, owls, a tiger heron, and African crested cranes, all for $.50. You might be interested in stopping at some of the *viveros* (greenhouses) near the Zoo-Ave. To get there by bus, go to Alajuela first from a 2, c 12/14, and take a La Garita bus from there.

Zarcero is one of the most charming Costa Rican towns. Perched on the hills that divide the Central Valley from the San Carlos plain, Zarcero's climate is fresh and invigorating. Its ruddy-cheeked inhabitants are famous for their peach preserves and homemade white cheese, but Zarcero's real claim to fame are the fancifully sculpted bushes in front of its picturesque little church. Gardeners shape them into gigantic green rabbits, horses, oxcarts and elephants. When we were there, a huge rainbow guided us down the country roads above Zarcero to the town plaza, then remained in a perfect arc directly over the church. There are no real hotels in Zarcero, but if you ask around, you'll probably find a family who will put you up for a modest fee.

The Zarcero bus leaves from the corner of c 16 and a 3 near Coca Cola at 9:15 every morning, or you can take any of the hourly San Carlos buses in the Coca Cola. The trip lasts two hours. It's easy to catch a bus back to San José, or on to Volcán Arenal and the hot springs at Tabacón. Just before you reach Zarcero, there is a group of restaurants and stands selling cheese, candied fruit and flowers. **Restaurant La Montaña** on the right specializes in hearty Italian dishes. If you want to stop for something to eat, any restaurant in that area is better than what is offered in Zarcero itself. By car, Zarcero is 1.5 hours from San José. Take the Naranjo-Ciudad Quesada exit on the highway to Puntarenas.

The **Grecia** area offers many possibilities for day trips, alone or including La Garita and Volcán Poás. Grecia was voted the cleanest town in Latin America, and its citizens take pride in maintaining that reputation. From its airy red metal church with delicate wooden filigree altars to the well-kept homes of its farmers, the area still exudes the goodness and simplicity which other parts of the country have lost.

West of Grecia is the small town of **Sarchí**, home of Costa Rica's traditional brightly-painted oxcarts. You can watch craftsmen turning out beautiful wooden bowls, plates, furniture, and walking sticks with the heads of animals and birds. You can buy the same things in San José and Moravia, but its nice to go to the source. The most inexpensive place to buy is at the cooperative, on the right at the end of town.

To get to Sarchí, take the hourly Grecia bus from the Coca Cola. In Grecia, connect with the Alajuela-Sarchí bus. You can catch the latter bus in Alajuela, but it takes a long, roundabout route to Grecia. By car, take the Grecia exit on the Puntarenas highway, 30 min. west of San José.

Sugar cane and coffee are the main crops in Grecia area. A winding road through the hills to the northwest takes you to **Los Trapiches**, where you can see how *tapa dulce*, the flavorful hard brown sugar of Central America, is made. A waterwheel activates the huge gears of a venerable Victorian cane press, imported 110 years ago from Aberdeen, Scotland. The cane juice is collected in enormous cauldrons (*pailas*), set into a brick vault in which a fire is built. As the liquid boils, it reaches different stages of consistency until it is poured into the flower-pot-shaped molds. At one point the sugar can be whipped into different shapes, called *sobado*. It is quite an interesting process to see, and you can spend the day there, picnicking or eating *comida típica* in their restaurant. There are swimming pools, and a small lake for boating. Nothing is very fancy--ticos love to go there on weekends. To get there, drive 300m past the church in Grecia and turn left, winding through the hills to Santa Gertrudis Sur, following the Los Trapiches signs. Call to make sure the *trapiche* is operating: 44-6656.

Los Chorros are two beautiful waterfalls protected by the National Park system. To get there, take the road going west from Alajuela, about 15km to Tácares. Turn right at the Tácares church and bear to the left for a couple of kilometers, until the road dead-ends near a cyclone fence on the right. There is a sign prohibiting you from entering. Just ignore it like the ticos do, and walk about 10 minutes downhill until you come to a quarry. Walk to the left into the quarry and you'll see a path to the right. Follow the muddy footprints and soon you'll see the National Park signs. As you can guess, Los Chorros is not very developed, which is fine. Bring good hiking shoes because the trail to the waterfall is steep and muddy at the beginning and at the end. Take the little trail that goes up to the left. It's only a ten-minute hike to the falls. Halfway down the trail, a sign indicates another branch to a lookout point (*mirador*) across from the top of one of the cascades. The main trail takes you to the bottom of a second magnificent waterfall. The many little jets of water that look like they are pouring from the rocks give the place its name. There is a covered camping area and a rickety bridge which takes you to the other side of the river. If you want to enjoy the waterfalls in peace, go during the week, as Los Chorros is crowded on weekends. On the way back, you might want to stop at **Las Tinajitas**, a clean, nicely decorated place with good food a few minutes outside Alajuela on the road to Tácares and Grecia.

Poás is one of the few active volcanoes on the continent that is accessible by a good road. The 37 km trip from San José is full of beautiful scenery, with lookouts over the Central Valley. It is the most developed of the national parks, with a visitors' center and well-maintained nature trails.

The main crater of Poás is 1.5km wide and 300 meters deep. There was a hot, sulphurous lake at the bottom, but it recently evaporated due to increased volcanic activity. Geysers and active fumaroles are visible from the lookout point above the crater. A 20-minute uphill hike takes you to another lookout over jewel-like Botos Lake, which fills an extinct crater.

Volcan Poás is entering an active phase, apparently part of a 40-to 45-year cycle. The volcano spewed a 4000-meter column of water and mud in 1910, sending ash as far as Puntarenas. Lava flow increased also in 1953. In May 1989 Poás shot ash a mile into the air, but still it is quiet compared to Arenal and former explosions of Irazú.

Scientists believe that Poás has a relatively open passage from its magma chamber to its huge crater, so it can let off steam more easily than other volcanos and doesn't build up the pressure that causes large eruptions. Nevertheless, the volcano is under close observation these days, and the park is sometimes closed to visitors because of sulfur gas emissions from the cra-

133

ter which combine with steam to make sulfuric acid. Local residents have experienced breathing problems and irritation to their eyes, skin and stomachs due to the sulfur gas, and the local coffee crop has suffered.

It is recommended that visitors not stay more than 20 minutes at the crater. You should take glasses to protect your eyes, and a handkerchief soaked in a vinegar and water solution to neutralize the effect of the sulfuric acid if it becomes difficult to breathe. The park is open daily 9am to 3:30pm.

Poás National Park protects the headwaters of several rivers which feed the Río Tárcoles to the southwest and the Río Sarapiquí to the north. While the active crater is full of subtle, moonscape colors, the rest of Poás is intensely green, with a great variety of wildflowers, bromeliads, ferns, mosses and lichen. One of the most interesting plants there is the *sombrilla del pobre* (poor man's umbrella) which has thick fuzzy leaves up to two meters in width. Hummingbirds are among the 26 species of birds most easily seen along the road or on the trails. Quetzals also frequent Poás. As you approach the park, you pass a cyclone-fence gate. *Aguacatillo* trees, favored by quetzales, grow in the pasture land along the dirt road to the left of the gate.

The average temperature on misty Poás is 50°, dropping as low as 22° and climbing as high as 70°, so it is important to dress in layers. Bring raingear. If you get there too late in the day, clouds will have covered the crater, so the earlier the better. When it's clear you can see Poás on the horizon to the northwest of San José. If you can't see it, it's probably too late to go. There are no restaurants at the park, but local ladies sell homemade food there on Sundays.

If you do go to Poás, be sure to stop at **Chubascos,** one of the nicest places we know for native Costa Rican food. Set in a hillside garden with covered outdoor tables, their large *casado* can't be beat, especially accompanied by *refrescos* made from local strawberries and blackberries, and topped off with homemade cheesecake. It's about 16 km above Alajuela. **Los Jaules**, **El Recreo** and **Restaurant Volcán Poás**, farther up toward the volcano, are also nice places to stop for a snack. **Churrascos Steak House** is in Poasito, about 10km from the park entrance. There is a little supermarket there also. **Lo Que Tu Quieras** is 5km from the park entrance. They have an incredible view from their mediocre restaurant, and several cramped cabinas (E, pb, hw, 48-5213).

About 14km east of the Park, near Vara Blanca, is **Albergue Volcán Poás** (LL, 55-3486, hw), a bed-and-breakfast especially for hikers and birders who like to get out and roam around the countryside. Nearby **Restaurant Vara Blanca** is recommended for generous servings and friendly service. Vara Blanca is the junction of the Heredia-Sarapiquí road, and the road approaching Poás from the east.

Getting there: Take the Alajuela turnoff about 15 minutes from San José. It leads you past Alajuela's Central Park and the Juan Santamaría Museum. Stay on the same road till you get to Fraijanes Lake and Chubascos. About 1.5 km beyond the restaurant you connect with the road from San Pedro de Poás, which leads you to the volcano.

If you are near Heredia, take the Barva-Birrí road to Vara Blanca and turn left for 6km, then right at Poasito. If you are in Grecia, go east to San Pedro de Poás and turn left. You can make a nice circular route, entering through Alajuela, and returning through Vara Blanca and Heredia. On the way down, take forks to the left, following little signs to El Pórtico. Ignore the third El Pórtico sign and keep to the right.

A **bus** to Poás leaves *Sundays only* from Parque de la Merced in San José (a 2, c 12) at 8:30 am. Buses leave from Alajuela's Parque Central continuously between 8 and 9am Sundays (41-0631, $3.30 roundtrip). Get there early to assure yourself a seat. The bus arrives at the volcano around 11 am. Check with the driver for departure time. Many tour companies offer day trips to Poás for $15-25.

You can also catch a bus any day from Alajuela to San Pedro de Poás. It leaves from the Parque del Cementerio every hour on the hour. From there you can take a taxi (about $10 one way), a bus that leaves for Poasito at 5am, noon and 5pm, or hitchhike the remaining distance.

Founded in 1706, **Heredia** has retained a friendly, small town atmosphere. Its colonial church built in 1796 has a pretty facade and a peaceful garden. There are concerts Thursday nights in the music temple in the Parque Central. In the **Mercado Florense** (300 m. south and 50 m. west of the Church) there's an inexpensive place to have a good seafood lunch. Near the National University are some popular student bars, especially **La Choza** and **El Bulevar**. **Hotel Verano** (F, 37-1616, cb, cw, c 4, a 6) on the west side of the market in Heredia is clean, friendly and very inexpensive. **Buses** to Heredia leave every 5-10 minutes from c 1, a 7/9 in San José from 5:20 am to 10:30 pm (through Tibás) and from a 2, c 12 every 20 minutes (through La Uruca).

La Posada de la Montaña is a new bed-and-breakfast above **San Isidro de Heredia**. Rooms are sunny and clean and guests can use the kitchen (B incl. breakfast, pb, hw, cable TV, fireplace, $10 airport pickup, tel/fax (506) 39-8096, cabinas with private kitchenettes and fireplaces, LL). The Posada is 1.2km to the right before the metal bridge behind the church as you enter San Isidro. On the way up you will pass the **Cerámica Chavarría** where doña Frances turns out her sturdy, ovenproof stoneware and blends her own non-leaded glazes. A mug we bought from her fell out of the car on the way back, and, true to her claims, it didn't break. Call first, 39-8455. She will give pottery demonstrations to groups. **Buses** leave San José for San Isidro every half hour from c 4, a 7/9. By **car**, take the San Isidro exit, on the left about 14km down the Guapiles Highway.

The mountains above Heredia are full of evergreen forests and pastureland. It's exhilaratingly chilly there all year round, and a bright, sunny day can turn into a rainy one in minutes, especially after noon. From these mountains you can see the sun glinting off the Gulf of Nicoya in the west. A hike to **Monte de la Cruz** gives you an incredible panorama of the entire Central Valley and beyond. Take a picnic lunch, an umbrella and a sweater. There is a restaurant there, open 10am to 11pm every day, but the menu is not too interesting. If you wish to enjoy the view in a more formal setting, visit **El Castillo,** a posh country club with an ice-skating rink, pool, gym, barbecue pits, go-carts, and a miniature train. The $5/person entrance fee lets you use all facilities and entitles you to a free lunch in the dining room, which overlooks the skating rink as well as the Central Valley. The small, wrought-iron sign at the entrance to El Castillo is hard to spot, but you'll see its well-manicured lawns on the right a few hundred meters after a large sign for Residencial El Castillo.

Before you get to El Castillo, there is a sign for **Bosque de la Hoja.** Go left, down a beautiful wooded road 2 km. The entrance says "Bar las Chorreras". Bosque de la Hoja protects the water supply for Heredia. It is not developed for tourism and the roads are terrible, so leave your car where a guard requests a minimal entrance fee. There are trails through cool, fresh forests of *ciprés*, and lovely meadows for picnics. Camping is allowed.

After your hike you might want to stop for a tasty lunch or dinner at **Stein Biergarten**, down the road to the left just before you get to Bosque de la Hoja. They offer tasty German food including meat, sausage, chicken, sauerkraut and kartoffel-salat. Not the place for weight-watchers, but even they can sip a club soda and enjoy the beautiful view and classical music. Once a month there is a live Tico and German band. Open Friday eves, and from noon onwards on weekends, 39-7021.

The turnoff to Bosque de la Hoja is 5 km north of **San Rafael de Heredia.** El Castillo is 1 km farther, and Monte de la Cruz is 2 km beyond that. An hourly bus leaves from behind the Mercado Florense in Heredia from 8am to 8pm. The 9am, 12 and 4pm buses go to a fork in the road 1 km from the entrance to Monte de la Cruz.

Going *left* at that fork takes you in about 1km to **Hotel Chalet Tirol,** charming 2-story vine-covered cabins with hand-painted Tyrolean designs and an elegant French restaurant (A, bathtubs, hw, electric heating, room service, airport pickup, 39-7070, 39-7050). The hotel, at 1800m (5900 ft) is surrounded by a cloud forest reserve that borders Braulio Carrillo National Park. Two hiking trails are accessible from the reserve, one of which leads to a moss-covered cliff where a dozen small water-falls cascade into as many small pools before joining the river below. It's a beautiful place to be, and amazing for being so close to San José. Another trail follows the Río Segundo into Braulio Carrillo amidst a carpet of ferns and ancient trees covered with orchids and bromeliads. A great place for a day hike or for a weekend, and you can warm up with a hot chocolate and *quiche lorraine* or pastry on the second floor of the Chalet's restaurant, or stay for their excellent *nouvelle cuisine* specialties.

All the above-mentioned places are about 35 minutes from San José by car. Take the San Isidro exit to the left about 14 km down the Guápiles highway. When you reach San Isidro, turn right in front of its pretty, white church and go 2 km to Concepción (ignore any previous Concepción signs). This area has a real flavor of *campesino* life, since these towns were pretty much off the beaten track until the highway opened in 1987. San Isidro and San Joaquín de las Flores, to the west of Heredia, are known for their colorful Easterweek processions. Con-

THE CENTRAL VALLEY AND SURROUNDINGS

tinue a few minutes more to San Rafael, where again you turn right at the church to reach Bosque de la Hoja, El Castillo, Chalet Tirol, and Monte de la Cruz.

The town of **Barva**, 2km north of Heredia, is one of the oldest settlements in the country. Its historic church and the houses near it have been restored. **Galería Huetar**, on the NW corner of the plaza, sells local arts and crafts and native food. Open 9am to 9pm every day (38-0802).

The **Instituto de Café** has its research station in San Pedro de Heredia, northwest of Barva. During the coffee harvest in December and January, you can see how the *grano de oro* (the golden bean) is dried and processed, and take a look at their collection of antique coffee grinders. Open weekdays, 7am to 3pm. To get there, turn left as you reach the square in front of the Barva church, and continue 2km to San Pedro, bearing to the right. The Institute is 400m beyond the San Pedro church. By bus, take the *Santa Bárbara por Barrio Jesús* from Heredia.

La Rosa Blanca, near the entrance to Santa Bárbara de Heredia, is certainly one of the most comfortable and beautiful bed-and-breakfasts in Costa Rica. Each room has a theme, and the architecture and hand-crafted furnishings are full of fantasy and delightful, creative touches. The honeymoon suite features a tower room with a 360 degree view and a bathroom painted like a rainforest, with the water for the bathtub bubbling out of a rocky waterfall (XL, pb, hw, breakfast incl., 39-9392, fax: (506) 39-9555). They also rent a 3-br house for families (XL).

Hotel El Pórtico is graciously designed, offering quiet rooms with large windows, a lovely lounge, a pool, sauna, jacuzzi and restaurant (L, 37-6022). Down the road are **Cabañas Las Ardillas,** cozy, ivy-covered cabins with kitchens, fireplaces and views of hilly pastureland. A round restaurant serves Costa Rican specialties (B, hw, lower weekly and monthly rates, 22-8134). Across the road is **Hotel Cypresal,** with cabins, pool, and restaurant (A, 37-4466). There are two ways to reach these hotels. North of Barva, there's a fork in the road. Take the left fork 4 km to Birrí, turn right at Las Delicias, and continue 5 Km, all on good road. Or, take the right fork above Barva to lovely **San José de la Montaña,** and continue 5 km beyond it. You'll see signs for Braulio Carrillo National Park on the right. Continue past the signs about 1 km to the hotels. The road has quite a few potholes, but goes through less developed country than the road from Birrí. The Barva-Birrí road continues north 1/2 hour to Vara Blanca, where you can turn left to go to Volcán Poás.

Hourly buses leave for San José de la Montaña from behind the Mercado Central in Heredia. At 6 am, 12 and 4 pm, they continue up to Paso Llano, the start-off point for hikes to Volcán Barva.

Quetzal

Volcán Barva is on the western edge of Braulio Carrillo National Park. Follow the road above the town of Barva through San José de la Montaña to Paso Llano and on to Sacramento. The country people who live in those foggy mountains sell fresh eggs, sour cream and baked goods along the way. There are now camping facilities at the entrance to the park, about a half hour hike from Barva's scenic crater lake.

Quetzales are sometimes visible there. They migrate to forests over 3600 feet above sea level, where they nest in the hollows of the tallest and oldest trees. Males and females share the incubation of eggs and feeding of their hatchlings. The females sit on the eggs at night and at mid-day, and the male sits with his beautiful green tail hanging out of the nest during the rest of the day. They cannot live in captivity. Also heard on Volcán Barva is the black-faced solitaire, which has been compared to the nightingale for the sweetness and delicacy of its song.

To climb Volcán Barva you should catch the 6am San José de la Montaña-Paso Llano bus from behind the Mercado Central in Heredia. At Paso Llano (Porrosatí), you'll see signs for the park entrance 6.4 km to the left. Bring raingear, a compass, and waterproof shoes or boots even in the dry season (see p. 83). Be sure to make it back for the 5 pm Paso Llano bus to Heredia. By car, go to San José de la Montaña (see above) and continue beyond it until you see signs to Sacramento and Braulio Carrillo. Jungle Trails, (55-3486, fax: (506) 55-2782), specializes in leading hiking and birding trips to Barva.

139

The founding of **Braulio Carrillo National Park** in 1978 represents a compromise between ecology and development. Environmentalists were concerned that the opening of a highway between San José and Guápiles would result in the ecological disasters that have followed the opening of other roads: indiscriminate colonization and deforestation. The government agreed to make 80,000 acres of virgin forest surrounding the highway into a national park.

The Guápiles highway, opened in May 1987, makes Braulio Carrillo the national park most accessible by car. The scenery is inspiring. Hopefully it is an education in itself for all the motorists who pass through it on their way to the Atlantic coast--mountains of untouched rainforest as far as the eye can see. And just 30 years ago, most of Costa Rica looked like that!

In order to hike the trails accessible from the highway, you must stop and pay a minimal entrance fee, either at the administration buildings before the Zurquí tunnel, or at the station on the right as you leave the park (coming from San José). The trail before the tunnel is steep and strenuous; the La Botella trail 17 km beyond the tunnel is easier. Parts of the trail are muddy, and snakes are a danger, so wear boots. Porcupines, margays, tapirs, monkeys, coatis, kinkajous, peccaries, pacas, ocelots, sloths and raccoons live in Braulio Carrillo though chances are you won't see them. More visible are the 500 species of birds there.

Take the hourly Guápiles bus (c 12, a 7/9, Coopetragua, $1). The La Botella trail is 2.5 km before the Quebrada Gonzales station at the far end of the park.

Rancho Redondo is a beautiful place to go for a drive and a view of the Central Valley. Just follow the main road through San Jose's northeastern suburb of Guadalupe. Soon the houses start to thin out and the crowded thoroughfare becomes one of Costa Rica's charming country roads, lined with the famous "living fenceposts". The volcanic soil is so fertile that fenceposts sprout and turn into trees. About 15km from San José, just before you reach Rancho Redondo, is a place to stop and look at the view. Rancho Redondo is the site of **Polestar,** the Costa Rican headquarters of a Florida-based addiction treatment center. Help for alcohol, drug and food problems is provided by a bilingual, bicultural team of MDs and psychologists, who use the Twelve-Step Program as a base. Stress-reduction workshops are also held there, in a large, comfortable lodge on a 2000-acre dairy farm. The climate is invigorating, the streams are clear, and the atmosphere is serene. Many different modalities of treatment are offered, some of which include family members. Call 29-1094; in US (305) 669-1888, fax: (305) 669-1777.

Though **Cartago** was the birthplace of Costa Rican culture and the capital for 300 years, many of its historical buildings were destroyed in the earthquakes of 1823 and 1910. The 1910 quake prevented the completion of a cathedral in the center of town. The ruins of that church have been made into a pleasant garden. On August 2, every year, thousands of Costa Ricans walk from San José to Cartago in honor of *La Negrita,* the Virgin of Los Angeles, who appeared to a peasant girl in 1635. She has become Costa Rica's patron saint, and her shrine is surrounded by offerings from grateful pilgrims she has miraculously cured. Tiny metal arms, legs, hearts, etc., decorate the walls near her statue inside the **Basílica,** an imposing structure on the east side of town.

Buses to Cartago leave often from c 13, a ctl/2 in San José, west of the Plaza de la Democracia (half-hour trip).

Volcán Irazú is 32 km north of Cartago. On a clear morning, the trip up its slope is full of breathtaking views of farmland, native oak forests and the valley below. The craters are bleak and majestic. On March 19, 1963, the day John F. Kennedy arrived in Costa Rica on a presidential visit, Irazú erupted, showering black ash over the Central Valley for the next two years. People carried umbrellas to keep the ash out of their hair, roofs caved in from the weight of piled-up ash, everything was black. Since then, the volcano has been dormant. Some gases and steam are emitted from fumaroles on the northwestern slope, not visible from the crater lookouts. It is said that you can see both the Atlantic and the Pacific from Irazú's chilly 3800 m (11,000-foot) summit. This is true on occasion, but often the Atlantic side is obscured by clouds.

A good place to go for a day hike is **Area Recreativa Jiménez Oreamuno,** a reforestation project started after the 1963 eruption. It's located about halfway up the west side of the volcano, near **Prusia.** The hike to the forest is very beautiful, through steep hills covered with oak and pine. Once there, you'll find trails and picnic tables.

Buses to Irazú leave weekends and holidays at 7:30am across the street from the Gran Hotel Costa Rica, returning at 1:30pm ($3). Other days you have to drive or take a tour. If you want to try to catch the view of both oceans, it's a must to go early. Bring warm clothes, raingear, food and something to drink. The first place on your right as you come down is a good place to stop for breakfast. About a third of the way down the mountain is **Hotel Gestoria Irazú** (D, 53-0827, cw, cb), a large, charmingly gloomy building that has seen better days. Call for reservations. Their restaurant is not recommended.

Developed by English botanist Charles Lankester, **Lankester Gardens** display the hundreds of varieties of orchids and bromeliads for which Costa Rica is famous. The gardens are run by the biology department of the University of Costa Rica.

Take the Paraíso bus from Cartago. Ask the bus driver to let you off near the gardens. There is a cube-shaped sign on the highway. The entrance is about 100 meters down a road to your right, then right again. The gardens are open every day from 9:30 to 3:30.

Orosi Valley, south of Cartago, is one of Costa Rica's jewels. You can visit the peaceful ruins of Costa Rica's oldest church at **Ujarrás,** then walk about 1/2 hour to **Charrarra,** ICT's tourism complex on the banks of Cachí Dam. Charrarra offers lakeside trails, a swimming pool, basketball courts, picnic facilities, a pleasant restaurant, and access to boating on the lake. Take the Cachí bus from Cartago and ask to be let off at Ujarrás. On Sundays, the buses go all the way to Charrarra at 8 am, 11 am, 2 pm.

South of Cachí Dam is the town of **Orosi,** with its colonial church, whose beautiful wooden altar and shrines were carved with a special grace. It is one of the few places in Costa Rica that has survived enough earthquakes to preserve its original atmosphere. A small museum of colonial religious history next door is open Tues-Sun 9-12, 1-5.

From Orosi, nature lovers can hire a jeep-taxi, hike, or drive the 10 km full of potholes to **Tapantí Wildlife Refuge.** Tapantí protects the rivers which supply San José with water and electricity. There's great birdwatching, trout fishing (see p. 80 re fresh-water fishing permits) and river swimming. There are some cabinas near the entrance--ask guards about them.

Motel Río (E, cw; D, hw, kitchens, pools, 73-3128, 73-3057), about 3km beyond Orosi on the Río Palomo is the famous, traditional place to go for a fresh fish lunch. It's open 8:30-5 every day. Signs indicate the turnoff to the left. The Orosi minibus goes all the way to the motel about once an hour on weekends, and at noon weekdays.

Getting there: All Orosi buses are 100 meters east of the church ruins in Cartago, and 300 m south. Cachí buses are on the same street.

If you rent a car for one day and start off early, you can easily visit Irazú, Lankester Gardens, Ujarrás, Charrarra and Orosi, stop for lunch at Río Palomo and continue on to Tapantí. Lankester is SE of Cartago on the road to Paraíso. Ujarrás and Charrarra are 6 km east of Paraíso; Orosi, Motel Río and Tapantí are south. A gravel road between Palomo and Cachí circles the dam and connects Orosi with Ujarrás, but it's not worth the wear and tear on your kidneys. There is a *mirador* on the way to Orosi with picnic and barbecue spots and a beautiful view.

Turrialba is becoming known worldwide as the perfect winter training ground for kayakers. The town, which used to be the main stopping place on the old San José-Limón road, suffered an economic depression with the opening of the Guápiles highway, which bypassed the zone completely. Now, however, it is a haven for international whitewater fans who rent houses there or stay with local families. Young Turrialbans are becoming interested in kayaking but most of them do not have the means to outfit themselves for the sport.

Turrialba is definitely "off the beaten track", and offers many possibilities for an interesting day or weekend trip, especially now that the road to Guayabo National Monument is paved. If you have a car, you can take a delightful, paved back road which starts slightly south of the town of Cot on the slopes of Volcán Irazú, and skirts Volcán Turrialba, passing through the towns of Pacayas and Santa Cruz before arriving in Turrialba itself. The trip takes less than 2 hours from San José. Once in Turrialba, there are several restaurants worth visiting:

The charming and folkloric **Turrialtico** is high on a hill about 8km east of town. As you drive up, you'll see wonderful gargoyles popping out of carved branches of coffee wood bordering the spacious open-air diningroom with its magnificent view of the valley. Native food is their specialty. Above the restaurant are comfortable rooms with the same great view (D, 56-1111, hw, pb, playground equipment.)

Two km farther down the road is **Pochotel**, on an even higher hill with an almost 360 degree view of the entire area, including Cerro de la Muerte and Chirripó to the south, and volcanoes Irazú and Turrialba to the north. You can climb up their observation tower and see even more. They'll send your refreshments up to the tower on a mini-ski-lift contraption they've invented. They also rent cabinas (D, 56-0111, pb, hw, playground equipment, camping allowed) and specialize in native food.

Just outside Turrialba is **Restaurant Kingston,** whose Limonese owner and chef has made it famous. If it's hot, you might just want to take a dip at **Balneario Las Américas**, two large pools for kids and adults (adm. $.75) with a bar-restaurant. You'll see signs for it on the main road, a few blocks toward town from Kingston. To the west of town, 600m from the church, is **Parque La Dominica**, a pleasant place to stop for a picnic. There are swings, basketball courts and a swimmable river.

Turrialba is the home of the Centro Agronómico Tropical de Investigación y Enseñanza **(CATIE)**. Established in the 1930's, it is one of the five major tropical research centers in the world. Its extensive library houses Latin America's largest collection of agricultural literature in English.

CATIE's 27,500-acre facilities include greenhouses, orchards, forest plantings, experimental agricultural projects, a dairy, an herbarium, seed conservation chambers, a nuclear reactor and housing for students and teachers. Seeds of fruit and nut trees, tropical forest species suitable for lumber, ornament, erosion control, shade and pulpwood are available by writing CATIE, Turrialba, Costa Rica. They also sell livestock well-adapted to the tropics. CATIE publishes a monthly newsletter in English. You can request it or arrange a visit to the Center by calling 56-64-31.

Birders will find the purple-crested gallinet and other rare waterfowl around the lagoon at CATIE. There is a trail from behind the administration building to the Río Reventazón, also a favorite with birders. You can catch a bus to CATIE where the main road crosses the tracks in Turrialba. Ask about schedules at the Almacén González.

The **Hotel Wagelia,** at the entrance to Turrialba, 150 m west of the central park, offers an elegant menu with reasonable prices (B, hw, no fans; A, a/c, TV, fridge; clean, small rooms, 56-1566, 56-1596). **Hotel Interamericano** (E, pb; F, cb, saggy mattresses but clean, friendly, cw, kitchen privileges, 56-0142) is near the railroad station.

Rancho Naturalista, high in the hills above Tuís, east of Turrialba, offers nature trails through virgin rainforest, habitat of four species of toucans, the snow-capped hummingbird and many other bird and butterfly species. Their comfortable lodge (hot water, good mattresses) overlooks the wide valley. Their creative cookery is a special attraction. $500 for a week's stay includes meals, lodging, transportation, and guided birding trips; $400 June to November (Apdo. 364, 1002 San José, 39-7138).

Guayabo National Monument on the slopes of Volcán Turrialba is considered the most significant archaeological site in Costa Rica. It is a glimpse into the harmony between man and nature that existed in precolumbian times. Birds abound in the ruins, which are set in premontane rain forest and dotted with the guava trees that give the town its name. *Oropéndolas* (related to our orioles) hang their sack-like nests from tree branches. Water sings its song in ancient aqueducts.

Archaeologists have excavated only the central part of a 10,000-inhabitant city that existed from 1000 B.C. to about 1400 A.D. The exposed area is composed of circular mounds which were the floors of large buildings raised to keep them dry; paved sidewalks, some of whose stones are decorated with petroglyphs; a large stone carved with stylistic representations of two Indian gods: the jaguar, god of the forest, and the crocodile, god of the river; a system of covered and uncovered aqueducts which still functions well; and the oldest bridge in Costa Rica, a flat rock now broken in several places, which crosses one of the aqueducts. Several roads radiate out from the center of the town. Spot excavations verify that some go on at least 8 kilometers. It's theorized that the most important people--the chief, his family, and priests--lived in the center while common people lived outside.

Many mysteries remain about the civilization that inhabited Guayabo. No one knows why the people left (just before the *conquistadores* discovered Costa Rica), nor why Spanish explorers never found or never kept records of finding the site.

Yet the peace and beauty that reign in Guayabo echo a wise and gentle people.

From the *mirador* (lookout-point) you can see the green grassy mounds and stone sidewalks nestled within the rainforest. Hawks and vultures swoop and sail in front of the striking four-layered backdrop of mountains. Across the road from the site, behind the campground, a steep trail leads down to the fast-flowing Guayabo river where you can sit bathing your feet and looking for birds. You can also walk up the road past coffee and sugarcane fields for views into the green Guayabo valley.

oropendolas

In an effort to preserve the ruins, visitors are requested to tour Guayabo with a guide along specified routes only. Guides will meet you at the exhibition room. The park is open 8am-4pm, but because park personnel and volunteers are working full-time on restoration and protection of the ruins, it is requested that visitors come on weekends only. Camping is allowed. Bring raingear.

Hotel La Calzada, (E, 56-0465, cb, hw, 400m before the entrance to the Monument), is a pleasant country inn, with comfy, light-filled rooms overlooking a large pond, a homey common area and good *campesino* food in their open-air restaurant. Whether you stop there during the rainy season to warm up with an *agua dulce* or decide to spend a few tranquil days birding and writing in your journal, it's a nice place to be. There is no phone there, so you leave a message at 56-0465, and they contact the hotel by radio, then call back to confirm your reservations. You can get discounts at La Calzada with an IYHF card (see p. 70).

Getting there: San José-Turrialba buses leave every hour from c 13, a 6 ($.75, 2-hr trip). By car, follow signs from Cartago to Turrialba, or take the above-mentioned back road from Cot, heading at first toward Volcán Irazú. Both are scenic and about equal in distance. The main road has more curves.

To get to Guayabo, take the Santa Teresita bus from the main bus stop in Turrialba at 10:30am or 1:30pm. It leaves you 4km from the entrance to Guayabo. José Miguel, the friendly owner of Hotel La Calzada, runs a once-a-day taxi service to meet the 10:30 Santa Teresita bus at the crossroads. Call to let him know when you are coming. The 19km trip to Guayabo takes about 40 minutes by car from Turrialba, a bit longer by bus. The road is paved except for the last 4km.

Most people hike downhill to the crossroads to catch the 12:45pm Santa Teresita bus back to Turrialba. You can also hitch back with families returning by car.

On the way back to San José on the main road, there are a couple of curious little places: **La Posada de la Luna,** west of the church in Cervantes, halfway between Cartago and Turrialba, serves *comida típica* and delicious homemade desserts. Their dining room is surrounded by cases full of antique memorabilia: Spanish swords, precolumbian artefacts, Japanese *netsuke*--you name it, they've got it. At the entrance to Paraíso, on the right coming from Turrialba towards Cartago, is the **Auto-vivero del Río,** a combination greenhouse and mini-zoo of native animals, including quail, *tepiscuintles, guatuzos,* ducks, turtles and a monkey. There is playground equipment for kids. Admission is free, but they ask for donations to support the animals. Besides plants, they sell rabbits and colored volcanic stones.

THE ATLANTIC COAST

Much of Limón province is a jungle-covered lowland. The coast is dotted with beautiful white and black sand beaches. A trip to Limón is a chance to enjoy the area's wild beauty and the distinct culture that characterizes it. Afro-Caribbean peoples migrated to the Atlantic coast before the turn of the century to work on the railroad, to fish and to farm *cacao* and coconut. Several kinds of English are spoken there, including an elegant Jamaican English and the patois that black people use with each other. "What happen" is the common greeting, but it is pronounced "Whoppen". Instead of saying *"Adios"* when they pass, people say "All right" or "Okay". For a fascinating history of the region, read Paula Palmer's *What Happen,* in which the elders of the black community tell their life stories.

Puerto Limón is Costa Rica's Atlantic port. Its main attraction is the annual carnival that coincides with *El Día de la Raza,* October 12. Brightly costumed *Limonenses* parade to the rhythm of drums, tambourines, pots and pans, maracas and whistles. You're part of the parade too, drawn in by the irresistible Afro-Caribbean beat. The drinking, dancing and carousing last several days. Another annual event in Limón is the surfing championship that takes place on Playa Bonita, a touristy beach a few km north of town. Like Puntarenas, Limón is in transition from funky seaport to gateway to some of the country's most beautiful beaches. The streets are full of people, bicycles, dogs and an occasional vulture.

A few km to the north, in a more scenic area between Limón and the container port of Moín, is the **Hotel Matama,** with shady gardens, pool and international restaurant (Caribbean specialties served on Sundays only). Rooms are clean and tastefully decorated. There is no cross-ventilation, so you have to use air conditioning (L incl. breakfast, a/c, hw, friendly staff, 58-1123, fax: (506) 58-4499). **Hotel Maribú Caribe** (LL, a/c, hw, pool, tel, 58-4010, fax: (506) 58-3541) is about 1km towards Limón from the Matama. Coming from the north you see its white, circular thatched cabinas on a hill like a tribal fort. It is perched on the only cliff in the area, so it has a great ocean view from its breezy restaurant. The rooms and pool are spotless, and the whole place has a sterility that makes it seem foreign to the Atlantic coast. The parking lot guards carry small sidearms. The restaurant is a bit overpriced, but the view makes it a worthwhile place to stop after the long drive to Limón. Just north of Limón is **Hotel Las Olas,** a large, monolithic structure built on rocky coral at the ocean's edge (B, a/c or cf, hw, pool, rest, sauna, 58-1414, fax: (506) 58-1678). To get to these hotels you can avoid Limón altogether. Take an exit that goes diagonally to the left from the main highway. You'll see the signs advertising the hotels. The road signs marking the exit to Moín are confusingly placed. Turn right just before the entrance to the port facility. You'll pass the beaches of **Portete** and **Playa Bonita** before you come to the hotels. We have heard that food is good at the big restaurant on Playa Bonita. Just as you enter Limón from the north, on the right, is **Restaurant Arrecife**, specializing in fresh seafood. A bit further on is **Springfield**, a favorite with locals for Caribbean cooking.

In Limón, the **Hotel Acón** (C, 50m. E of market, a/c, hw, TV, rest, 58-1010, fax: 58-2954) is the best equipped. The **Park** (E, a/c and hw in some rooms, 58-3476), with a certain aging charm, is next to the sea wall, so receives the ocean breezes. The **Lincoln,** 200m N from the *mercado* is nothing special but reasonably clean (E, pb, tf, cw, 58-0074). The **International** next door has a/c in some rooms (D, pb, cw, 58-0434). There are lots of funky cheap hotels on the same street as the bus stop. One doesn't seem to be any better than another. You can stay just as cheaply in the more beautiful areas down the coast, so try not to get stuck in Limón for the night. If you do have to wait there, **Parque Vargas** is pleasant, with its huge palms, and you can take a refreshing walk along the sea wall. **Los Cuatro Mares** on the south side of the *mercado* is a nice, clean place to stop for a snack. Be careful in Limón after dark. Mugging is a danger. We were even stopped once by a uniformed person who seemed to be trying to trump up something about our identification in order to get a bribe. This is very rare in Costa Rica. We just played dumb and walked away.

We recommend going south to the **Talamanca** region. When we first went to Talamanca in 1975, there was no road. We took a two-hour train ride from Limón to Penshurst on the Río Estrella, where we were met by a man in a dugout canoe who ferried us across the river to a rickety bus. Then it was another hour on a dirt road to Cahuita, a small village where horses grazed on the grassy paths between houses. That has all changed, now that the roads have come. Cahuita's grassy paths have become dusty streets, and the people of Talamanca find themselves thrust uneasily into the twentieth century. Independent farming and fishing are giving way to a tourist-based economy, with some related drug culture and theft. Tour buses lining the streets of this small town during the dry season make local people feel that their home is lost to them. During the rest of the year, Talamanca reverts to its relaxed pace. The beaches are uncrowded and the weather, in September and October especially, is beautiful in contrast to the afternoon rains in the rest of Costa Rica.

At the Pacific beaches, the local culture takes second place to a tourist milieu created by highland Ticos and foreigners of all nationalities. Talamanca, however, is still *tierra incognita* for most Ticos. The area was opened after a 1975 law was passed prohibiting construction within 50 meters of the shore. Then the point below Cahuita was declared a national park. Recently, the area south of Puerto Viejo has been made into a wildlife refuge. For these reasons the beaches retain their pristine beauty, and the people their unique way of life. "Laid back" is definitely the style on the Atlantic coast. There are a few places that offer air conditioning and hot water, but service is generally very slow. Because of this, the Atlantic coast is a great place to relax. Bring along some snacks to eat while you're waiting in restaurants or dance with your waiter or waitress. We hope that somehow the people of Talamanca can preserve their unique flavor without being run over by "tourism infrastructure".

Cahuita is now a 45-minute ride from Limón. One entrance to the National Park is along the white sand beach at the southern edge of town, but the park campsites are at the **Puerto Vargas** entrance on the other side of the point, 4 km south of

Cahuita, and about 2 km to the left. There is water available there, as well as outhouses and picnic tables. The Park Service charges a minimal fee. Signs indicate the sections of Puerto Vargas Beach that are dangerous for swimmers.

Cahuita National Park protects a coral reef that extends 500 meters out from Cahuita point. Take flippers and a mask to enjoy the underwater garden of 123 species of tropical fish, as well as crabs, lobsters, shrimp, sea anemones, sponges, black and red sea urchins and sea cucumbers. In order to snorkel, you must enter from the beach on the Puerto Vargas side and swim out to the reef.

Several local residents have begun to take tourists out to the better snorkeling spots by boat; ask around. José McCloud (ext. 256) has been recommended as an excellent guide to the flora and fauna of the Talamanca mountains and can tell you a lot about the community as well. **Cahuita Tours** (ext. 232) can take you to the reef in a boat with a glass window in the bottom. The trip, which takes all morning, costs about $11. They also rent snorkeling equipment, bicycles, binoculars and scuba diving equipment. They're on Cahuita's main street, half a block from the Guardia Rural. **Moray's** (ext. 216) offers snorkeling tours, boat tours of the beaches south of Cahuita, hiking or horseback tours, and tours to Tortuguero as well as rental of equipment. They also rent rooms. They are on the road to the black beach next to the rural guard station.

Biologists observe that the coral in the reef has stopped growing. They attribute this to silt washed down by the river from the banana plantations inland which inhibits the coral's ability to reproduce. A further problem is that the blue plastic bags covering the fruit to protect it from discoloration are washed into the river and out to sea. They wrap around the coral and smother it. Sea turtles sometimes eat the bags, thinking they are jellyfish.

151

There is a shady 7km nature trail between the beach and the jungle. It's 4km by trail from Cahuita to the point, another 3km to the Puerto Vargas camping area. You might see iguanas, sloths, and howler and whitefaced monkeys along the trail. The freshwater rivers and estuaries are good places to spot caimans and herons. You can spend the day hiking and snorkeling, then come out on the highway at the Puerto Vargas entrance to the park and catch the 4pm bus back to Cahuita.

Hotels and restaurants: See p. 115 for hotel codes. There is only one telephone number for all Cahuita. Dial 58-1515 and ask for the extensions given below: **Hotel Cahuita** has cabinas (D, pb, tf, pool, ext. 201) and cheaper rooms (E, cb, nf) in the old hotel above their restaurant. **Cabinas Vaz,** across the street, are similar (E, pb, tf, rest, ext. 218). The **Sol y Mar Restaurant** next door offers local specialties and also has spacious, clean cabinas (E, pb, cw). The **Cahuita National Park Restaurant** features fresh seafood, fruit drinks and desserts. Open every day, 8am to 9pm. All the above places are at the park entrance. **Cabinas Palmer** (E, tf, communal fridge; D with kitchens, ext. 243) are very clean and homey. Owners are lovely, helpful people. Half a block from the bus stop. Down the street from Palmer's, and directly on the water, are **Cabinas Jenny,** with a new two-story building (D, pb, cw). **Surfside Cabinas** are behind the school. They also have four rooms with fridges right on the water and a restaurant, open every day 7am-9pm. Rice and beans served weekends only (E, pb, tf, ext. 246, 202, 218). **Cabinas Brisas del Mar** are near the sea, across from the school (ext. 267, clean, pb, cw, D).

In this area, we recommend that you **avoid drinking water**, juices made with water or ice, and raw fruits and vegetables that cannot be peeled. We always bring a large plastic jar of San José water on our trips. You might want to bring your own fruits and veggies too (previously washed, of course), because it gets a bit expensive to eat three meals a day on the coast. Also the food tends to be a bit greasy and salty, and lighter meals feel good in the hot weather.

You can have fresh coral crabs at **El Típico** near the entrance to town. Make sure you ask them how much their crab, lobster and fish costs. The price on the menu is for the smallest size. Our large crab, though delicious, was almost twice as expensive ($7.50) as the menu price. Near the Típico is a place to rent surfboards and snorkels. On the other side of town, one block to the right from the Guardia Rural, **Miss Edith** cooks up a storm, ladling out tasty, down-home Caribbean lunches. In response to the requests of her customers, she also includes vegetarian fare in her menu, as well as native medicinal teas like bayrum, guanabana leaves, sorosi, and lemon grass. Good for what ails you. Closed Tuesday and only open for supper on Sunday; breakfast served 7am-9am. If you want her to make rondon, a native stew, let her know early in the day so she can get it started. You can also buy fresh lobster on the beach and bring it to her to cook. Miss Edith's sister is starting a laundry service; ask about it.

North of town is a long, beautiful black sand beach. About 50 m. before the soccer field on the black beach is the entrance to **Cabinas Colibrí** (B, pb, hot water, kitchens, cf, ext. 263). **Atlántida Lodge** is diagonally across the ballfield (B, clean, tranquil, well-kept grounds, safe parking, pb, hot water, cf, screens, ext. 213). Continuing north, **Cabinas Black Beach** are charmingly designed 2-story stone and wood structures (D, pb, protected parking, ext. 251). One of the owners is Italian, so you'll find lasagne and other Italian dishes there. Next door, **Cabinas Brigitte** has cheap, dark rooms with mosquito nets (F, cb). She's Swiss, but cooks native-style for guests. **Cabinas El Ancla** are next (F, pb, basic). The big new **Hotel Jaguar** has spacious rooms with natural ventilation and its own private water supply (B, cw, nf, screens, restaurant with international menu, ext. 238). **Cabinas Algebra**, which serves some of the best Caribbean food we've had in Cahuita, is a few hundred meters beyond (D, pb, cw, 58-2623 for messages).

Club Campestre Cahuita, halfway between Limón and Cahuita, has pools and dark rooms with heavy-duty ceiling fans. Its generous but greasy restaurant is open all day, every day. Camping is allowed on the beach across the road from the hotel ($3). Rooms are only open to non-members during the off-season (C, pb, cw; D newer cabinas, pb, hw, 58-2861).

Aviarios Río Estrella is a privately owned wildlife sanctuary located 10km north of Cahuita. They offer tours in a pontoon boat down canals similar to those in Tortuguero, where one can see birds, monkeys, otters, caimans and river turtles. They rent canoes and rafts for the more adventurous. Camping is possible. You can see their signs on the road to Cahuita. Call for reservations: 24-7822, fax: (506) 24-6895

Hitoy Cerere Biological Reserve is definitely off the beaten track and has hardly been developed for visitors. Trails are overgrown and unmarked and there are no camping facilities. Park guards have to spend most of their time cutting down marijuana that people plant within the reserve. But for hardy explorers, there are beautiful views, clear streams, waterfalls and lots of birds to see. To get there you have to take a Valle de la Estrella bus from Limón which winds into the banana plantations and get off at Finca Seis, the end of the line. Jeep-taxis there will take you 10km farther for around $4, and leave you within 1km of the entrance. They will return to pick you up at an agreed-upon time, and can take you back to Cahuita if you want (1.5 hrs, $25).

Puerto Viejo is 19km south of Cahuita, on paved road except for the last 6km after the turnoff to Bribri. The town is smaller and less developed than Cahuita, and the beaches to the south are some of the most beautiful in the country. There is now bus service from Limón all the way to Manzanillo, 14km south of Puerto Viejo.

The area outside the reef in Puerto Viejo has become famous in surfing lore as "La Salsa Brava". Waves are world class from December to April. Another season opens up in June and July. In September and October the sea is calmer, better for snorkeling and swimming. Non-surfers will be able to enjoy Puerto Viejo a lot more in those months. Everything is less crowded and the weather is generally beautiful. Swimming is best at Punta Uva, a gorgeous beach 7km S of Puerto Viejo.

During the high season, surfers on their way out often sell their boards to new arrivals. This avoids the tremendous hassle of taking surfboards on the bus. Some surfers hire a taxi or truck to haul their gear from Limón ($25-30). This is cheaper than renting a car in San José, and most of the good waves are an easy walk from Puerto Viejo. We have heard that at least one surfboard per day breaks on the reef. La Salsa Brava is definitely not for neophytes.

The Puerto Viejo area is home to at least three different cultures: the English-speaking black farmers who grew cacao and coconut until a blight ruined the cacao harvest, the indigenous people of the Bribri and Cabécar tribes who live in the foothills, and Spanish-speaking immigrants who came to the area in search of land. The Talamancan Ecotourism and Conservation Association publishes an excellent pamphlet, Welcome to Coastal Talamanca, which describes the cultural heritage of the zone, as well as providing visitor information. Also look for Taking Care of Sibo's Gifts, in which the people of the Ké-koLdi indigenous reserve explain their way of life and their commitment to conserving nature.

Because Talamanca was so isolated from the rest of Costa Rica, many of its cultural traditions are still alive. Miss Dolly can prepare you a traditional Caribbean meal (ask her a day in advance) or take you for a walk to learn to identify medicinal plants and herbs. Mauricio Salazar of Cabinas Chimuri takes visitors on horseback through the Indian reserve to observe flora and fauna and learn about customs of the Bribri and Cabécar people (see below).

Ask local fishermen to take you ocean fishing. Daniel Brown at the Soda Aquario and "Papi" Hudson in Puerto Viejo arrange snorkeling trips. You can rent bikes and horses in Puerto Viejo, or walk the beach trail from Barra Cocles to Manzanillo (9.5km).

Note for drivers and bike renters: Do as the locals do and *get off your bike* to cross the small wooden bridges along the beach road. It's very easy to lose your balance on the uneven wooden surface, and there are no railings to keep you from falling into the rocky river below. If you are in a car, drive slowly, because the bridges are unmarked and you can be on them before you know it.

Stanford's Restaurant El Caribe is famous for fresh seafood. His disco is jumping Thurs-Sun. You can cash traveler's checks there, though the exchange rate may be less favorable than in San José. The **Soda Támara** is a popular place to eat (open 6:30am to 9pm, closed Tues), as is the **Parquecito**, right on the beach, open all day. Definitely the best breakfast in town is at the **Coral**. Heated homemade wholewheat and French bread accompany the eggs and omelettes. The rest of the menu ranges from yogurt and granola to *gallo pinto* to hearty wholewheat buttermilk pancakes. Breakfast is served every day except Mon from 7 to noon. They reopen at 7pm on Tues, Fri and Sat, for Margarita's famous and delicious pizzas. **Juices**, one block south of the Coral, is also a clean, pleasant breakfast spot with homemade bread, jam and cakes, good coffee and local herbal teas. Open every morning at 6am. **Johnnie's Place** serves cheap, hefty portions of greasy, salty "chinese" food and is also a disco (located next to the Rural Guard). Fresh fruits and vegetables are delivered to town on Wednesdays. You can buy them from the delivery truck as it makes its rounds, or at the vegetable stand near the bus stop and at the Parquecito. Miss Dolly makes bread with coconut milk which is good with her homemade guava jam. You can buy ginger biscuits, pineapple rolls, plantain tarts and *pan bon* from local ladies like Miss Sam and Miss Daisy. Little rounds of unsweetened *cacao* are on sale at the Soda Támara. Just the thing to take back for hot chocolate in town, which you can sip while you recall the misty beaches and reggae rhythms of the Talamanca coast.

As in Cahuita, **beware of the local water** (see p. 152).

Insects: Just to be on the safe side, we recommend that you invest in some mosquito coils (about $1 at your local pulpería) or bring mosquito nets. Whether you will be bothered or not depends on the climatic conditions and the location and design of your hotel. If there are mosquitos they will only bother at night. Worse than mosquitos are no-see-ums in the sand which bite your ankles around dusk. And watch out for mean biting ants in the grass. Read insect notes on p. 72-3.

Lodging: Cabinas Chimuri are down a road to the right, 300m before you get to the black beach that leads to Puerto Viejo. The typical Bribri constructions of thatch over bamboo are set on a hill in the cool, shady forest. A large, open-walled *palenque* serves as a common cooking area for the cabins (D, cb). Near the cabins are waterfalls with pools for a refreshing swim. Mauricio, the owner, is a Bribri Indian. His nature tours on horseback are a favorite with visitors ($25/person). Longer treks through the Atlantic side of **Parque International La Amistad** are possible if people come prepared with good shoes, sleeping bags, etc. These 3-day camping trips require advance notice and payment so that supplies can be bought and preparations for the boat trip out can be made. Mauricio also sells traditional Indian crafts. Chimuri is a great place to stay for those who like simplicity, doing their own cooking, living in nature, and getting to know the Bribri way of life. The best way to secure a place there is to send a deposit to Mauricio Salazar, Puerto Viejo de Talamanca, Limón, Costa Rica, keeping in mind that it takes about three weeks for letters to arrive, even within Costa Rica.

Cabinas Black Sands are located just before the road turns to go along the black beach that leads to Puerto Viejo. Turn left at Pulpería La Violeta and follow the road when it veers to the right (about 400m). The Indian-style thatch-roofed structure has three rooms and a shared kitchen (E, cb, cw). It's right on the beach, private and tranquil, about a 20-minute walk to Puerto Viejo.

Cabinas Playa Negra are about 300m back from the beach as you approach Puerto Viejo. They have breezy second story sleeping space for six and kitchens below (C, nf, cw, 56-1132, 56-6396).

El Pizote Surf Lodge preserves the natural wood style of most coastal cabinas, but has all the amenities--storage space, reading lamps by the beds, large comfortable mattresses, mirrors you can actually see yourself in, ceiling fans. There are rooms with shared baths (B) and individual bungalows with private baths (L). Bicycles, diving gear and horses are for rent, and there are nature trails into the forest from the quiet grounds of the lodge, which also has guanabana and Hawaiian papaya plantations. It is set back from the road about halfway down the black beach as you approach Puerto Viejo (25-2813, 29-1428).

Pensión Agaricia is a small family-style hostel run by a Costa Rican artist and his European wife. The second-floor rooms are clean and sunny with bunkbeds and shared baths. Breakfast is served for guests only ($5). The owners say they like to maintain a quiet, private atmosphere. They are right at the entrance to Puerto Viejo, across the street from the beach (D, tf, bike rentals and souvenir shop, possible lodging for pets, good for groups). One block further down are **Cabinas Grant** (C, new, cw, pb, tf, locked parking lot, 58-2845).

Hotel Maritza, one block to the left, used to be the only place you could stay in Puerto Viejo. Its small, ramshackle second story rooms (F, cb, nf) have been supplemented by newer, modern cabinas with private baths (D, hw, cf, 58-3844). One block north, at the bus stop are the **Cabinas Ritz** (E, pb, cw, nf, rather stuffy). A couple of blocks down and to the right are **Cabinas Manuel León** (F, pb, cw, run down but on a nice part of the beach, 58-0854).

Hotel Puerto Viejo caters to surfers. It has basic second-story rooms, most of which are well-ventilated (E, mosquito nets, nf, cb). The Brazilian manager, Adrián, knows a lot about the local waves. His neighbor, Lica, repairs surfboards. Bicycles are for rent behind the hotel. Next to it are **Cabinas Stanford**, rather dark, but fairly secure (D, pb, tf). Make arrangements at

Stanford's Restaurant. Farther down the same street are **Cabinas Tamara,** (C with stove, D without, clean, fans, cw, shady furnished porches, arrange through the Soda Tamara). All the above are one block from the beach. **Cabinas Jacaranda** (E, basic, cb, nf, mosquito nets) share the building with the Restaurant Coral, one block inland from Cabinas Tamara.

The **Kiskadee** is a real treat, five minutes up a path through the jungle in back of the soccer field. I'm a lousy birdwatcher, but even I couldn't help seeing scarlet tanagers and the yellow and black kiskadee for whom the lodge is named, flitting through the heliconias by the side of the trail. There are two second story rooms, one with double beds, one with bunks, and ample communal kitchen space below. It's clean, nicely decorated and run by a friendly retired American woman who charges very little for the dormitory-style accommodations (F, outhouses, nf, bring a flashlight, and boots if it's rainy). The soccer field (*cancha de futbol*) is to the right at the end of the block the Coral is on. Go to the far goalpost and you'll see the Kiskadee sign.

Out on the beach past Stanford's are **Cabinas La Salsa Brava** (E, pb, cw, basic). About 450m down the road to Punta Uva is the **Escape Caribeño**, tidy cabinas with a communal cooking area (D, pb, cw, cf, some with fridges, bring your own utensils). The office is on the left, cabinas on the right.

Communicating with Puerto Viejo in order to make reservations is not easy. You can leave messages for the hotel of your choice at either Manuel León's *pulpería* or the Hotel Maritza (numbers above), but having your call confirmed is another story. The phones are often out of order or constantly busy because they are the only phones that residents and visitors can call out on. You might just have to take your chances. Do not go without reservations during Christmas or Easter. Try to go on weekdays in the high season.

There are new hotels and cabinas all along the road to Punta Uva, most of which were under construction when we were there. **Cabinas Dasa** rents two 2-story cabins on the beach at Punta Uva with furnished kitchens (B, weekly rates only, pb, cw, nf). For info, look for their yellow sign on the left, 4km south of Puerto Viejo. About 200m beyond the sign is **Maracú**, primitive Indian-style cabins with cooking area, (F, cb, cw, nf). Next on the right is the entrance to **Hotel Punta Cocles** (A, pb, hw, cf, a/c, some with kitchens, pool, snack bar, 34-

34-0306, fax: (506) 34-0614), the most developed lodging in the area. Their well-designed bungalows have private porches facing the jungle. A nature trail identifies the local trees and plants and offers a chance to birdwatch. Guests can swim at Playa Chiquita, about 300m from the hotel. Bikes, snorkeling equipment, binoculars, surfboards and horses are available for rent. A few meters beyond is **Miraflores Lodge,** a rustic bed and breakfast surrounded by a tropical flower plantation (B, some rooms with pb). About 1 km further on the left are **Selvyn's Cabinas** (F, basic, cb, nf, cw; larger separate cabin, D). His restaurant is open all day, every day. Punta Uva is a short walk from there. **Cabina Punta Uva** (C, pb, kitchen, cw) is at the next entrance to the beach, about lkm from Selvyn's. A road on the left another km down takes you to the other side of Punta Uva, not as spectacular, with a couple of bar-restaurants on the beach, Cabinas Dasa (see above) and, **Hotel Punta Uva,** solidly built cabinas (L, pb, cf, hw, 55-3939, fax: (506) 55-3737).

Seven km beyond Punta Uva is the small fishing village of **Manzanillo.** The **Manzanillo-Gandoca Wildlife Refuge** protects a 9km beach where four species of turtles lay their eggs, including the giant leatherback (*baula*). The main nesting season is January through April. Villagers are given a certain number of eggs to sell; the rest are raised in incubators to protect them from human and animal predators, and released. The refuge also includes two swamps important as wildlife habitats, a 300-hectare forest, and coral reefs. The Gandoca River estuary is a nursery for tarpon; manatees, crocodiles and caimans are also seen there. Talk to Florentino Grenald, the enthusiastic Refuge administrator in Manzanillo, about hiring local guides. He can also provide you with a list of the 358 bird species which have been identified in the area.

Maxi's Cabinas are the only place to stay in Manzanillo (F, basic, cb, nf); locals gather to play dominoes in his bar/disco. Sightseeing or snorkeling tours of the coast in motorized dugout canoes can be arranged through Willie Burton. Miss Marva, Miss Alfonsina, Miss Edith and Doña Cipriana will prepare meals for you in their homes (with advance notice). Miss Alfonsina can also share her knowledge of local medicinal plants with you.

Getting there:

By bus to Limón: The Limón bus stop is on a 3, c 19/21 in San José, near the northeast corner of Parque Nacional. Buses leave almost every hour, but buy tickets in advance if it is a weekend or holiday ($1.90, 23-7811, 21-5917).

Limón-Sixaola: The Sixaola bus leaves for Cahuita, Puerto Vargas and Puerto Viejo at 5am, 10am, 1pm and 4pm. The stop is one block north and half a block west of the Mercado Central in Limón. Get there early to buy a ticket. If you catch the 7am bus from San José, you should be able to make the 10am bus down the Talamanca coast (one hour to Cahuita, half an hour more to Puerto Viejo). Buses leave Puerto Viejo for Limón at 6am, 1pm and 4pm (no 1pm bus on Sundays). They enter Cahuita about 30 min. later.

Limón-Manzanillo: There is also a bus from Limón all the way past Punta Uva to Manzanillo. It leaves Limón at 6am and 2pm, and returns from Manzanillo at 9am and 4:30pm.

San José-Sixaola: There is a **direct** San José-Sixaola bus that leaves from a 11, c 1/ctl each day at 6am, 2:30pm and 4:30pm (3.5-hr trip, $4, 21-0524, 58-1572). It can leave you either at the entrance to Cahuita or at the Bribri turnoff, about 6km from Puerto Viejo. It reaches the same Bribri-Puerto Viejo *cruce* around 6:30am, 9:30am, 11:30am and 4pm on its way back to San José from Sixaola and Bribri. There's not much to see in the town of Bribri. It is an administrative center more than anything. If you want to experience Indian culture, talk to Mauricio Salazar at Cabinas Chimuri.

By car: Driving to the Atlantic Coast is fairly easy and enjoyable. The first part of the drive is through the beautiful mountains of Braulio Carrillo National Park. It is hard to believe that when it is raining cats and dogs in San José, it can be clear and hot on the other side of those mountains. It's true, though, especially in September and October, usually the heaviest months of the rainy season. Try to go early in the day to avoid fog and rain. And if it has been raining a lot, ask around about landslides in Braulio Carrillo before you set out. Once you emerge from the park, there are numerous places to stop for a break. We can't recommend the food in one place over the other. The two restaurants on either side of the 24-hour gas station at the entrance to Guácimo are clean, and the **Centro Turístico Pacuare,** just south of Siquirres, is a good place to stop for a snack and a swim. To get to Talamanca, take a right at the first intersection you come to as you enter Limón. Cars are often stopped and checked as they leave Talamanca. The police are looking for contraband from Panamá.

green sea turtle

Tortuguero National Park: The area north of Limón, like most of the Atlantic coast of Nicaragua, is a water-based society. All travel is by boat. Roads are planned for the future but still do not exist. In 1974, a series of canals were built to connect the natural inland waterways between Limón and Barra del Colorado, thus allowing coastal residents to get to Limón without the hazards of sea travel. In 1979 the government established a twice-weekly launch service up the inland waterway. Tortuguero got its first electric generator in 1982. In the information kiosk near the center of Tortuguero village, there is a fascinating exhibit on the cultural history of the area, illustrated by our own Deirdre Hyde.

Tortuguero has been famous for turtle shells, meat and eggs since the 1600's when the Spanish set up *cacao* plantations on the Atlantic coast. Turtles were valued as a meat source on ships because they would stay alive on board if they were kept out of the sun and sprinkled with water. Turtle soup became a delicacy in England. Large-scale turtle export started in 1912. By the 1950's the green turtle faced near extinction.

Long-term biological research on the green turtle, started by the Caribbean Conservation Corp. (CCC) in 1954, has helped greatly in the understanding and preservation of this species. Dr. Archie Carr, the founder of the CCC, wrote an entertaining and informative book about his wanderings in search of the green turtles' nesting ground (see p. 256), which finally led him to Tortuguero. Thanks to international interest in his work, Tortuguero was declared a National Park in 1970 by the Costa Rican government.

Tortuguero is the largest nesting area in the Caribbean for the green sea turtle. They return to Tortuguero every two to four years to mate offshore and dig their nests. Although their feeding grounds can be as far away as Florida and Venezuela, none of the 26,000 turtles tagged in Tortuguero has ever been found to mate at any other beach.

Green turtle nesting season is from July through September. The leatherbacks usually nest in May and June. But you can usually see nesting turtles at any time of year. Their flipper marks look like tractor treads, which show up as wide black lines on the beach at night.

When we were in Tortuguero in March, we saw two huge leatherback *(baúl)* females laboriously digging holes in the soft brown sand by the light of the full moon. Witnessing this age-old ritual left me with a deep respect for the primordial instinct in all creatures, including humans. The turtles lay about 100 eggs at each of several nestings per season. The eggs incubate for approximately 60 days, then the baby turtles bite through the rubbery shells and clamber up out of the nest, heading straight for the ocean before dawn. Their instinctive navigational powers direct them into the open sea.

Recognizing that no conservation effort can succeed without full support from the human community, the Caribbean Conservation Corp. has begun an outreach program to Tortuguero village. Besides employing several townspeople in their research station (locally called Casa Verde, about 2km north of the town), the CCC in partnership with the National Parks Service has trained local people as turtle guides. Young men who in earlier times might have become expert turtle hunters are learning a new way to make their living from the town's unique natural resource. They have formed a cooperative, and take visitors onto the beach during nesting season. The guides instruct you when to take flash pictures, how to approach the turtles, etc. Tickets go on sale from 4 to 6 every afternoon in the information kiosk (¢200, plus ¢100 park admission).

Local guides will not take more than 10-15 people onto the beach at one time. Some of the lodges do not use local guides and try to crowd 30 to 50 people around a nesting turtle at once. The National Park is trying to make this illegal.

The CCC training program is one of a handful across the country that strive to involve local residents in tourism in a productive, autonomous way. CCC is also training naturalist guides who can show people around when it's not nesting season.

Sea turtles and tourists are not the only animals that abound in the area. The National Park is also home to fresh water turtles, crocodiles, sloths, howler, spider and colorado monkeys, toucans, *oropéndolas*, parrots, morpho butterflies and many others. In addition, it is known as one of the world's richest fishing grounds for tarpon and snook.

Dugouts: The best way to enjoy the exuberant vegetation and abundant wildlife of Tortuguero's canals is to rent a dugout canoe *(cayuca)*. Miss Eva, Rubén Aragón ("Bananero"), Mister Dama, and Juan José Artencio ("Mille", who owns a friendly bar, Bayby Doll 2, on the water 100 meters south of the dock) are some of the villagers who currently rent out cayucas. Ask about current rates. Paddle around for awhile to see if your dugout is the right size for you, and make sure it is of solid, one-piece construction and not caulked together. Cayucas are quite stable and easy to paddle. Check to see that you have a plastic bailer for your boat.

You have to pay ¢100 admission to the park at the administration (300m. S of the information kiosk) before you paddle off. The main waterway of the National Park is inland from the canal that comes from Moín. Paddle south. You will see smaller waterways branching off which you can explore. If you go out alone, without a guide, ask where the currents are most gentle. The current in the Río Tortuguero can be quite strong. If you would like to hire a guide, try Mr. Dama, Bananero, or Jim.

Motorboats to tour the canals of the National Park are also available in town and from the lodges. These are okay for going places fast, but the noise disturbs the quiet beauty of the jungle streams, and you might scare away wildlife before you can see it.

To make your boat trip more comfortable, make sure to bring the following:

Thick-soled running shoes and socks
Insect repellent
Sunblock
Broad-rimmed hat or visor cap
Umbrella for sun or rain
Lightweight plastic poncho for rain or picnic cloth

Lightweight longsleeved and shortsleeved shirts
Towels
Lunch in waterproof bags
Water
Swiss army knife
Flashlight (don't ask why, just take it)

Camping is allowed in the National Park, but remember that Tortuguero has one of the highest annual rainfalls in the world: over 200" a year. The beach at Tortuguero offers little shade, has rough, unfriendly surf, and is frequented by sharks. *Terciopelo* (fer-de-lance) snakes are not uncommon on land, especially at night. There is a nature trail on the narrow piece of land between the large canal and the sea. It is a bit less swampy in the dry season.

Hotels: There are several inexpensive hotels right in the village (for descriptions of the more comfortable lodges, see next paragraph). **Brisas del Mar** (known as Bochinche in honor of a memorable fight that took place there once), has inexpensive, dark cabinas right on the beach (F, cb, cw, nf). They do not serve food, however they run a bar and hold dances there Saturday and Wednesday nights. Next door, where most foreign tourists go, is **Sabina's**. She also has a bar, but it's less noisy. Her cabinas are clean and vary in price according to size (F, cb, cw, nf). She has a few new, more modern cabinas too (C, tf, pb). Pastor Centeno runs the new **Meryscar**, 200 meters south of the information kiosk in town. His wife cooks meals for guests. Family atmosphere (F, cb, cw, screens, some rooms with tf. D-E per person with three meals). More remote and pleasant is **Tatané**, with individual mini-A-frame cabins 5 minutes by boat from town, on the canal to Barra. Owner Marcos Zamora is an authorized turtle guide; he can also take visitors on trips through the canals. He will transport visitors to and from town free of charge; (E, cb, cw). When you arrive in the village, ask around for him, or hire a boat to take you there. Marcos and Centeno often greet the Gran Delta. It's a good idea to make reservations at the hotel of your choice, as all work with tour groups, and can be crowded. Call 71-6716--that's a pay phone at the *pulpería*--and leave a message for your hotel with Olger Rivera. The hotel owners should call you back to confirm your reservation.

Getting there: Many people prefer to splurge on a tour to Tortuguero due to transportation difficulties. However, remember that if you choose a tour, your time and activities in Tortuguero will probably be planned for you. There are budget tours available; do enough research so that you know exactly what you'll be getting and paying for (meals, extra tours, etc). If you're very adventurous and wouldn't mind waiting hours or a day or two for a ride up or down the canal, you might be happier doing it on your own, and you'll spend a lot less money.

We'll describe the tours first, then tell you what we know about doing it alone.

All the lodges offer 2 and/or 3-day packages which include some or all of the following: day or night tours of the canals via motorboat or cayuca (some charge extra for this), ascent of Cerro (Mount) Tortuguero, and night-time turtle nesting tours. Though most tours include bus and boat transportation between San José and Tortuguero, all offer an air transport upgrade. Though some of the lodges have offices in Limón, call for reservations before you leave San José.

Mawamba Lodge (pb, some fans, 33-9964) is a new hotel with pleasant cabinas and a large, airy dining room one km north of Tortuguero village on the ocean side of the canal. Food is very good. They have a 2-day, 1-night package for $140, which includes 4 hours of tours, and a 3-day, 2-night package with 6 hours of tours for $165. Mawamba picks up guests in speed boats at Moín and can whiz them to Tortuguero in as little as 2 1/2 hours. They also have a large old launch with showers and bar on board for charters.

Cotur takes you by bus to Moín (2.5 hrs) and up the canals in launches. The trip is supposed to take 5 hours, but if the water level is low in the canals, the boats get stuck on sandbars and everyone has to jump out and push. The 3-day trips include transport, guided tours, meals and room at the shady **Jungle Lodge,** across the canal from Mawamba (pb, cf, 33-0155, 33-6579, 33-0133, 33-0226, fax: (506) 22-0568). You can also go with them by plane and boat back in one or two days. Prices range from $132 to $186 plus tax. Cayuca tours on the canals are $5 extra.

Costa Rica Expeditions flies 5-passenger planes directly to and from their comfortable **Tortuga Lodge** (pb, hw, cf, 22-0333, fax: 57-1665). The lodge is on 50 hectares of the forested spit, 2 km from the village across the canal from the Casa

Verde. Prices for 2- or 3-day nature tours range from $130 to $249. They also offer a 1-day 1-night fishing trip that includes 6 hours of canal or ocean fishing for $195-$299.

The **Hotel Matama** in Limón offers 2-day boat trips to Tortuguero (3 hrs) for $50/person (transportation only, minimum 6 people, 58-1123). Agencia Mitur takes people via bus and boat to **Ilan Ilan**, a new hotel 1.5 km. north of Tortuguero across the canal. Rooms are basic though comfortable, each with its own ice cooler (cw, pb, tf, 55-2031, 55-2262).

Depending on space, most of the above tour companies will include non-tour passengers in their flights and cruises. Call ahead of time, or check with the lodges for a ride back once you are in Tortuguero.

Other options: the cheapest but slowest and most iffy is the **Gran Delta**, the main means of transportation for the people who live along the canals ($3). This old, flat-bottomed boat is crowded and noisy, and the trip takes at least 7 hours. Because of frequent mechanical problems the Gran Delta often does not function. Call JAPDEVA, the Atlantic Port Authority, at 58-1106 for current information. When the Gran Delta is not sick, she leaves Moín early Saturday and Thursday mornings. She spends the night in Tortuguero and leaves early the next day. If the Gran Delta is too full to take you, other boats sweep the Moín dock soon after. Be careful when discussing prices--ally yourself with other travellers going to Tortuguero and offer to pay collectively. Boat captains have been known to charge vastly higher rates for people who don't barter or who ask for an individual price. If you buy a round trip passage, try to get a receipt that confirms that you've paid your way back.

Another option: SANSA has 1/2-hour flights to **Barra del Colorado,** N of Tortuguero near the Nicaraguan border. The landing strip there is presently being repaired, so call SANSA for current information: 21-9414, 33-0397, 33-3258). From there you can hire a boat from the municipal dock to take you the 1- or 2-hour trip to Tortuguero. Prices vary according to the price of gas; in August 1990 the boat captains were asking about $65 for the trip. Again, if you are going to do this, ally yourself with other travellers to get a better price. Coconut barges leave Barra for Moín by way of Tortuguero; they might have room for you.

Barra del Colorado is a sleepy, rainy, car-free town on opposite banks of the Río Colorado, near its mouth. There is excellent fishing in the river, nearby canals, and the Caribbean sea. All the hotels here specialize in fishing.

Tarponland, right next to the airstrip, is the most modest (D, pb, cf, cw, 71-6917). Owner Guillermo Cunningham will take guests fishing ($55/day) or to Tortuguero ($65-70). He will also arrange group tours of the area.

Archie Fields' **Río Colorado Fishing Lodge** has become an institution (LL per person w/3 meals and free drinks at happy hour, cf, hw, pb, $225-245/day per person including all-day fishing trips). The maze of hallways and rooms winds around courtyards full of caged animals (monkeys, a deer, a tapir, pheasants, parrots, scarlet macaws), a bar with a dart board, popcorn during happy hour, daiquiris and piña coladas, a TV room with US channels thanks to an 18-foot satellite dish, a dining room which overlooks the town and the rest of the hotel, and the best-equipped kitchen north of Limón (with Pearl, an outstanding cook). The Lodge's fleet of boats is brand new, with new motors. They are all outfitted with sonar fish finders, radios, and skilled guides. Now that there is no contra activity on the Río San Juan, Costa Rica's northeastern border with Nicaragua, the Lodge is again offering their famous San Juan tour, which ends in the town of Puerto Viejo on the Río Sarapiquí (see Northern Zone section).

Isla de Pesca is 5 min from Barra by motorboat. Guests are housed in several A-frame cabins with thatched roofs that share a grassy palm-filled court ($999 for 3-day fishing tour, $225 for 3-day Tortuguero tour; cf, pb, hw, 23-4560, fax:21-5148). A few minutes farther down the waterway is the homey **Casamar**, well-designed, comfortable duplex cabinas. Mango trees shade the grounds, howler monkeys provide the sound effects. Open only during peak fishing season--Sept-Oct, Jan-March ($900 for 3 days of fishing, plus airfare to Barra, 43-8834, fax: 43-9287).

Getting there: See p. 166.

Elephant ear (tiquisque)

THE NORTHERN ZONE

Puerto Viejo de Sarapiquí was Costa Rica's main port in colonial times. Boats embarked down the wide Sarapiquí River north to the Río San Juan that forms Costa Rica's border with Nicaragua, and from there to the Atlantic. Now that *contra* activity has been stopped in Costa Rica, tourists can follow the same river route, then turn down the Río Colorado to Barra del Colorado Wildlife Refuge and go from there to the canals of Tortuguero (contact Río Colorado Lodge, 32-8610, or Cabinas Oro Verde, 23-7479).

La Selva, the research station and biological reserve of the Organization for Tropical Studies, has brought fame to Sarapiquí because of the enormous variety of tropical plants and animals found there. Recently, the 3500-acre research area was made part of a "protected zone" which connects it with Braulio Carrillo National Park to the south, in an effort to secure the large hunting territories needed by jaguars and pumas. Over 450 species of trees have been identified there so far, as well as 81 reptile species, 48 of amphibians and 113 of mammals. Over 400 species of birds either live in or migrate to La Selva from the highlands, including toucans, *oropéndolas*, tinamoos, and umbrella birds. Over 300 different species were observed in a single day in the "Birdathon", an annual event in which people pledge money for each species observed by Audubon Society birdwatchers. The money goes to establish an endowment fund which will protect Braulio Carrillo on a permanent basis, and hopefully will serve as a model for funding conservation projects worldwide.

One of the many courses offered at La Selva is not for biologists, but for "decision makers": government and business leaders from around the world who need to understand tropical ecology in order to guide their countries along the soundest path in the future.

Tourists can roam freely on the 50 km of well-kept nature trails, but the scientists there want visitors to understand that research and education are La Selva's top priorities. In order to assure this, all visitors, whether for a few hours or a few days, must make reservations through the OTS office in San José (40-6696, 40-5033). It is no longer possible to drop in. La Selva is expensive to visit, which makes it an attraction mostly for those with an interest in natural history. A day on the trails, three meals at the reserve's cafeteria, and a night in "rustic but comfortable" accommodations cost $76. There are special rates for card-carrying graduate students in tropical sciences. A less expensive way to visit is by spending just a day there, which includes lunch, for $15. A bus leaves the OTS for La Selva three times a week ($10).

Hotel La Selva Verde in **Chilamate**, 5 minutes by car west of Puerto Viejo, has one of the most beautifully designed lodges we've seen (L/person, incl. meals, double occupancy; A in the older lodge near the road, less w/o meals). Their forest reserve along the river is great for birdwatching. They will arrange trips down the San Juan, or rafting, tubing and kayaking trips on local rivers for you. Make reservations in advance (20-2121, 71-6459, fax: (506) 32-3321).

Rancho Leona (71-6312), 12km southwest of Puerto Viejo in the village of La Virgen offers a varied menu from shrimp creole and eggplant parmesan to BLTs and cheeseburgers. They will also take you on an all-day kayaking trip down the Río Puerto Viejo. No experience necessary. More challenging trips can be arranged for experienced kayakers. Included in the $75 fee are two nights free bunkbed lodging, if you so desire. Small groups can include tree-planting along a deforested stretch of riverbank in their trip ($115). Leona and Ken make beautiful necklaces, earrings and lovely hand-painted T-shirts, depicting native birds and animals. They can also take you on hiking, camping and horseback riding trips, and know all the good swimming holes in the area.

A few km to the east of Puerto Viejo is **MUSA**, a cooperative of local ladies who grow and sell native medicinal herbs.

They will give you a tour of their farm and explain the uses of the different plants. They also offer excellent rosemary *(romero)* and chamomile *(manzanilla)* shampoos and natural clay preparations. The farm is in El Tigre, on the road to Horquetas.

Also to the east of Puerto Viejo is **El Gavilán**, a former cattle ranch which has been converted into a lodge. Tours of the rainforest and rivers by horseback and boat are offered. Arrangements must be made in San José because lodging, transportation, meals and tours are included in a package deal ($150/person, 23-7479, fax: (506) 53-6556, shared rooms and baths, hw, jacuzzi).

Getting there: The Río Frío bus leaves four times a day from c 12, a 7/9 in San José for Sarapiquí. The 6:30am and 12 noon buses go on the scenic route above Heredia that winds around the northeast side of Poás volcano to the northern plain and passes through La Virgen, Chilamate and Puerto Viejo before reaching La Selva. Don't go this route if you tend to get carsick. Otherwise, it is one of the most beautiful rides you can take, passing by the powerful La Paz waterfall on a hairpin turn, with vistas of the forests of Braulio Carrillo to the east. By bus it takes 4 hours, 2.5 hours by car, all on paved road. The 9am bus goes on the Guápiles highway through Braulio Carrillo and turns north to Horquetas, La Selva and Puerto Viejo. The 4pm bus takes the same route but continues on through Chilamate, ending about 8pm in La Virgen. It is a good bus to take if you want to go kayaking at Rancho Leona.

If you are coming from Monteverde or Guanacaste and want to avoid going back to San José, you can take buses from Cañas to Tilarán and Tilarán to San Carlos. To do this, you will have to spend the night in San Carlos or La Fortuna (see p. 177). The San Carlos-Río Frío bus leaves at 6am, 9am and 3pm, taking about 2 hours to reach Puerto Viejo.

By car, Cañas to La Fortuna takes about 2 hours, including 45 min on bad road on the north side of Lake Arenal. You can get from Volcán Arenal to Puerto Viejo in under 2 hours, avoiding San Carlos, if you turn left at El Tanque, a few km out of Fortuna, then take the turnoff to Muelle (route 4), following signs to Aguas Zarcas and always turning right. At Aguas Zarcas, 23 km W of San Carlos, turn left to San Miguel, and left again to La Virgen, Chilamate and Puerto Viejo, all on good road.

Many people are appalled at the destruction of vital rain-forests, but few do something about it. Amos Bien, an ecologist and former manager of La Selva, decided that the best way to convince people not to cut down rainforests is to demonstrate that conservation through tourism and ecologically sound management is the best use of land from an economic standpoint. The result is **Rara Avis,** a 1500-acre forest reserve near Las Horquetas, southeast of La Selva. Rara Avis is the site of biologist Don Perry's research on the rainforest canopy, which he writes about in his fascinating book, *Life Above the Jungle Floor* (see p. 257). Brave visitors can observe the forest from the tramway from which he does his research, traveling 300m through the jungle and going as high as 50m off the ground. The ride involves the signing of a release and a $35 donation per hour to further canopy investigation. The new, 8-room Waterfall Lodge is 500 feet from a gorgeous 3-tiered waterfall, and is the most comfortable place to stay at Rara Avis (LL/person double, pb, hw). El Plástico Lodge is more rustic but comfortable as well (A/person double, cb, hw). Both prices include 3 hearty meals, guides and transportation from Horquetas. From

171

Horquetas to El Plástico it takes about 3 hours to go 9 miles on very bad road. Once there, visitors must be willing to put up with muddy trails to experience the rainforest's pristine beauty. Experienced biologists accompany small groups to explain rainforest phenomena and point out wildlife.

Because of its isolated location, transportation must be arranged in advance by calling Rara Avis at 53-0844 (fax: (506) 21-2314). You can get substantial discounts at El Plástico with an IYHF card (see p. 70). Toruma in San José sometimes arranges low-cost group trips to member hostels (24-4085).

Ciudad Quesada (San Carlos) is located in the San Carlos plain of central Alajuela province, one of Costa Rica's most agriculturally-productive zones. As is true in many areas, its forested hills and family farms have been bought up by large-scale cattle farmers, some of them expatriate North Americans. Although increasing export capacity, this contributes to Costa Rica's serious deforestation problem.

Ciudad Quesada is a midpoint for trips north to Volcán Arenal and Tabacón thermal spa. You can also go east to connect with highway 9 to La Virgen and Puerto Viejo de Sarapiquí. **Hotel La Central** (D, 46-0766, 46-0301) and **Hotel El Retiro** (F, 46-0463) are both clean and comfortable with private baths on Parque Central in San Carlos. There is a crafts cooperative on the northwest corner of the park. **Balneario San Carlos** has a large swimming pool, kids' pools, a tico-style restaurant, roller skating twice a week, dances on Sundays, and a small lake for boating and fishing. Their somewhat rundown cabinas have fridges and hot water, no fans (D, 46-0747). You'll see signs for the Balneario 5 blocks northwest of Parque Central.

El Tucano, set back from the road in a shady forest, offers swimming pools, a sauna and a small, lukewarm, circular pool with jacuzzi, fed partially by a thermal spring. The grounds are beautifully kept, and an elegant restaurant offers an international menu including seafood and Italian specialties. Their new cabinas have bathtubs, a rarity here (LL, pb, hw, 46-1822). Use of pools and sauna costs about $2 for non-guests. It's 20 minutes northeast of Ciudad Quesada on the road to Puerto Viejo. Take a Río Frío, San Miguel, Aguas Zarcas, Pital or Venecia bus from the terminal in San Carlos.

You can continue east from El Tucano 32 km to San Miguel at the junction of Highway 9. Go left to Puerto Viejo and La Selva, or right to San José via Heredia, one of the most beautiful drives in Costa Rica (see p. 170-1). The return trip takes about 3 hours.

San José-San Carlos buses leave almost every hour from 5am through 6pm from the Coca Cola (3 hours, $1.50). Try to get a Directo bus--it makes less stops.

Arenal fulfills the volcano stereotype. Its perfectly conical shape emerges from Alajuela's gentle green hills. From time to time, loud explosions are heard and a mushroom cloud of grey, brown, orange or blue smoke billows out of the top. Although the volcano is capable of inspiring intense fright and awe in visitors, inhabitants of nearby Fortuna de San Carlos and the dairy farms at its base seem to live with relative peace of mind. If you ask, they will tell you with surprising tranquility about the time it erupted.

Since Arenal was dormant until 1968, the only people who suspected it was a volcano were those who had scaled it and found a crater and steam vents at the top. But few listened to them, until an earthquake shook the area on July 29, 1968. Twelve hours later, Arenal blew, sending out shock waves that were recorded as far away as the Boulder, CO nuclear explosion monitoring center. All damage was 5 km west of the volcano, where people were knocked down by shock waves, poisoned by gases and struck by falling rocks. Three new craters formed during the eruption sending down lava flows which eradicated the town of Pueblo Nuevo. At the end, 78 people had died. Since then the volcano hasn't erupted; it just rumbles and explodes, and shoots out rocks, soot and smoke.

Arenal is the most impressive at night. In the dark you can see the bursts of fire and red-hot rocks hundreds of feet into the sky. In the day you only see smoke and hear the volcano's terrible roar. Incandescent material cascades down the sides, especially on the north. Explosions happen every few hours during active phases, but the volcano can also go for months without an explosion.

Although the volcano is not dangerous if you keep your distance, it is very dangerous to climb. One tourist was killed and another burned in July 1988 when they hiked too near the crater, foolishly trusting the volcano's placid appearance in between explosions. If they had seen it explode before climbing, they probably never would have attempted it. They also unwittingly risked the lives of 15 Costa Rican Rural Guards and Red Cross workers who heroically searched the volcano to retrieve the body of its victim. Please do not climb this volcano.

It *is* wonderful to watch, though, and there are several places you can watch it from. You can camp out at **Tabacón**, the thermal pools 6 km east of Lake Arenal. There are showers and dressing rooms on the other side of the stream, as well as a ringside view of Arenal's performance.

Tabacón's thermal waters spring out of the volcano. They are channeled down a tiled slide into a pool. A more natural pool with some shade trees over it is in the back, as well as an amazing warm waterfall that will give you the massage of your life. I'm not sure if it was designed to massage you or only to be looked at, but I recommend that if you have stiff shoulders or a tense back you maneuver yourself over the rocks into a relatively comfortable position and hang on tight--the water comes down with a lot of force. The whole complex is surrounded by the area's brilliant vegetation, and of course, smoking Arenal serves as a stunning backdrop. Open every day, morning to evening. It's most crowded weekends ($1.50 adm., restaurant).

The **Arenal Volcano Observatory**, sometimes used by Smithsonian investigators in their vulcanological research, has recently been conditioned for guests. Located on a private macadamia farm, it offers a closeup view of the south side of the volcano and part of Lake Arenal. Accommodations are simple, with 3 bunkbeds per room, and a common dining area serving hearty *campesino* food (pb, hw, A/person incl. meals). New cabins with fireplaces and a great view of the lake are also available for up to 4 people. The climate at the observatory is cool and fresh, in contrast to that of La Fortuna, which can get a little muggy. Visitors must make reservations through Costa Rica Sun Tours (55-3518, 55-3418, fax: (506) 55-4410) although you do not have to be part of a tour to go there. You have to ford two rivers on the road up the mountain, but bridges are in the process of being built, so check with Sun Tours for exact directions

Beyond Tabacón is **Lake Arenal,** a large reservoir. The original Laguna Arenal was the source of a river whose waters flowed east to the Atlantic. But dams built for a hydroelectric energy plant enlarged the lake and diverted the waters. Now they flow out the NW side of the reservoir to irrigate the dry Pacific coast. Many people enjoy boating, fishing and wind-surfing on the lake. The east side, near Tabacón, retains its original lush greenery, but as you travel west, you see the dev-astating effect of cattle ranching, as the exuberant vegetation gives way to grassy pastureland.

Arenal Lodge is partially owned by Peter Gorinsky, the famous fishing guide. It is a large, comfortable house with a library, billiard table, and a lovely view of Arenal in the distance (LL/person, cb, hw, $265/day incl. fishing, 28-2588, 46-1881, fax: 28-2798). It's 4km up a gravel road near the north-eastern tip of the lake.

Lago Cote Ecoadventure Camp is an elegant new lodge which offers hiking, horseback riding, mountain biking, water sports, windsurfing, and volcano trips with all equipment in-cluded, even backpacks, binoculars, etc. The entrance is well-marked, a few km west of the town of Nuevo Arenal on the shore of Lake Arenal, and 4km north, near heart-shaped Lake Cote. To call it a camp is a misnomer--attention to detail, qual-ity and comfort are evident in everything there, but baths are shared, dormitory-style, which fits in with the outdoor emphasis of the place. Their rainforest nature trail is completely lined with wooden planks so you don't slip and slide. Large, well-padded armchairs in front of a fireplace await those who want to relax with a drink and a book. In short, it's a place for those who want to be in nature but want their creature comforts too. LL/person incl. meals and transportation, $20 less if you get there on your own. An 8-day-7-night package costs $599 in-cluding transportation to and from San José. Call Tikal Tours, 23-28-11, fax: (506) 23-1916.

You can get there either from the Interamerican Highway via Cañas and Tilarán (paved except for the entrance road to the Camp) or from La Fortuna, going over the 9km of unpaved road on the northeast side of Lake Arenal.

A few km to the west of the entrance to Lago Cote is **Mirador Los Lagos**, simple cabinas and a restaurant high on a hill overlooking Lake Arenal (C, pb, hw, 69-5484, restaurant open every day 8am-8pm).

Twelve km east of Tabacón is **La Fortuna**, the closest town to Arenal. **Hotel Las Colinas** (D, clean, hw, pb, tf, 47-

9107, 100m W, 50m S of the gas station) and **Cabinas San Bosco** (E, clean, pb, nf, 47-9050, 200m N of gas station), are the nicest places to stay in La Fortuna. **Hotel La Central** is basic, fairly clean and friendly (F, cb, nf, 47-9004, 100m beyond the gas station). **El Jardín,** across from the gas station, has good Tico-style food and playground equipment for kids. **La Vaca Muca,** 3 km W of La Fortuna, on the road to the volcano, offers generous *casados* and other local dishes. **El Coquito,** 2/3 of the way to Ciudad Quesada, is a good place to stop for a *refresco* and *ceviche*.

The **Catarata La Fortuna** is a beautiful waterfall 5.5km from the town. You'll see a sign pointing south on a road at the back of the church. Go 1km and turn right down a country lane. There is one hill, roughly paved with rocks, about halfway there that you can drive up if your engine is powerful enough and you don't mind a few dents in your chassis. If you have the time it's a nice walk from La Fortuna--if you drive you'll have to abandon your car at a series of muddy hills about 20 minutes by foot from the waterfall (don't get your rear wheels stuck in a rut on the left when you're parking). There's a fork about 100m before you get there. Take the left fork and soon you'll see the sign pointing to the *mirador*, where you can see the falls cascading on the other side of the ravine. If you want to walk down to the bottom of the falls (about 10 min), keep to the right on the ravine trail. At one point a fork goes sharply down to the left but it is treacherous and only takes you to the river. The force of the waterfall is such that swimming is not possible. The Río La Fortuna is going to be diverted in order to boost the level of Lake Arenal. We don't know what will become of this lovely waterfall when that happens. Ask at your hotel.

Getting there: The 5:45am San José-San Carlos bus (leaves from Coca Cola) continues on to Fortuna every day, returning at 2pm. You can also catch a Fortuna bus in San Carlos at 6, 9, 1, and 4:30. From Fortuna it's 13 km to Tabacón. Buses leave San Carlos at 6am and 3pm for Tilarán, passing through Fortuna and Tabacón around 8am and 4pm.

By car, you can take a circular route turning north at San Ramón de Alajuela, 55 min west of San José on the highway to Puntarenas. There, ask directions for the road to La Tigra, paved except for a 12km stretch in the middle. It borders a reserve which protects a beautiful stand of rainforest southeast of

Monteverde and conserves the water supply for the town of San Ramón. A few km beyond La Tigra, turn right at a large gas station to go 4km on bumpy gravel road to Jabillos, where you connect with the San Carlos-La Fortuna road. You can return to San José via San Carlos, Zarcero and Naranjo, all on paved road. The San Ramón-La Tigra road winds less than the Naranjo-Zarcero route. Both are picturesque and take about 3 hours travel time from San José.

Zarcero is the midpoint on the trip to or from San Carlos. You will probably want to stop and see the famous gardens in front of the church where bushes are pruned in the shape of elephants, airplanes, a bullfight, etc. If you want to eat though, stop 5 min. south of Zarcero where there are a few nice restaurants, and kiosks selling preserves, carnations, sour cream and cheese. Food is better there than in Zarcero itself.

You can also come from the west, combining a trip to Guanacaste or Monteverde with a visit to Arenal by taking a half hour bus ride from Cañas to Tilarán, and catching the Tilarán-San Carlos bus at noon, which reaches Tabacón around 3:30pm. It takes a lovely route around the north side of Lake Arenal, paved except for the 9 km strip. By car, it's 1.5 hours from Tilarán to La Fortuna (see map, p. 171).

olive ridley turtle

GUANACASTE PROVINCE

Guanacaste was a separate province of Spain's Central American empire until 1787, when it was given to Nicaragua. It was taken away and given to Costa Rica in 1812, when Costa Rica's population was too small without it to be represented in the colonial government that ruled from Guatemala. After independence, both Costa Rica and Nicaragua claimed Guanacaste. *Guanacastecos* were divided too. Liberians, whose founders were Nicaraguan cattle farmers, wanted to join Nicaragua. Nicoyans were in favor of joining Costa Rica. Nicoya won in a vote, and an 1858 treaty declared Guanacaste part of Costa Rica.

Its long period of autonomy, the high indigenous population and its geographic isolation from the Meseta Central have contributed to make Guanacaste a unique part of Costa Rica. Many "Costa Rican" traditions originate in Guanacaste. The people, dark-skinned descendants of the Chorotega Indians, are possibly closer to their cultural and historical roots than other Costa Ricans. There is a special *campesino* richness in their friendly manner.

Most of Guanacaste has been converted into pasture land for beef production. The deforestation the region has suffered has altered its climate and ecosystems, causing occasional droughts. Brahma bulls lounge under the graceful, spreading shade trees that gave the province its name. The brilliant yellow blossoms of the *corteza amarilla* dot the plains in February, and in March the light red blossoms of the *carao* or carob tree brighten the landscape.

The clear, gentle waters of Guanacaste's beaches attract Ticos and foreigners alike. The dry climate helps keep mosquitos to a minimum.

178

Centro Ecológico La Pacífica, 4 km north of Cañas on the Interamerican Highway, is a shady, green oasis in the midst of Guanacaste's heat. Over 200 different bird species have been observed in its woods and near the Río Corobicí, which flows through the ranch. Trees are labeled with their scientific and common names, and birdlists are available to guests. They have tastefully designed cabinas (A, cf, hw, lovely pool, 69-0050, fax: 69-0555) and their restaurant offers an international menu.

Rincón Corobicí, right on the river just after the entrance to La Pacífica, is also a cool, pleasant place to stop for a few hours or the whole day. Their Swiss-owned restaurant specializes in beef, seafood and fish. They have a souvenir shop, a playground, clean bathrooms, a small campground, and a trail along the riverside. They offer a 3-hour rafting trips down the Corobici ($33) and a 5-hour trip bordering Palo Verde National Park ($50 incl. gourmet lunch). Mountain bike tours also available. Make reservations in advance at ph/fax: 69-0303.

Many *campesinos* feel that environmental concerns interfere with their livelihood rather than supporting it. This makes ecology and community development enemies, creating an impossible situation for both. By involving the community in the formation of its reserve, **Lomas Barbudal** is actively trying to bridge this gap. Local school children, for example, are helping plan the visitors' center and clearing trails. Rivers you can swim in, shaded by graceful trees and waterfalls you can hike to, are the reserve's main attractions.

The dirt road to Lomas Barbudal is on the left, 20 minutes N of Cañas, right after Bagaces. After 6km on the dirt road, you come to the entrance (adm. $1). The reserve guardhouse is across a little stream, refreshments are about 200m to the right and the swimming hole is about 200m to the left. Camping is allowed. Bring insect repellent during the rainy season. Call 67-1062 for more information.

Palo Verde National Park is one of Central America's last natural refuges for the thousands of birds that pass over this region on their annual migratory paths. North American ducks and egrets rest there during their migration. Birds from the Guanacaste plains touch down, too. In addition to the 260 species of birds that visit, Palo Verde is a habitat for mammals, amphibians and reptiles, many of which can be observed relatively easily. During the dry season, animals stay near the few permanent springs in the area, one of which is only a hundred meters from the park's administration building and campsite. The best observation spot for birds is about one km before the administration building, in the swamp.

Palo Verde is on the east side of the mouth of the Tempisque River. Stretching along the banks of the river is a plain that floods during the rainy season and dries to a brown crisp in the dry season. Further from the river rise bluffs dotted with limestone cliff outcrops. The park administration is set in an old *hacienda* at the base of the bluffs; there are a couple of trails that set out from there and climb to lookout points.

You can sometimes join the park rangers on their daily horseback patrols around the park. Once a week they go to the **Isla de Pájaros,** a bird-filled island in the Tempisque. Because the park has relatively few visitors, the rangers are usually willing to take people along ($25 for the boat ride).

Camping is allowed in the Park. If you notify the administration beforehand, they might also be able to offer meals, transportation or lodging for a fee (67-1062).

The Organization for Tropical Studies has a research station in the northern part of the park where visitors can stay. Arrangements must be made in advance through OTS in San José (40-6696, A/person, bring your own food).

Getting to Palo Verde: Turn left at the gas station in Bagaces, N of Cañas. The Park is 35km from there. Signs mark the way.

During the dry season you can enter the area from the Nicoya Peninsula. Take a bus from Nicoya to Puerto Moreno. Local boatmen there will take you across for a minimal fee and indicate which way to hike to get to the park station. Don't try this route in the rainy season--the whole plain is swamped.

Most bus transportation to Guanacaste is by way of **Liberia,** 45 minutes north of Cañas on the Interamerican. Even though it looks farther away on the map, a trip to Liberia from San José (4 hours) takes less time than a trip to Nicoya by way of the Tempisque ferry. You can take a circular route through Liberia, Santa Cruz and Nicoya, the gateways to the Guanacaste beaches, and come back on the ferry. Roads are paved along that circular route, making it a 2-hour trip by car from Liberia to the Tempisque.

About 2km before you get to Liberia, on the right, is **Hotel Las Espuelas** (A, 66-0144, hw, a/c, pool, rest.) the most pleasant and well-maintained in that area. There are three gas stations where the main road into Liberia intersects the Interamerican highway. They are the surest place to get gas on holidays. At this intersection are **Hotel Boyeros** (B, 66-0722, hw, a/c, pool, tel, rest.) and **Hotel Bramadero** (D with fans, C with a/c, a bit run down, quieter rooms in back away from pool, 66-0371). **Hotel El Sitio** is about 100m to the west (A with a/c, B with fans, spacious grounds, pool, hw, rest, 57-0744, 66-1211). **Hotel La Siesta** is 5 blocks into Liberia and 2.5 blocks to the right from the Farmacia Lux (B, a/c, small pool, rest, clean, quiet, 66-0678). Make sure you have reservations for all above hotels during the dry season. See page 115 for hotel codes. **Las Tinajas** on the W side of Liberia's Parque Central has tender deep-fried fish and chicken.

Coatimundi (pizote)

Rincón de la Vieja is one of Costa Rica's richest, most varied and little known parks. Volcanologists say that Rincón de la Vieja volcano, although active, is unlikely to erupt because the geysers and mudpots in the area help it "let off steam". It is a compound volcano made up of nine craters which melded together one million years ago. Rincón's most recent violent activity was in 1966-67. The volcano erupted frequently, destroying trees and pastureland. Some of the rivers that spring from the volcano's slopes were polluted by the poisonous gases.

The park is a watershed for 32 rivers, many of which empty into Guanacaste's major river, the Tempisque. Three hundred species of birds have been identified there, as well as deer, collared peccaries, coatimundis, pacas, agoutis, raccoons, ja-

181

guars, two-toed sloths, and three species of monkeys. *Las Pailas* (The Cauldrons) is a 50-hectare wonderland of pits of boiling hot water, vapor geysers that stain the rocks around them red, green and yellow because of the iron, copper and sulphur in the steam, a mini-volcano that formed a couple of years ago, and the *Sala de Belleza* (Beauty Salon), seven bubbling pots of grey mud. You dip a stick in the smooth glop, let it cool, and make yourself a rejuvenating face mask. On the eastern side of the park are *Los Azufrales*, hot sulphur springs of perfect bathtub temperature, right next to a cold stream to splash in (don't let the sulphur water get in your eyes, and don't stay in longer than 5 minutes without alternating with the cold water).

The park is great for hiking because it is largely untouched, not too steep, and the trails are dry most of the year. Unlike the slippery, muddy cloud and rain forests, Rincón is a transitional area between dry and cloud forest. The trails get a bit muddy only at higher altitudes before the forest gives way to rocky, windblown volcanic terrain.

If you want to hike to the volcano craters and Laguna Jilgueros, a scenic lake where sometimes tapirs and *quetzales* can be seen, it's best to camp overnight. March and April are the best months for this, but it is always wise to bring rainsuits, warm clothes, several changes of clothing wrapped in plastic, good hiking boots, waterproof tents, and a compass. We saw a well-prepared group of campers who made the trip in July with no problem.

It is wise to hire a guide if you are going to the volcanoes, because paths are not clearly marked in the rocky terrain, and thick mists come up frequently. A guide is almost necessary also in Las Pailas because the dry, crusty earth around the mudpots is brittle and thin in some places. We know two cases of people who were severely burned when the ground under them gave way and they fell into boiling mud or water. The unsafe areas are not clearly marked.

One of the reasons that Rincón has been thought of as inaccessible is because the road to the park entrance is in bad condition, and lodging was unavailable. Now, Alvaro Wiessel, grandson of a German immigrant who named a crater of the volcano after himself when he "discovered" it in the 1850's, has made his country home into a warm and friendly hostel from which visitors can set out to explore the park. Las Pailas is 30 min west of the hostel, Azufrales is an hour to the east, the campground from which to explore the craters and Jilgueros is a beautiful 2.5 hour hike through virgin forest to the north, with the craters 1.5 hours beyond. Horses and guides are also available. Room and board are L/person including guides, A/person with an IYHF card (see p. 70). Horses are extra. Because **Albergue Rincon de la Vieja** is isolated, you must call for reservations so that they have time to buy provisions (66-0473, cw, cb, bunks, Apdo. 114, Liberia, Gte., CR).

To get to the Albergue, go 4.5km N of Liberia on the Interamerican till you see yellow bumps in the road which indicate a school zone. Turn right onto a lovely old gravel road which leads in about 10km to the small town of Curubandé. Continue 2km farther to the entrance to Hacienda Guachipelín, then through the gate 2km to where you see a sign saying "Albergue". Turn left at the sign and go another half hour to the river, leave your vehicle, wade across, walk up the hill, and there you are. If you don't have a vehicle, the lodge will pick you up in Liberia for $15/person. Actually, it takes just about as long to get to the lodge as it takes to get to Monteverde, because even though the turnoff is an hour farther north, you spend more time on paved highway and less time on gravel roads. The road to the Albergue is in the process of being paved, because a fancy hotel is being built near there, so travel time will be even shorter.

You need 4-wheel drive and about 2 hours to get to the park administration building if you decide to go by the official access road. The park boundary is 25km N of Barrio Victoria in Liberia. Depending on time and space available, park guards might be able to help you with transportation, meals and lodging. Headquarters in Santa Rosa can make radio contact with them (69-5598).

While most of Costa Rica's parks aim to preserve virgin forest, **Santa Rosa National Park** not only protects the little remaining tropical dry forest, but tries to promote its regeneration. This park encompasses almost every ecosystem that occurs in Guanacaste. The most recent addition to the park is a large tract of pastureland, overgrazed and biologically bankrupt, where biologists are applying research findings about how forests propagate themselves. Seeds for forest regeneration are primarily carried by the wind, and by mammals and birds who eat seeds and then defecate in treeless pastures. Encouraging this kind of

183

seed dispersal, and burning firelanes to control the spread of wildfires, will allow the dry forest to renew itself. Instead of making the park off-limits to *campesino* families who formerly eked out an existence as ranch hands, the park incorporates local people as caretakers, research assistants and guides. In addition to receiving a salary, they live and farm within the park, so that their social framework, as well as the environment, is preserved. The new addition, by the way, includes the area where the clandestine airstrip, which figured in the Iran-Contra fiasco, was located.

The three times that Costa Rica has been militarily invaded, the invaders were defeated at the Hacienda Santa Rosa's *Casona* (big house). These days the Casona is a museum with commemorative historical and environmental education exhibits. Near the museum is a trail you can follow for a short natural history jaunt.

There is **camping** in a central area with water, outhouses and nice big shady trees (for a minimal fee). The ranger will tell you which areas of the park are especially rich in wildlife at the moment.

A 13 km trail will take you to **Playa Naranjo,** a long stretch of white sand which you can usually have all to yourself. At *Argelia* house, right off the beach, there is a camping area, an outhouse and a windmill-pumped well. There is another camping area at *Estero Real,* which you can reach by bearing right at a fork in the trail to Playa Naranjo. It is shady, close to the beach, and has water and latrines. Off Playa Naranjo is Witch Rock, famous with surfers the world over for creating the perfect wave.

Santa Rosa is home to a wide variety of easily-observed animals. There are three types of monkeys. Howlers emit deafening growls through enlarged voice boxes. Spider monkeys owe their remarkable agility to a long tail with something like a fingerprint on its end which helps them grip tree branches. Whitefaced monkeys, whose varied diet allows them to live in several ecosystems, are the most inquisitive of the three.

You'll see vultures, falcons and a blue and white jay with a feather on top of its head that looks like a curled ribbon on a birthday present. This bird's beauty is contradicted by its obnoxious squawk. Twenty-two species of bats inhabit the park, including two vampire varieties (they rarely attack humans--their victims are almost always livestock). Pelicans, gulls, herons and sandpipers are the most easily-recognized birds on the beach. Cicadas buzz from tree branches, so loud that sometimes you have to shout to be heard.

There are collared and whitelipped peccaries whose reputation for ferocity is misleading, a Santa Rosa biologist told us. Peccaries are actually afraid of humans and flee when we are near. White-tailed deer wander in the savanna land and coatimundis prowl around forests. As in most areas of the Pacific coast, iguanas are everywhere. Caimans live in the estuaries of Playa Naranjo.

Collared peccary (zahíno)

One evening we came across a Pacific Ridley turtle digging a hole to lay her eggs. Some 500,000 turtles nest on the Pacific coast of Costa Rica, of which 200,000 choose **Playa Nancite,** a two or three-hour hike from Playa Naranjo. Their largest *arribada* usually takes place in October. After an approximately 60-day incubation period, the baby turtles hatch and crawl into the sea. An estimated 2 percent survive all the hazards of turtle-hood and become adults.

Playa Nancite is covered with turtle eggshell fragments and a few shells and skeletons of unfortunate mother turtles who didn't make it. You can't stay at Nancite overnight without a permit--it serves mainly as a biological research station. To hike there from Argelia, walk north along the beach. Go at low tide so that you can wade across the river. During high tide, you have to swim across and currents are strong. Find the trail that traces behind the estuary and you'll arrive at the Estero Real picnic and camping areas. Inland from Estero Real, the trail turns off on the left and climbs over a ridge to Nancite. Take water for the hike.

The formerly inaccessible **Murciélago** sector of Santa Rosa is now easier to get to. Keep on the Interamerican 5-10 minutes beyond the Santa Rosa turnoff, and turn left on the road to Cuajiniquil. About 15 min down the winding road to the park is the **Restaurant Cuajiniquil**, where you can have a good fresh fish lunch for about $3. Once you get to the administration buildings at Murciélago, there are swimming holes and a camping area. In the dry season you can reach Playa Blanca, a beautiful beach on the tip of the Santa Elena peninsula. You can buy meals from the park cooks if you let them know in advance that you're coming (69-5598).

Guanacaste National Park was opened on July 25, 1989. It was created to protect the migratory paths of animals that live in Santa Rosa, so it extends from the Interamerican highway to Orosi and Cacao volcanoes to the east. Many moths procreate in the high mountains during the dry season, then fly down to spend the rainy season at a lower, warmer altitude. The *jabalí*, a wild pig, goes down from the volcanoes to the dry forest in January to search for seeds of the *encino* tree. Scientists studying wildlife in Santa Rosa found that it is impossible to protect these animals if the environments so necessary to their existence are not also protected.

Although Costa Rica has about .001% of the world's landmass, it has 5% of the world's biodiversity. For instance, an estimated 3800 species of moths live in Santa Rosa alone. Studying all of them would take years. However, now, in an exciting new project, local park employees are trained in biological inventory techniques by some of the best scientists in the world. By all reports, the program is a tremendous success, due to the sharp powers of observation of the *campesinos*, their familiarity with the region and its wildlife, and their motivation to learn a new career that would never have been open to them a few years ago. People are now being brought to Guanacaste from parks all over the country, to be trained in the same techniques. All specimens will be turned over to the new **Biodiversity Institute** in Santo Domingo de Heredia, which hopes to be able to identify every plant and animal species in the country.

Three different biological stations exist in the new park to aid in this effort: one on **Volcán Cacao** has a rustic wooden lodge in cloud forest with a fantastic view. The **Maritza** station is a newly-built structure with dormitories, a lab and a dining room on the skirts of Volcán Orosi. The **Pitilla** station is on the northeast side of Volcán Orosi at a lower elevation in rainforest similar to that found at La Selva in Sarapiquí. All lodges accept visitors and can prepare meals if given enough advance notice. Guanacaste, Santa Rosa and Rincón de la Vieja parks are all administered from Santa Rosa headquarters (69-5598), so call there for reservations and directions.

Getting there: Buses that go to Peñas Blancas on the Nicaragua border pass the entrance to Santa Rosa. They leave San José at 5am and 7:45am (c 16, a 3, 55-1932, tickets in advance, 4-hour trip, $3.50). Or catch a La Cruz (*not* Santa Cruz) bus from Liberia at 5:30am, 9:30am, or 2pm and ask to be let off at the "*entrada a Santa Rosa*". You must walk or hitch 7.2km to the Casona and camping area before you start the 13km hike to the beach. The trail to Estero Real is probably a creek in the rainy season. We made it down to the beach in a huge 4-wheel-drive jeep once, but the boulders made it a harrowing trip. A tank would be the appropriate vehicle.

By car, Santa Rosa is only 20 min north of Liberia on the Interamerican. The entrance to the Murciélago sector, thru Cuajiniquil, is about 5 min beyond, also on the left.

Los Inocentes is the large estate of the Víquez family near Volcán Orosi in northern Guanacaste. They have converted their old family *hacienda* into a lodge from which visitors can ride horses to the forests surrounding the volcano to observe birds, monkeys and other native animals. Trips to nearby beaches and Santa Rosa are also offered. Food and service are excellent, and one gets a sense of the graceful way of life of traditional Costa Rica (39-5484, 66-9190, A/person incl. meals, pb, hw, pool; horses and guide extra). To get there, turn right at the security post about 5 minutes north of the turnoff to Cuajiniquil (the sign points to Upala and Santa Cecilia). After 14.5 km on paved road, you'll see a "Los Inocentes" sign, and a store to the right. The hacienda is the first gate after the store.

Beaches near Liberia (See p.115 for hotel codes).

Playa del Coco is the most central of the beaches near Liberia. It has some of the least expensive cabinas in the area, most of the dancehalls, and its waters are full of small craft. It

187

is not the place to go if you want solitude and relaxation. **Hotel Anexo Luna Tica** (C, 67-0279) has breezy second floor rooms with fans. **Cabinas Luna Tica** (D incl. breakfast, 67-0127, pb, cw, cf) are also a block to the left as you near the beach. **Cabinas El Coco** are right on the beach. The sound of the waves muffles the noise from the neighboring discotheque somewhat, but not completely (D, 67-0167, fans, relatively clean, cw, rest; cheaper, less breezy and noisier rooms in back, best to get front room on 2nd floor). The **Flor de Itabo** is about 1km from the beach as you enter town, in a very quiet area. It is a well-designed hotel with a lot of nice touches (L, 67-0011, fax: (506) 67-0003, hw, a/c, pool, rest, sportfishing).

El Ocotal is the most elegant hotel in the area, perched high on a hill 4 km south of Coco (XL, 67-0230, 22-4259). Even if you can't afford its sport fishing, tennis and swimming facilities, you can visit its restaurant for breakfast or lunch and enjoy the beautiful view. A dirt road to lovely, shady Ocotal cove is to the right of the hotel gate, a 40-minute walk from Coco. **Bahía Pez Vela** (LL, 21-1586), right after Ocotal, has a small black-sand beach and comfortable cabinas for dedicated sportfishers.

Playa Hermosa, 9km to the north, is quieter and cleaner, with gentle waves and clear water. The turnoff is to the right before you get to Coco. Follow signs to Condovac. **Cabinas Playa Hermosa** are quiet, fairly comfortable and right on the beach (C, 67-0136, fans, hw, good fish dinner for $5). Right next door are three campesino restaurants that offer a whole fish for $2. Halfway down the beach is **Aquasport,** where you can rent kayaks, windsurfing boards, sailboats, etc, or have an excellent seafood dinner (*paella* is their specialty). They won't rent windsurfing boards during the dry season, because heavy winds on that beach make windsurfing dangerous. **Los Corales** are cabinas with kitchens (L on weekends, C during the week, pools, jacuzzi, a/c, conference room, 57-0259, 55-4978, fax: 55-4978). Posh **Condovac La Costa** overlooks Playa Hermosa from the north. If your beach experience requires a discotheque, there it is, plus sportfishing facilities, windsurfing, waterskiing and snorkeling rentals, tennis courts, and little golfcart-like vehicles that transport you up and down the hill (XL, hw, a/c, kitchens, pool, cable TV, rest., 21-8949, 33-1862, fax: (506) 22-5637).

Best for camping is **Playa Panamá,** 3km north of Hermosa. A wide bay makes for very gentle water, especially at low tide when tide·pools form near the north end of the beach. Watch out for sea urchins! There are a couple of bars and *pulperías* on the south end, but the north end has beautiful shady trees. You'll have to bring your own water, or ask for it at the bars. You can hire a fisherman at any of the beaches to take you across Bahía Culebra to **Playa Nacascolo,** where many Indian artefacts have been found. You can camp there, but there is no water.

Getting to Playa del Coco: A bus leaves San José (c 14, a 1/3) every day at 10am and returns at 9:15am ($2.10). Buses leave Liberia for El Coco (30 min trip, $.60) at 5:30am, 12:30pm and 4:30pm, returning at 7am, 1:30pm and 6pm.

Hermosa and Panamá: Buses leave Liberia for both beaches at 11:30am, returning at 4pm. You can also take a bus from Coco to the turnoff and walk or hitch 5 km to Hermosa or 8km to Panamá. A bus leaves San José (c 12, a 5/7) for Playas Hermosa and Panamá at 3:30pm and returns at 6am. Condovac also has a direct bus all year (21-8949, $20 r.t.).

By car, Coco, Hermosa and Panamá are about a half hour from Liberia. There is a gas station on the road to Coco after the turnoff to the town of Sardinal.

Beaches near Santa Cruz (See p. 115 for key to hotel codes).

If you want to continue south, take any of the above-mentioned buses from the beaches and get off at Comunidad (also called Tamarindo Bar), where the road from Coco meets the road from Liberia. There you can intercept a Santa Cruz or Nicoya bus. In 15 minutes you'll be in Belén, where a bus passes around 10:30am and 2:30pm for Playas Brasilito, Flamingo and Potrero. You'll see the turnoff for the beaches about a block after you pass the plaza of Belén. A winding road leads to the village of Huacas, where you turn off to the right. Turn right again after about 200 meters to go to Playas Brasilito, Flamingo, Potrero and Pan de Azúcar. Go straight to get to Conchal and Playa Grande. The trip from Belén to Brasilito, the closest beach, takes about 1/2 hour by car, an hour by bus, all on paved road. The road is unpaved after Playa Flamingo, as is the road to Playa Grande. There are a couple of gas stations in Filadelfia, about halfway between Comunidad and Belén.

Brasilito is a small town on a grey-sand beach. Rooms at **Mi Posada** (E, cw, nf, 68-0953) are basic, clean and have private baths and a soda. Two second floor rooms catch the sea breezes, all others are ground floor. The ever-present juke box in the dance hall across the street might be a problem for some. To the left of Mi Posada on the beach are shady trees to camp or park under. To the right are restaurants and bars. El Rancho has a spigot you can get water from. The beach itself is no great shakes, but the people are very friendly. Half an hour south on foot is **Conchal** (see next page) a beach remarkable for its hill of shells. Leaving Brasilito you'll pass the entrance to **Villas Pacifica**, fancy condominiums on a hill (XL, restaurant, pool, a/c, cable TV, access to sportsfishing facilities at nearby Flamingo Beach, 68-0932).

Five minutes down the road is the entrance to **Playa Flamingo,** one of Costa Rica's most exclusive beaches, sporting its own marina and landing strip. **Hotel Playa Flamingo** (XL, 39-1584, fax: (506) 39-0257) is huge, has a bar you can swim up to in its pool, boutiques, fancy restaurants, etc, and is right on the beach. The **Presidential Suites** (XL, same numbers), up the hill offer spacious, comfortable, nicely-decorated apartments, with great views, breezy cross-ventilation on the top floor, a pool, maid and laundry service. The nearby **Flamingo Marina Resort** (XL, 68-0996, fax: (506) 21-8093, 68-0928) has a jacuzzi and bar on the terrace of its suites plus regular rooms and 5-person apartments. It overlooks the marina and bay, 300m away from the beach. All the above hotels have a/c, cable TV, restaurants, and private terraces. They will arrange transport from the airport in Tamarindo ($20 round trip), or air charter service. Air-conditioned buses leave the Hotel Herradura near San José Mon, Wed, Fri at 9am for Flamingo and return Tues, Thurs, Sat ($40 round-trip, 4.5 hours). Car rental is available as is windsurfing and scuba diving equipment. **Flamingo Bay Pacific Charters** offers well-equipped sportfishing. **Marie's Restaurant** nearby has good omelettes for breakfast.

A Tralapa bus ($3, c 20, a 3, 21-7202) leaves San José every day at 10:30am, arrives in Santa Cruz at 2:30pm and continues to Flamingo, returning at 7am.

Across the bay from Flamingo, 6 km from Brasilito, is **Playa Potrero. Bahía Flamingo Beach Resort** offers large, simple rooms with good mattresses on a rather barren strip of

Great blue heron
(garza azul)

beach (LL, kitchens, pb, hw, cf, restaurant, small pool, 68-0976). **Cabinas Cristina** are 250m inland (C, quiet, kitchens, small pool, cf, cw, 68-0997).

Buses leave Santa Cruz for Brasilito and Potrero at 4am, 10am and 2pm. The 10:30 Flamingo bus from San José goes all the way to Potrero (see above).

Fifteen minutes by car farther north is **Playa Pan de Azúcar** and **Hotel Sugar Beach** (L, hw, a/c, 68-0959, fax (506) 21-8245, in US: (818) 905-5605). It's a pretty beach with some shade, a rocky part for snorkeling and a sandy part for swimming. There's a great view from the restaurant and bar which is open every day. Pet monkeys, iguanas and a scarlet macaw entertain the guests. A charter boat is available for fishing and snorkeling trips. The hotel is 15 km from the turnoff at Huacas. There is no bus service beyond Potrero.

Getting there: See p. 189-90.

If you do not take the Brasilito turnoff on the road from Huacas you will soon reach the village of Matapalo. Follow signs 5km to the **Condor Club**, perched on a hill above the southern end of Playa Conchal. Each solidly built cabina is almost totally taken up by a huge, incredibly firm mattress with a heavy-duty fan right over it. The elegant but moderately-priced restaurant, disco and pool all have a stunning view of the coast. A beach shuttle, regional tours, tennis, basketball and volleyball courts are available for guests (LL, cf, a/c, TV, hw, pb, 31-7328, fax: 20-0670, make reservations well in advance).

The leatherback sea turtle is the largest reptile in the world, 5 feet long, some weighing over a ton. Around 80 leatherbacks come every night to nest in the beach at **Playa Grande** during November, December and January. Playa Grande is also becoming a favorite spot for surfers, because of its long waves. In a project called Friends of Playa Grande, Costa Rican boy and girl scouts are trained to count turtle eggs, to keep campers off the dunes where the turtles nest, and to warn tourists against the use of flashlights and flash attachments on cameras, which can scare the turtles and interfere with their nesting. The young conservationists have had a very positive impact on the visitors. The same scouts also protect turtle nesting sites on the Caribbean coast.

To get to Playa Grande, go straight ahead on the road going west from Huacas instead of turning right (north) for Playa Brasilito. Turn left at the village of Matapalo. The 10am and 2pm Santa Cruz-Flamingo buses stop in Matapalo first. From there it's a few minutes by car or taxi to Playa Grande. Half a km before you get there are **Cabinas Playa Grande** (C, cw, pb, cf, kitchen, 37-2552). They will meet your bus in Huacas if you give a few days notice of your arrival. Another hotel is opening soon on the beach, and there are plans for large developments at each end. As of this writing, conservationists are trying to make Playa Grande and neighboring Tamarindo and Langosta beaches into a protected zone, hopefully giving the turtles a voice in future touristic undertakings.

Tamarindo is a wide, white-sand beach with a large estuary--a favorite with surfers and windsurfers. The estuary has been made into a wildlife refuge. Leatherback (*baúla*) turtles nest on the beach, August to February. Many baby turtles have been crushed as they scramble to the ocean by inadvertent tourists because it is hard to distinguish them in the dry, loose sand high up on the beach. Be sure to walk near the water line, where it is easier to spot the baby turtles.

Tamarindo is also an active fishing village, something to be valued since many Guanacaste beaches have lost their traditional activities to tourism. You can watch the fishermen *zarpando* (sailing out to sea) at dawn, and you can eat their catch at the **Fiesta del Mar** and **Tercer Mundo** restaurants or the hotels. **Johan's Bakery** is open from 6am daily with European bread, pastry and pizza. The **Supermarket El Pelícano** is open 9-5 daily, closed Sunday. Next to it you can rent scooters, boogie boards, beach chairs and umbrellas, or find out about houses and rooms for rent. Across the street, the **Coconut Cafe** serves fondue, grilled meats, tropical fruit drinks and ice cream.

As you enter Tamarindo, **Cabinas Pozo Azul** has a pool but not much atmosphere (C, pb, cw, a/c, fridges, 68-0147). The **Pueblo Dorado** has small, clean, comfortably-furnished rooms (LL, hw, a/c, pool, ph/fax: (506) 22-5741). **Pensión Doly** (E, pb; F, cb, small, cement rooms) is definitely basic but it's clean, friendly and right on the beach. Don't go swimming there; that section of the beach is dangerous. The large **Tamarindo Diriá** is a comfortable place to stay. It has lovely, shady grounds and two pools, but can get crowded during tourist season (LL, smallish rooms, a/c, fans, cable TV, hw, tennis, game room, rest., 68-0652, 33-0530, fax: (506) 22-0568). Local people sell jewelry and animals made out of shells at the entrance to the beach from the hotel. **Cabinas Zully Mar** are in "downtown" Tamarindo, where the road ends in a clutch of bar-restaurants on the beach. The rooms are clean and the management friendly (D, pb, cf, 26-4732). The American-owned **Tamarindo Resort** has a pool and restaurant at the south end of town plus dozens of cheaply-built bungalows in a shady area back from the beach (L, hw, cf, kitchens, maid service, 68-0883, 55-2263, fax: (506) 55-3785).

Getting there: SANSA flies to Tamarindo from San José Mon, Wed, Fri and Sat at 8am, returning at 8:50 ($20, check schedules at 33-0397, 33-3258, 21-9414). Most hotels in the area arrange transport for guests from the Tamarindo airport.

Empresa Alfaro buses to Tamarindo leave San José at 3:30pm from c 14, a 5, and return at 5:30 am ($4, 22-2750, tickets in advance). Tralapa buses leave at 4pm from a 3, c 20 and return at 5:30am ($4, 21-7202, tickets in advance). Buses leave Santa Cruz for Tamarindo daily at 3pm, and at 10am also on weekends.

The turnoff for Tamarindo is 13 km S of Huacas on paved road, about an hour from Liberia by car. There are gas stations in Filadelfia, between Liberia and Belén. There's an outdoor tire repair shop on the left on the dirt road to Tamarindo, on a rise after a little bridge.

Junquillal is a wide, almost deserted beach. It has two comfortably elegant hotels with nice pools, tennis courts and spacious two-unit bungalows. **Villa Serena,** (XL, 68-0737) is smaller, intimate, with three excellent meals included in its rates. Sauna and videos also available. **Hotel Antumalal,** farther

193

down the beach, does not include meals in its rates (LL, pb, a/c, hw, 68-0506). **Hotel Junquillal**, at the entrance to the beach, has a restaurant and three funky cabinas (D), and charges campers $4 per night for use of their facilities, such as they are.

Getting there: To reach Junquillal from Tamarindo, continue south 18 km to a crossing called "27 de Abril." Turn right onto an unpaved road and go another 12 km. Turn left at Paraíso. The hotels are a short distance from there. If you are coming from Liberia, it is faster to take a turnoff to the right just before you reach Santa Cruz (follow signs). From there it's 19 km to "27 de Abril." Turn left, and proceed as above.

A direct San José-Junquillal bus leaves from the Tralapa station at 2pm daily, arriving around 8pm and returning at 5am ($4, a 3, c 20, 21-7202). Daily Tralapa buses to Santa Cruz leave at 7:30am, 10:30, 12, 4 and 6pm and return at 4:30, 6:30, 8:30 and 11:30am, and 1:30pm. Most San José-Nicoya buses also pass through Santa Cruz (c 14, a 5, 22-2750).

If you need to spend a night in **Santa Cruz**, the **Diriá** (B, 68-0080) and the **Sharatoga** (C, 68-0011) both offer a/c and swimming pools, almost a necessity in the inland heat.

The old road to Nicoya goes to the left after you cross a bridge leaving Santa Cruz. It's a bumpy but interesting drive through the hills that are the heartland of the province. You'll pass through **Guaitil,** where local artisans have been reviving the art of pottery-making in the Chorotega style. They re-create every known original style and design, using native clay, with little or no use of a wheel and no artificial paints or colors. Pottery is displayed at the local shop and in front of peoples' houses. Stop for a chat with them and you'll feel the warmth and goodness of the Costa Rican *campesino*. San Vicente, 2km SE also has a pottery shop in the center of town. Buses leave Santa Cruz for Guaitil every two hours between 7am and 5pm. By car it's 12km SE of Santa Cruz and 19km NE of Nicoya.

Beaches near Nicoya

While Liberia is the transportation and commercial capital of Guanacaste, **Nicoya** is the cultural capital. Its church, dedicated to San Blas, was built in 1644 and is presently undergoing restoration. It's open 8-12 and 2-6, closed Weds and Sun.

Next to the church is a lovely, shady square abloom with flowers. **Hotel Jenny** (D, 68-5050, a/c, cw, TV) and **Las Tinajas** (E, 68-5081, pb, cw, tf) are both pleasant places to stay in the center of town. The **Pensión Venecia** has no fans, but is clean and very cheap (F), across from the church. **Restaurante Jade,** 100m east and 75 north of the church, offers tasty Chinese food. **Hotel Curime,** south of town on the road to Playa Sámara has a pool, restaurant, and modern cabinas with fridges and the world's noisiest air conditioning (A, hw, 68-5238).

Nicoya is about 20 minutes from Santa Cruz on the paved road, an hour on the old road.

The **ferry** ride across the Tempisque is a pleasant 20 minutes. It crosses continuously, but if you get there when it is pulling away, you have to wait, which is why it sometimes takes as long to go by the ferry route to or from Nicoya as it does through Liberia (5 hours). If you do not buy your ticket ($.10) quickly and jump on the ferry when it is there, your bus will leave without you. Buses that go to Nicoya by way of the ferry leave San José at 8am, returning at 4pm. Buses to Nicoya through Liberia leave San José at 6, 10, 1:30, 3 and 5pm (Empresa Alfaro, c 14, a 5, 22-2750, $3.50, tickets in advance). The ferry also takes 12 cars at a time ($2.25).

Playas de Nosara is an international community with many North American and European residents. About half the land in this 12 square km development has been set aside as a wildlife reserve and park. The maritime zone fronting 4km of beach is protected by the forest service. Because of these reserve areas, Nosara is generally much greener than the rest of Guanacaste. No hunting has been allowed there for 18 years, so birds and wildlife are plentiful. It is common to see coatimundis, armadillos, howler monkeys and even the jaguarundi, a cat with a grey diamond pattern on its fur which looks black from a distance. Parrots, toucans, cuckoos, trogons and pelicans are also easily observed. Humpback and grey whales can be seen offshore during the northern winter months. The beaches have community-maintained shelters for picnicking and camping. There are coral reefs and tidepools on Playa Guiones for snorkeling. Surfing is best there and at the Nosara River mouth. A small restaurant on **Playa Pelada** offers fresh fish and provides water for campers.

195

The views from the very pleasant **Hotel Playa Nosara** are magnificent (LL, hw, cf, pool, rest., 68-0495). The hotel is high on a point, so you can see long Playa Guiones on one side and beautiful Playa Pelada on the other. The **Gilded Iguana** is famous for their Black Panther cocktail (named after the local jaguarundi), and serves soup and sandwiches Weds thru Sun, with a traditional bridge game on Sat. They rent furnished efficiency apartments (LL, 68-0749). Some of the more than 80 homes of the community are rentable by the week or month ($600-800/mo. incl. utils., maid service, 68-0747). The new **Condominio de las Flores** offers completely equipped apartments ($500/wk, $1500/mo. during high season, 2-br, 2-bath, 68-0696). A few km to the north is the village of Nosara, where there is a gas station and a *pulpería*. **La Lechuza,** 2km N on the road to the village, is a favorite gathering place for residents, open for lunch Mon-Sat. **Cabinas Chorotega**, next to the gas station, are very clean, with fans and shared baths (E, 68-0836).

Getting there: SANSA flies Tues, Thurs and Sat to Nosara at 6am, returning at 6:50am ($20, check schedules at 21-9414, 33-0397, 33-3258). Hotel Playa Nosara picks guests up at the plane. Regular buses leave Nicoya for Nosara at 12 noon and return at 6am. The trip takes about 2.5 hours by bus, and 1.5 by car on dusty, bumpy gravel roads.

Instead of going back to Nicoya, we explored the coastal road through Paraíso to Santa Cruz. The going was rough, with several river beds to cross, but it got a bit smoother after Marbella. The trip took 2 hours and wasn't that exciting.

Ostional Wildlife Refuge, just north of Nosara, protects the breeding grounds of *lora* or olive ridley turtles, which arrive in great numbers between the third quarter and the new moon from April to December, with peak activity in August and September. The people of Ostional are allowed to harvest turtle eggs during the first 36 hours of the *arribada* since the eggs laid during that period are usually dug up and crushed by subsequent waves of mother turtles. The eggs are sold to bars across the country to be gulped raw as *bocas*. After the first 36 hours, community members guard the beach to make sure that the rest of the eggs are laid without disturbance. They will be glad to show you around and tell you about their cooperative. You can stay in simple cabinas there (F), and buy meals from local families. Call the village *pulperia* (68-0467) to reserve cabinas and find out if the turtles are active.

Getting there: During the dry season, you can ford the river between Nosara and Ostional, but the road is smoother going southwest from Santa Cruz via Marbella, at least through July. A bus leaves Santa Cruz at noon each day during the dry season and arrives at Ostional at 3:30.

Villaggio la Guaria Morada is a very elegant beachside hotel a few km south of Nosara at Punta Garza. Italian-owned, known for good food (XL, 68-0784, 33-2476).

Playa Sámara, 1 hour S of Nosara, is the perfect long white sand beach with shallow, gentle waters. It's a favorite with swimmers and windsurfers. Many Ticos have summer homes there. **Hotel Las Brisas del Pacífico** is a well-designed hotel at the southern end of the beach (L, cf, hw, jacuzzi, pool, 68-0876, 55-2380, fax: (506) 33-5503). A number of cheap cabinas and *hospedajes* are at the north end of the beach. Residents of the north end are good about letting visitors camp and use their facilities. **El Acuario,** 100m south of the soccer field, rents camping space and use of its facilities for $1. They have a good fish dinner for $4.

Getting there: A direct San José-Sámara bus leaves from Empresa Alfaro, a 5, c 14/16 at noon daily ($4, 6-hour trip, 22-2750, 23-8227, 23-8361, buy tickets several days in advance on 3-day weekends). Buses leave for Sámara from Nicoya at 3pm daily and also at 8am on weekends, returning from Sámara at 5:30am daily and again at 2pm weekends during the dry season. During the rainy season, there is one bus at noon only.

SANSA flies to Sámara Mon, Weds and Fri at 6am, returning 6:50am ($20). Check with SANSA about schedule changes and buy your ticket 2 weeks in advance during the dry season (21-9414, 33-0397, 33-3258). To drive to Sámara from Nosara, you have to ford an ankle-deep river about halfway there. The trip from Nicoya by car is about 1.5 hours.

About 5 minutes south of Sámara by car is **Playa Carrillo,** another beautiful white sand beach whose waters are kept calm by a reef at the entrance to the bay. There is not much shade for camping at Carrillo, nor are there facilities, but there is a large bar and restaurant with a great view at the entrance to the village, up on a cliff where it receives the sea breezes (good breakfasts for $1.50 and fish for $3). Next door are some rather unattractive cabinas (D, for up to 3 people). Carrillo also boasts an airstrip and an ice factory--the exclusive sportfishing hotel **Guanamar** (XL, cable TV, phones, a/c, hw, some with kitchens, pool, restaurant, 39-4433, fax: (506) 39-2405) is located there.

If you travel south from Carrillo by car, you must ford the Río Ora at low tide. It's good to purchase a tide table if you travel the unpaved coastal roads in Guanacaste (see p. 80).

About two hours south of Carrillo is **Playa Coyote.** It is long and deserted and was very windy when we were there. We were told that **Playa Caletas,** one beach to the south, has 15-foot waves. There are primitive showers and a bar at Coyote. It is most easily reached by gravel road from Jicaral, which is an hour northwest of Playa Naranjo, where the Puntarenas ferry lands. The trip takes 1.5 hours.

El Cerro **Barra Honda** is part of a flat-topped ridge that juts up out of the dry cattle-grazing land of the Nicoya Peninsula. People used to call the ridge a volcano because it's covered with large white limestone rocks piled around deep holes that look like craters. In the 1960's and 70's speleologists discovered that the holes were entrances to an intricate series of interconnected caves, some as deep as 200 meters, and the area was made into a National Park.

When the region was under the sea millions of years ago, marine animals deposited calcium carbonate that hardened and became⁻ limestone. Later, when the land was pushed up out of the sea, rainfall combined with carbon dioxide and dissolved the limestone to hollow out the caves. In a process similar to how icicles grow, dripping water carrying calcium carbonate formed stalactites and stalagmites in the form of curtains, organpipes, fried eggs, etc.

Within the caves a whole habitat flourishes--bats, insects, birds, blind salamanders and fish. In the *Nicoa* cave, speleologists discovered human skeletons. They had been there a long time; a stalagmite was growing on one skull. It is assumed that they were Indians from the region since some Indian artifacts were found near the skeletons.

Fortunately, the caves have suffered almost no vandalism. The deep vertical drops at the entrances have discouraged all but the best-equipped from entering. The park rangers can take you down into *Terciopelo,* the cave with the most beautiful formations of all. A visit requires a week's notice to the National Parks regional headquarters in Bagaces (67-1062). They won't take you down in the rainy season or during Holy Week.

Ríos Tropicales runs spelunking tours into the caves. They have better equipment, and can go places the park rangers can't (33-6455).

Even if you can't get down into the caves, a visit to Barra Honda is rewarding. You can explore the flat top of the ridge. The biggest trees are full of howler monkeys. Iguanas stand motionless, birds screech. The look-out point reached by following the *Sendero al Ojoche, la Trampa, la Terciopelo* affords wide views of the peninsula and the gulf of Nicoya. The *Sendero al Ceibo* leads to a waterfall decorated with lace-like calcium carbonate formations. It's about 6 km from the trailhead.

In the dry season it's very hot, so bring a canteen with you as you explore. The campsite is up the road to the right, on the left side of the trail. There are picnic tables and water.

Getting there: Barra Honda is a half hour from Nicoya by car. Take the main road east and make a left when you see signs for the village of Barra Honda. You can also come from the east via the Tempisque ferry and turn right at the Barra Honda turnoff. The road to the village is paved. Beyond that, the dirt road to the park gets narrower and bumpier, but National Park signs clearly mark the way. You can take a bus at noon from Nicoya to the village of Santa Ana (1.5-hour trip) and walk 2km to the park. Buses leave Nicoya for Barra Honda village at 10:30am and 3pm, leaving you 6km from the park.

Frigates

THE CENTRAL PACIFIC ZONE

Puntarenas was Costa Rica's main port for most of the 1800's. The treacherous terrain between San José and the Atlantic Coast made an eastern port impossible, until the railway was completed in 1890. So oxcarts laden with coffee rumbled down to Puntarenas, where the precious beans were shipped to Chile, then re-exported to Europe. In 1843, English Captain William Le Lacheur landed in Puntarenas on the way back from a business failure in Seattle. Worried about the danger of sailing with an empty ship, the captain traveled five days by mule to San José, hoping to find some cargo for ballast. It turned out that coffee had been over-produced that year, and growers were desperate for new markets. Even though he was a stranger and had no money to give them, the growers entrusted him with a weighty shipment. He came back two years later with the payment, and a lively trade with England was established.

Puntarenas is no longer a commercial port, since the inauguration of Puerto Caldera a few years ago, but it is still the closest beach to San José. According to a recent study by the Ministry of Health, swimming is not recommended at the beaches in and near Puntarenas, but it is pleasant to stroll along the Paseo de Turistas, feel the sea breezes, and watch the sun set behind the mountains of the Nicoya Peninsula.

The town is only four blocks wide for most of its length, because it is built on a narrow spit. Fishing boats and ferries dock on the estuary side; a beach runs along the gulf side. For visitors, Puntarenas has two distinct characters that the season determines: it is lively and full of people in the dry season, sleepy and tranquil in the rainy season.

In summer, people-watchers will enjoy the never-ending parade of tourists up and down the wide sidewalk next to the beach. Kiosks there serve snacks, *refrescos* and ice cream. There's a great, inexpensive series of concerts and plays at the Casa de la Cultura during the summer. We enjoy Puntarenas more in the rainy season when it is uncrowded, breezy and refreshed.

The new 174-room **Hotel Fiesta** in El Roble, a few km before Puntarenas, is designed to cater to the big-time tourist trade (XL, a/c, hw, cable TV, pools, restaurants, casino, tennis, volleyball, gym, fishing, water sport equipment rentals, conference rooms, 63-0185, fax: (506) 39-0217, 63-1516). The green, residential San Isidro area near the hospital, has many cabinas with kitchens that can be rented by the day or week. **Cabinas Los Chalets** are the nicest (B, cw, pool, 63-0150). Frequent buses connect San Isidro with Puntarenas.

The loveliest hotel in Puntarenas is the **Portobello,** about three miles from downtown on the estuary. Its lush, colorful, beautifully-tended gardens create a sense of privacy and tranquility, and attract many birds (A, 61-1322, a/c, hw, pools, good restaurant, cross-ventilated rooms). The Portobello and its nextdoor neighbor, Hotel Colonial, offer free mooring and use of facilities to sailboats passing through. **Hotel Colonial** (A incl. breakfast, a/c, cf, cw, hw in some units, pools, swings, pingpong, etc., 61-1833) appeals to a younger crowd. The **Yacht Club,** just before Portobello, has cabinas (D, hw, a/c, pool, 23-4224, 61-0784). Downtown, near the bus stop, are the **Chorotega** (D, pb; E, cb, rest, 61-0998, c 1, a 3) favored by backpackers, **Las Hamacas** (D, cw, a/c, cf, pool, rest, 61-0398, a 4, c 5/7), and the **Cayuga** (D, cw, a/c, rest, 61-0344). The **Ayi Con** is probably the cleanest of the cheap hotels near the market (E, cb or pb, cw, cf; D, a/c, 61-0164, c 2, a 1/3). The **Imperial** (D, cb or pb, cf, cw, 61-0579) is a nice old building right across from the beach near c ctl. The upstairs rooms have more light. **Cabinas El Jorón** (C, hw, fridges, a/c, dark, noisy, 61-0467, c 25, a 2) has a restaurant known for its steaks. **Hotel Tioga** (C, 61-0271, a/c, hw, indoor pool, cafeteria, breakfast included) is a favorite with visitors. It was *the* place to stay 25 years ago, and is still comfortable and well-maintained. **Las Brisas** (B, 61-2120, a/c only, cw, small pool, 3 blocks west of ferry landing) has large, clean rooms with no cross-ventilation. **Hotel La Punta** is probably the most convenient for those who

Downtown Puntarenas

want to catch the ferry in the morning. It's just around the corner from the terminal (C, cf, cw, pool, rest., clean, 61-0696). The fancy **Hotel Yadran** is on the ocean side of the point (L, carpets, a/c, TV, hw, bathtubs, pool, rest., 61-2662, fax: (506) 61-1944). **La Caravelle** on the oceanfront is recommended for good food. **Restaurante Miramare** specializes in Italian sea-food.

Camping on the beach is not recommended.

Getting there: San José-Puntarenas **buses** leave from c 12, a 9 continuously from 6am to 7pm. Get there early on week-ends and holidays. *Directo* buses take 2 hours ($1.50, 22-1867). The **train** takes a beautiful route through mountains, across gorges, over farmland ($.80, 4 hrs, many stops). It leaves from the Pacific station on a 20, c 2 in San José at 1pm, with an additional train at 6:30am weekends. Trains return from Pun-tarenas at 6am daily with an additional run at 4pm weekends, 26-0011).

Calypso Tours takes you around the Gulf in their luxurious yacht, provides fresh tropical fruit and ceviche to nibble, serves a gourmet seafood buffet on Tortuga Island where you can swim or snorkel, and provides fishing tackle for the trip back to Puntarenas. They pass close to an island which is one of the main refuges for pelicans and frigate birds ($70, incl. trans. to and from San José, discounts with OTEC card, 33-3617, fax: (506) 33-0401). You can combine the Calypso cruise with trips to Carara Reserve, Monteverde, or rafting down the Corobicí River. They also offer a romantic two-hour sunset cocktail cruise every Saturday. **Bay Island Cruises** and **Fantasy Yacht Tours** are recent clones of Calypso, which has been doing the cruise for 16 years.

A huge, rusting **ferryboat** leaves from the estuary at the far end of Puntarenas at 7am and 4pm every day with an 11am trip Thurs, Sat and Sun (61-1069, $.80/adult, $5.50/car). It returns at

9am and 6pm daily, plus 2pm Thurs, Sat and Sun. The hour-long ride takes you between verdant islands and makes you feel adventurous. *If you have a car, be sure to get in line at least an hour before the ferry leaves from either end*, as only a limited number of cars can fit. Drivers only are allowed to enter the ferry in their cars. Passengers must walk on. For some reason, drivers have to give their passport or *cédula* number when buying a ticket, plus the license number of the car. The ferry has booths, overpriced snacks and lousy bathrooms on its second level, which tends to be hot and stuffy. Most people ride on the open third deck, so be prepared for sun, wind, and possible rain. Hungry seagulls follow the ferry and catch thrown tidbits in mid-air. We arrived too late to get on the returning 1pm ferry one Sunday, so parked our car in the line for the next ferry, locked it, and went swimming in the lovely pools of Hotel Oasis (see below). We were then treated to a beautiful moonlit trip back across the gulf, which transformed the aging ferry into a romantic ocean liner.

If you have a car, you can continue south from the ferry landing at Playa Naranjo to Paquera, Tambor and Montezuma on the gulf side of the Nicoya Peninsula. There is no bus between Playa Naranjo and Paquera (see below). There are several cheap and good *sodas* at the peninsula landing, and a gas station. A Nicoya bus meets the ferry but it's a bumpy 3-hour trip. It's better to take the Tempisque Ferry to Nicoya (see p. 195).

Hotel Oasis del Pacífico, on Playa Naranjo to the left from the ferry landing (A, 61-1555, cf, pool, rest) offers sportfishing, horses, tennis. Their restaurant is a bit overpriced, but a stop at their swimming pools ($3/person) can make the difference between a pleasure trip and a hot, dusty ordeal. They provide transportation to and from the ferry landing.

Hotel de Paso, inland and to the right from the ferry landing is clean and pleasant, and also has a pool. Its restaurant is open Dec-May (C, pb, cw, some with a/c, some cheaper rooms with shared baths, 61-2610).

Hotel Bahía Gigante, about 15 minutes south of Playa Naranjo on gravel road, has condos on a hill overlooking the bay of the same name. Its restaurant, pool and regular cabinas are behind the hill, making them rather land-locked and buggy (A w/kitchens, views, C below, cw, fans, 61-2442).

Paquera is a small town 45 minutes from Playa Naranjo by car. **Cabinas Ginana** are clean and inexpensive (E, pb, cf, cw, rest., 61-1444, ext. 119). There are also gas stations, food and clothing stores, and pharmacies in Paquera. A boat leaves the dock behind the market in Puntarenas at 6am and 3pm for Paquera. A bus meets the boat and continues to Tambor and Cóbano, near Montezuma.

Curú Wildlife Refuge is located on a private farm 7km south of Paquera. Its beach is home to thousands of phantom crabs, one of which stole my watch while I was enjoying the warm, gentle waters of its picturesque, cup-shaped bay. Luckily we could see the watchband at the bottom of the nearest crab-hole, and we fished it out with a stick. Snorkeling is supposed to be good there too, but we didn't stay long enough to find out because no-see-ums and other nasty biting bugs were making mincemeat of us. Fortunately the effects of the bites were not long-lasting. The farm has banana plantations that are specifically for the wildlife, so its not hard to see howler and white-faced monkeys, pizotes, iguanas and 115 species of birds from the five different hiking trails. Three kinds of turtles nest on the beach. Because the reserve is on private land, it is necessary to call before arriving (61-2392, 26-4333). Leave plenty of time to do this because the phone connections are very bad. There are primitive showers and toilets near the beach, and very rustic accommodations for groups of students and researchers.

Bahia Ballena is a deep, round bay on the southeast end of the Nicoya peninsula. Its waters are gentle and warm, but they are not clear near the shore. **Hotel La Hacienda** (L, cw, cf, pool, rest, horses, 61-2980) is a peaceful resort. Their main claim to fame is their beautiful, non-chlorinated, fresh-water pool, near shaded cabañas where you can relax and look out over the ocean, which is nicer to look at than to swim in. Air transport can be arranged to their airstrip.

In the village of **Tambor** on the southern rim of the bay is **Hotel Dos Lagartos** (D, pb; E, cb, cw, clean, some rooms with fans, friendly, low-key, quiet, good mattresses, 61-1122, ext. 236). From the beach in front of the hotel you can see two points in the distance which resemble crocodiles or lizards, hence the name. The beach is nice for kids because the sand is spongy, and the bay is shallow and has gentle waves. A river to the north fills the water with leaves, but beyond the breakers it's cleaner. The hotel is a great place for those on a budget, but there's no place to store or hang anything, and you should bring your own soap, towels, a universal plug for the sink, and a flashlight in case of power failures. There's a very annoying water pump that goes on and off every 30 seconds during the night, affecting the rooms that face the ocean. We've never noticed any bugs there. **Pulpería Los Gitanos**, down the beach from the hotel, is well-stocked and friendly. Meals are plentiful, cheap and good at **Cristina's**, across form the school. **Restaurant La Bahía** at the wharf on the southern end of the bay serves seafood. You can walk there along the beach or take the turnoff to the left as you leave Tambor. Half a km beyond La Bahía, the road dwindles to a trail. You can walk around the point 8km to Tango Mar, and see monkeys, iguanas and sea birds on the way.

The wharf has gas and diesel tanks to service boats, and a marina is being built. We were told that yacht books recommend going 250 miles out to sea to avoid the Papagayo winds off the northwestern coast of Costa Rica, then tacking in to the Gulf of Nicoya to refuel. This new marina will eliminate the need to go all the way to Puntarenas. Contact Tango Mar (see below) to make sure marina is ready.

Tambor is about 1.5 hours south of Playa Naranjo by car and 1.5 hours from Paquera by bus. Tango Mar has signs out marking the road, so follow them to get to Tambor.

Tango Mar is a unique resort on a beautiful stretch of beach south of Bahía Ballena. Its thatch-roofed cabinas are well-designed and comfortable (XL, hw, kitchens) and its new hotel rooms right on the beach are clean and well-ventilated (XL, hw). There are larger condos with shared kitchens. Its restaurant is run by Bob, an experienced Cajun chef from Louisiana. The food is a lot more interesting than most beach hotel fare, and the huge salads bring tears of joy to the eyes of those who have had one too many french-fries at the beach. Tango Mar boasts the only seaside golfcourse in Costa Rica, and offers sportfishing, sailing, surfing, windsurfing, waterskiing, beach volleyball, and 4-wheel motorcycle, van and golf-cart rentals. They will pick you up in Paquera, or you can fly in from San José to their airstrip (23-1864, 61-2798, fax: (506) 55-2697). By car, follow signs south of Tambor. Reservations only.

Montezuma is a backpacker's paradise. The beaches are varied and beautiful, the hotels are cheap, camping is common.

The sun rises from behind the sea, which provides a challenging exercise in figuring out how the Pacific Ocean got to be east of you.

For a tour of the various beaches, walk north (left) along the coast. The first few rocky bays you pass have very strong currents, especially during high tide. Playa Grande, about 30 minutes away by foot, is calm and shallow, the best and safest place for bathing. There's fresh water in a shower in the park behind Chico's Bar, and a few fresh water streams near pleasant campsites that you'll see as you walk north along the beaches. Beware of hungry monkeys who will steal your food if you don't keep it in your tent. That ominous sound coming from under the dry leaves is probably just hermit crabs.

There's a gorgeous waterfall about 20 minutes south of town where you can swim, cliff-dive, and talk with local people. Walk along the road to Cabo Blanco for 300 meters. At the bridge, head upstream half a kilometer or so.

You can stay at the following hotels or camp. If it's the dry season, call for reservations beforehand (61-1122 is the number for the whole town, plus the extensions given below). At the entrance to town are the **Casa Blanca** on the left, with kitchen privileges and a balcony with hammocks, and **Las Praderas** on the right (D, fans, cw, pb, ext. 284). As you turn towards the beach you'll see **Cabinas Karen**, a white house with simple rooms and cooking facilities (F, no fans). Doña Karen, who, with her late husband, was responsible for founding the Cabo Blanco Reserve, also offers simple cabinas (F) with shared kitchens and baths set back in the forest on a beach north of town. Next comes **El Sano Banano**, a vegetarian restaurant which shows videos on a large screen at night. They also prepare sack lunches and sell filtered water. **Hotel Moctezuma** (D, pb; E, cb, fans) tends to be noisy because of Chico's bar next door, but has a good restaurant. In back of Chico's are **Cabinas Mar y Cielo** (D, pb, fans, right on the beach). **El Pargo Feliz**, 50m N of Chico's has good fish and lobster dinners. On the inland side of the church, is **Hotel Montezuma Pacific**, the only place in town with air-conditioning. Present rooms are rather small, larger rooms are under construction (C, some hw, some cw, pb, ext. 200, or 22-7746, 21-0182). There are peaceful cabins in the woods behind the second beach to the north (B, kitchens, fans, ext. 272). They have a spigot of spring water that campers can use. The owners run **El Sano Banano**.

El Caracol, 100m south, serves seafood and *casados* and rents primitive thatched-roofed huts on stilts (F). **Cabinas Las Arenas** (F, cb, small rooms with natural breeze or fan, grill and firewood for guests) on the beach to the south are okay if you have quiet neighbors. On the other side of the point to the south are **Casa de Huespedes Alfaro** (D, pb, cw, fans, soda, ext. 259), and **Hotel Lucy** (F, cb, cw, could be cleaner, ext. 273) with breezy rooms upstairs, fans downstairs, and access to a kitchen and clothes-washing area.

Fresh fruits and vegetables are delivered to Montezuma on Wednesdays and Saturdays. If you come later in the week, it's best to bring your own. **Pulpería Manantial** will prepare fileted and seasoned fish for you to grill (be careful of gringo prices there).

Getting there: Take a bus to Puntarenas. From the dock behind the Mercado in Puntarenas take the *lancha* (boat) to Paquera--it leaves at 6am and 3pm ($1). A bus waits for the *lancha* at Paquera, and makes the trip to Cóbano down a bumpy road, through beautiful country, in about 1.5 hours ($3). During the dry season the bus goes all the way to Montezuma. Otherwise, take a jeep-taxi the remaining 7km. If you want to take the 6am boat you'll have to spend the night in Puntarenas. The boat returns to Puntarenas from Paquera at 8am and 5pm. If you ask around in Montezuma, you might find a local fisherman who will take you all the way to Puntarenas in his boat.

If you have a car, take it on the big ferry from Puntarenas to Playa Naranjo (see p. 202-3) and follow the road south to Paquera. Turn left about a km beyond Paquera, at the Tango Mar sign. Continue one hour to Cóbano and turn left when you see the Cabo Blanco sign. The trip takes about 2.5 hours on gravel roads. Montezuma is about 45 min. S of Tambor.

Don't try to go in a regular car if it has been raining. You have to ford a couple of streams, and hills become treacherous. The worst is the last hill that goes down to Montezuma, which becomes a mountain of slippery mud. Regular cars are OK if it hasn't rained for a few days. If you are going to be camping, it might not be too wise to take a car, because there is no road that goes along the beach. You have to leave your car in town and hike across several beaches to get to the good camping spots. Sometimes you can find local people who are willing to put the car in a safe place for you, but at the height of tourist season that might be difficult.

We explored the road going west to Río Negro and Manzanillo from Cóbano on our way to Playa Sámara in Guanacaste. You have to ford several rivers, and sometimes the road
fades into little more than a trail, but we made it through. Just
keep asking people if you're going the right way--there are no
signs. We would have made it to Sámara in about 4 hours by
jeep if we hadn't hit the Río Ora at high tide (see p. 198).

Howler monkey (mono congo)

A road continues south from Montezuma through Cabuya
and on to **Cabo Blanco Wildlife Reserve.** You have to ford
two streams; the 12km trip takes over an hour by jeep. Stop at
the ranger station to get an entrance permit. You can take a
fairly strenuous 2-hour hike up the *Sendero Sueco* and down to
Playa Balsitas. Bring food and plenty of water. Hike left around
the point to Playa Cabo Blanco for another 2-hour hike back.
At high tide you won't be able to make it around the point,
so ask the guards about tides before you leave. You'll see lots
of howler monkeys. Don't stand directly underneath them--they
like to pee on sightseers. There are pelican colonies on either
side of the point, which has beautiful pinkish coral sand.

The road to **Monteverde** from the turnoff on the Interamerican highway is rough, steep and dusty. It's a two-hour climb
through sadly deforested country until you reach the green
pastures that lead to the famous cloud forest. Many Montever-
deans would like to keep the road that way: they not only want
to preserve the cloud forest in its natural state, they also want

to protect the simple, friendly lifestyle that has made their community such a special place. Many communities in Costa Rica have opened to tourism quickly over the last few years. The economy desperately needs the business that tourism brings, but things can be lost in the process. Monteverde, because it has always concerned itself with social issues, is perhaps more articulate about these problems than most rural villages that are being "invaded" by tourism.

A group of Alabama Quakers who felt that Costa Rica's disarmament policy was more in line with their pacifist tradition started dairy farming in Monteverde in the early 1950's. Visiting biologists found the cloud forest above their community rich in flora and fauna, and the Quakers, along with the Tropical Science Center, had the foresight to make it a reserve.

Monteverde is not a place you can visit in one day. You need a day for travel and recovery each way, plus at least one day to visit the reserve ($6 entrance fee, closed Oct. 6-7 each year). A self-guiding pamphlet is available at the field station for a few dollars, and guided tours are available from naturalists who have years of experience in the Reserve ($12.50/person for a 4-hour nature walk; meet guides at field station at 8:15am. Part of fees go to environmental education programs in the zone). In order to protect the forest, only 100 people can be in the reserve at one time. That means that if you arrive when several tour groups have entered, you might have to wait until some of them leave. One more reason to visit May-December instead of during the high season.

The cloud forest stretches from the lush ferns and mosses that cover the ground to the dark canopy formed by the tallest trees. Vines and web-like moss hang down and swing slowly in the breeze. Some of the trees look top-heavy because their branches are so densely enveloped with epiphytes and moss.

Quetzales feed on the tiny, avocado-like fruits of *aguacatillo* trees. They are most visible in the early morning from January through September, and especially during the mating season in April and May. Beautiful and strange frogs also live in the cloud forest, but they're very difficult for the average inexperienced forest-wanderer to spot. The Golden Toad is remarkable for its color and the poison glands behind its ears. An aquarium in the field station exhibits cloud forest wildlife. The animal of the week lives in the aquarium for a few days only and is released back into the wild.

The **Río Negro Tropical Reserve**, 6km north of Santa Elena, is similar to the Monteverde Reserve, but entrance is through guided tours only ($6 entrance, $12 tour). Call Giovanni Bello of the Monteverde Reserve for information on Río Negro (61-2655).

Slideshows: Each day at 6pm, a spellbinding slideshow by world-famous photographers Michael and Patricia Fogden about rainforest wildlife from all over Costa Rica is presented at the Fonda Vela, the hotel closest to the Reserve. The $3 entrance fee goes to efforts to preserve and enlarge *quetzal* habitat on the Pacific slope. A multi-media slideshow incorporating sounds of the rainforest is also shown several times a week at the Monteverde Lodge in Santa Elena.

Conservation: Children from all over the world have been inspired by the efforts of a group of Swedish fourth-graders who organized the first **Children's Rainforest** campaign in 1987, in response to a presentation at their school by a biologist from the **Monteverde Conservation League**. Since then, school children from Costa Rica, Europe, Japan and the US have raised money to buy 17,000 acres of rainforest on the Atlantic slope behind the Reserve and are negotiating the purchase of 24,000 more. Besides on-going programs in environmental education, reforestation, and protection, the League also has an ambitious plan to link up remnant patches of forest (especially near rivers) to make green corridors that will ensure habitat for migratory birds and butterflies. Their office is across from the gas station as you enter Monteverde (61-2953, fax: (506) 61-1104, open 8-12, 1-5 weekdays; Apdo. 10165, 1000 San José, CR. Donors of $25 or more receive their quarterly newsletter, *Tapir Tracks*).

Arts and crafts: On the right, next to the food coop as you enter Monteverde, is **CASEM**, a cooperative of local women who make beautiful embroidered and hand-painted clothing and souvenirs portraying quetzals, golden toads and other cloud forest flora and fauna. Across the street, above the stables, is the studio-gallery of Monteverde artists **Stella Wallace** and **Meg Laval**. You can also see their paintings at the Monteverde Lodge in Santa Elena. Watercolor paintings by resident artist **Sarah Dowell** are also exhibited in local hotels. Visitors are welcome to tour her studio, a short hike above the cheese factory. The **Hummingbird Gallery** near the entrance to the reserve exhibits Michael and Patricia Fogden's photographs from around the world. The Fogdens spend months at a time with sloths, frogs, snakes, insects and birds, trying to get just the right shot. You'll never see better wildlife photographs. They also sell beautiful and inexpensive Guatemalan textiles, tee-shirts and high-energy snacks for the trail.

Cheese: The famous Monteverde cheese factory offers tours 9-11am Mon-Sun and 1:30-3pm Mon-Sat. They sell delicious cheddar, jack, gouda and other cheeses there for less than San José prices. You can also buy great homemade wholewheat bread and rolls, fresh milk, and *cajeta* (scrumptious milk fudge) at the cheese factory. (Open 7:30am-12, 1-3:30pm Mon-Sat, 7:30am-12:30pm Sun.)

Hotels and restaurants: See p. 115 for hotel codes. After you've been chugging up the road for about 2 hours, you will see the huge, white **Monteverde Lodge** glinting from the hills near Santa Elena, a town 3km from Monteverde. The Lodge, built especially to accommodate tour groups from Costa Rica Expeditions, is spacious and comfortable. It features an indoor atrium with a large jacuzzi in which guests can relax after their trek through the chilly cloud forest, 6km beyond (LL, meals cost $35/day, bathtubs, hw, 57-0766, fax: 57-1665).

The bus from Puntarenas leaves you off in Santa Elena. Your hotel will send a taxi to meet you if you have made reservations. The bus from San José continues on to the cheese plant in Monteverde, stopping at various hotels along the way. In Santa Elena are some inexpensive *pensiones,* **Pensión Santa Elena** (F, basic but fairly clean, home cooking, 61-1151) and the **Tucán** (clean, nice touches, hw, cb, D/person including meals, quite a bargain, 61-1007). Both have shared baths, laundry service, will fix bag lunches for hikers, and are located on the street going downhill from the bus stop. The cloud forest is a windy 6km from Santa Elena, but there is usually enough friendly traffic to try hitching, at least part of the way. Taxi service from Santa Elena to the Reserve costs about $6.

The **Sapo Dorado** (Golden Toad) is a friendly hotel/bar/restaurant between Santa Elena and Monteverde. They have spacious, comfortable, well-designed cabins with fireplaces (L, pb, hw, ph/fax: (506) 61-2952). The restaurant is open all day every day, and features healthful and tasty cuisine. There's always a vegetarian selection on the menu. They serve elegant sunset suppers accompanied by classical music on their terrace overlooking the Gulf. At night they play a variety of good taped music for dancing. You'll see their sign shortly after leaving Santa Elena. It's about 300m up the hill to the left.

Next on the left is the new **Pensión Heliconia**, a wooden building with balconies and a comfortable, homey atmosphere (A, 61-1009, pb, hw, rest). A road to the right leads in about 1km to **Pension Monteverde Inn** (D incl. meals, pb and cb, 61-2756, cheap but poorly maintained). About 100m farther along the main road is **Hotel de Montaña Monteverde** (L, 61-1846, pb, hw, rest.) with views of the Gulf of Nicoya from its well-appointed rooms. The chalet-style **Belmar** (L, 61-1001, pb, hw) also has beautiful views, comfortable rooms, and a restaurant/bar. Its entrance is uphill from the gas station on the left.

You still have not arrived in Monteverde proper, and when you do you might not realize it, because Monteverde is not really a town. Most houses of community members are back in the woods where you don't see them, and are connected by footpaths. **Restaurant El Bosque**, on the right as you enter Monteverde, is a great place to go for lunch or dinner. A few meters down the road is a well-stocked food store and **CASEM,** the crafts cooperative. The next entrance on the right is to **Pensión Quetzal**, the oldest lodge in Monteverde, with cozy, wood-panelled rooms (C/person, cb, hw; B/person, pb, all rates incl. 3 meals, 61-0955). The Conservation League's Bajo Tigre Nature Trail is about 100m from the Quetzal ($1 entrance fee includes self-guiding map). Out on the road again, you'll see the cheese plant up ahead. The **Pensión Flor-Mar** is about 200m beyond the bridge to the right, where the road turns left to go to the Reserve (C/person incl. 3 meals, some pb, some cb, hw, friendly atmosphere, ph/fax, 61-0909). A few hundred meters up the hill toward the Reserve is the **Fonda Vela**, (A, meals extra, hw, pb, secluded camping area, restaurant, meeting room, views of gulf and forest, 61-2551). All above hotels will bag breakfasts and lunches for early birders. Laundry services, horse and boot rental, and transportation to the Reserve are also available.

The Reserve is a 30-minute uphill walk from the Fonda Vela. The **Reserve Field Station** sometimes has room in its dormitories for students or researchers (F, cb, hw, can rent kitchen space, reservations with 30% deposit 45 days in advance, 61-2655).

Many Monteverde hotels are completely booked by tour companies from December through May, which is really the best time to go there. Most hotels require a deposit in order to secure a room, usually the cost of one night's stay. Your best bet would be to call or fax the hotels, confirm the availability of space, and send your deposit at least 6 weeks before you plan to arrive. Christmas and Easter are booked months in advance. Write all hotels at Apdo. 10165, 1000 San José, CR.

Getting there: By **bus** there are three options:

1. A bus leaves San José (c 12, a 9/11, at the Tilarán terminal, $4, tickets in advance, 22-3854) for Monteverde at 2:30pm Mon thru Thurs, and Sat at 6:30am. It returns to San José Tues thru Thurs at 6:30am and at 3pm Fri and Sun. There is also a 3pm return bus on Saturdays during the dry season. Get there early for the return bus which leaves from the cheese factory. For current schedules, check with your hotel when making reservations.

2. There is a daily bus from Puntarenas to Santa Elena, 3 km from Monteverde. It leaves Puntarenas at 2:15pm, turns off the Interamerican highway at the Río Lagarto around 3:30, and arrives in Santa Elena around 5:30. You can leave San José on the 10am Puntarenas bus (c 12, a 9), arrive in Puntarenas around 12:30, have a leisurely lunch (be careful of the water) and catch the Santa Elena bus on the oceanfront, one block from the San José-Puntarenas bus station. If you are in Manuel Antonio you can take an early Quepos-Puntarenas bus to connect with the 2:15 Santa Elena bus, which returns to Puntarenas daily at 6am.

3. The 12:45 San José-Tilarán bus (c 12, a 9/11, 22-3854) connects with the Puntarenas-Santa Elena bus at the Lagarto turnoff around 3:15pm. Buy tickets 1/2 hour in advance. If you are coming from the north, any San José-bound bus will let you off at Lagarto where you can intercept the Santa Elena bus.

By car, turn off the Interamerican highway at the Río Lagarto, about a half hour north of the Puntarenas turnoff. Go straight up from there for 1.5 to 2 hours. **Chino's**, on the left a few km before you get to Lagarto is an inexpensive place to stop for a drink on your way up or down the mountain. They have clean, locked bathrooms. There is a pulpería and soda at Lagarto but their facilities leave much to be desired.

If you don't mind bad roads, you can also travel by car from Tilarán to Monteverde by way of Quebrada Grande, Cabeceras and Santa Elena. In Cabeceras you can choose to go straight, through Turín, or uphill to the left through Las Nubes. Both pass through beautiful scenery--the Las Nubes route is 2 km longer and gorgeous--both are in equally terrible condition. The trip takes 2.5 hours. Even though this route looks much shorter on the map, you don't save that much time because the roads are so difficult. From Tilarán to the Lagarto turnoff by way of Cañas and the Interamerican is only an hour and a half. Paved roads make all the difference.

During the school year (March-November) you can catch a milk truck from Santa Elena to Cabeceras. From there you can catch a bus to Tilarán. The whole trip takes about 3 hours. Check at the Restaurant Imán in Santa Elena for current info (61-1255). If you stay overnight in Tilarán you can catch a bus to San Carlos which passes Volcán Arenal. **Cabinas El Sueño** (D, hw, pb, 69-5347) or **The Spot** (B, 69-5711, pb, hw, nf) are recommended in Tilarán, a clean, pleasant town a half hour uphill from Cañas and much cooler.

Clothing: Bring raingear, warm clothes and good socks. Most hotels rent rubber boots. Be sure to dress in layers for the trip up and down. You forget when you are in cool, windy Monteverde how swelteringly hot you'll be by the time you get to the Interamerican Highway. If you can't pull off your flannel shirt or sweater you'll be miserable.

Playa Doña Ana is a small beach which has been developed by the Tourism Institute, 2km south of Puntarenas. It has covered picnic tables, dressing rooms and showers, and a restaurant with blasting music which competes with the sound of the waves. Surfers say the waves at Doña Ana and Boca Barranca are great. Buses from Puntarenas to Mata Limón, Jacó, Orotina and Quepos pass by the entrance. The turnoff for Playa Doña Ana is right before the overpass on your way out of Puntarenas. The signs are not well placed. **Hotel Río Mar** (D, 63-0158, pb, rest) is on the left just before Doña Ana.

Carara Biological Reserve is located near Orotina, southeast of Puntarenas, in a transition area between the dry climate of Guanacaste and the humid climate of the southern coast. It has wildlife common to both regions, like macaws, toucans, trogons, waterfowl, three kinds of monkeys, alligators and crocodiles, armadillos, sloths and peccaries. Jaguars, pumas, ocelots, jaguarundis and margays are present, but hard to see. You can get there on any Jacó or Quepos bus. No camping is allowed in the reserve.

Tourists are only allowed on certain trails, but professional guides can go with you into restricted areas. **Geotur**, in San José, specializes in guided nature tours to Carara (34-1867).

Playas Jacó and Herradura are the closest swimmable beaches to San José. **Playa Herradura** is right after the Río Caña Blanca, about 5 minutes north of Jacó, and 3km down a gravel road from the main highway. It is smaller than Jacó, the waves are gentler and there is more shade. Good trees for hammocks. Camping is allowed. There are sodas and a few cabinas on the beach.

Playa Jacó is long and wide, and much more developed than Herradura. The rip currents there can be dangerous, so don't swim alone (see p. 74-7). In a country full of tropical paradises, Jacó certainly does not stand out, but if you like sun and fun, surfing and beer-drinking contests, and you want to get to the beach and back as fast as possible, Jacó is for you. The ICT has created a *núcleo turístico* offering parking, locked closets, bathrooms and showers for $.60/person for those who want to visit for just the day. It's next to the **Pizzería Bribri**, to the right at the second entrance after Hotel Jacó Beach.

Surfers use Jacó as a base for trips to nearby beaches like Boca Barranca (very long left wave), Playas Tivives and Valor (rights and lefts), Escondida (accessible by boat from Jacó), Playa Hermosa (very strong beach break 3km south of Jacó, site of annual surfing contest) and Esterillos Este and Oeste, Bejuco and Boca Damas, all on the way to Quepos. Many hotels give surfers discounts from May to December.

Hotels: See p. 115 for hotel codes. There are plenty of hotels, cabinas and campsites. Many have kitchenettes complete with utensils. They give substantial discounts during the off-season, and Jacó is often sunny when it's raining in San José. All the following establishments are off Jacó's main street, which runs parallel to the beach. We'll mention them in order of their appearance, north to south. **Cabinas Antonio** (D, 64-3043, pb, cw, fans, next to the main bus stop at the entrance to Jacó) are clean and relatively quiet. The Belgian-owned **Hotel El Jardín**, on the beach 100m from the bus stop, is clean, comfortable, quiet and includes breakfast. Its restaurant has the reputation of being the best in Jacó (B, pb, hw, cf, pool, 64-3050). Next is **Hotel Jacó Beach** (LL, incl. breakfast, a/c, hw, large, circular pool, discotheque; cars, bikes, mopeds, surfboards, sailboats, kayaks, tennis equipment, etc. for rent, 64-3032, 64-3034). They are the center for most of the charter flights from Canada, so are very busy. **Tangerí Chalets** have 3 bedrooms, kitchens, and pools for adults and kids. They prefer to rent by the week. **Hotel Tangeri** is next door (LL, fridges, bp, hw, a/c, 42-0977). The Dutch-owned **Villas Miramar** is one of the loveliest and most tranquil places in Jacó (B, 64-3003, kitchens, hw, cf, pools, gardens, down the fifth road to your right). **Cabinas Zabamar** have fridges (C, pb, cw, pool, 64-3174). **Hotel Cocal** is on the beach (B, clean, pb, hw, cf, pools, rest, 64-3067). **Las Gaviotas**, 250m from the beach, is new, clean and pretty. Rooms have patios and kitchenettes (A, hw, pool, 64-3092). **Cabinas Alice** (C, pb, cw, cf, 64-3061, 37-1412, toward the beach from the Red Cross) are dark and poorly ventilated. Doña Alice serves good food at shady outdoor tables. **Apartamentos El Mar** are secure, clean and spacious with kitchens and pool (B, cf, pb, hw, 25-7132, 64-3165). **Casas de Playa Mar Sol** are nice for families because each has a small wading pool in front of the house (C and B, 64-3008, cw, tf, kitchens).

Hotel Jacofiesta is new and probably the best in Jacó. Cheerfully painted on the outside with a broad blue strip at the base of white walls in the style of a *casa típica*, the rooms are light and airy, with efficiently-designed kitchenettes (L, a/c, hw, pool, rest, cable TV, 64-3147, fax: 64-3148). The **Marparaíso** (L, fans, cw, pb, rest, pools, jacuzzi, 21-6544, 64-3025) is on the far end of the beach. It's very popular, but its design gives a crowded, closed-in feeling. Beyond it are **Cabinas Madrigal,** funky rooms (E, pb, cw, 64-3230), greasy restaurant, shady campsites with toilets, showers, makeshift tables and barbecue pits ($1/night). About 2 blocks inland from Madrigal's, where the street connects with the main highway to Quepos, is **El Bosque**, a nice place for breakfast.

Getting there: San José-Jacó **buses** leave the Coca Cola at 7:30am and 3:30pm, returning at 5am and 3pm (64-3074, 3.5 hrs). Get to the bus stop early on weekends because you'll be waiting with a big crowd of *josefinos*. A bus from Quepos to Puntarenas passes Jacó on the main road around 6am and 3pm. All Quepos and Manuel Antonio buses pass Jacó on their way to and from San José ($3.50-4). Look at schedule on p. 222 and add or subtract 1.5 hrs. for arrival times. Get off at Restaurant El Bosque, 2 blocks from the beach at the southern end. Get Puntarenas-Quepos buses to Jacó at 1:30 near the Puntarenas train station. Hotel Irazú has a comfortable mini-bus to and from Jacó every day (2.5 hrs, $11 one way, 32-4811). Leaves Irazú 9:30am, returns 2pm. Make reservations in advance.

By car, Herradura and Jacó are a 2-hour drive from San José on a winding road through beautiful countryside. Take the Atenas turnoff on the highway to Puntarenas. The road is in fairly good repair most of the way through the mountains, and offers some magnificent views. Near Orotina you can buy watermelon, mangos and sugar cane juice. After Orotina the road is excellent, with sea views on one side and green rice fields on the other. You also pass the entrance to Carara Biological Reserve (see above) about 20 minutes before Jacó. A new section of highway now connects Puntarenas and Jacó in an hour. You can continue on to Quepos (70km), Dominical and San Isidro de El General on the same road.

When you first glimpse the sea from the hills above **Manuel Antonio,** the word *paradise* might cross your mind. The lovely beaches were made into a national park before they could be turned into another Acapulco. So far, the hotels that have sprung up in the last few years have taken advantage of the beautiful views without calling too much attention to themselves. But as Manuel Antonio becomes more well-known, the influx of tourism is taking its toll on the delicate environment.

Manuel Antonio is one of the few remaining habitats of the squirrel monkey, *mono tití.* Howler and white-faced monkeys, two-toed sloths, coatimundis and raccoons frequent the beaches, which are shaded by leafy trees. Iguanas pose like statues unless they are moving their heads up and down like pumps (a territorial sign made only by males).

There is a trail that takes you through the jungle to the top of Cathedral Point, where you can look down the vertical cliffs to the blue ocean 300 feet below. You start from Playa Espadilla Sur (the second beach) and take a circular route, about an hour from start to finish. At low tide you can also begin or end on Playa Manuel Antonio, the third beach. The trail is very steep in some parts and muddy and slippery in the rainy season, so don't go alone, and wear hiking boots if possible.

Manuel Antonio

The wedge-shaped piece of land that is now Cathedral Point used to be an island. As you can see from the illustration, a neck of land connects it to the beach. This rare phenomenon is known as a *támbalo*: a deposit of sand which builds up over thousands of years and finally connects an island to the mainland. Northern-flowing currents pushed water and sand through the opening between the island and the beach, and then flowed on to Punta Quepos, farther north, which forced the water back. The sand-bridge was formed after about 100,000 years of this action. Grass and shrubs gained a foothold on it, followed by the present-day trees that keep the formation from returning to the sea. The Manuel Antonio támbalo is one of the most perfect in the world.

The Indians who lived in Manuel Antonio 1000 years ago observed that while female green turtles were laying their eggs in the sand at high tide, the male turtles were waiting for them in the water. The Indians fashioned balsawood models of female turtles to attract the males into an area surrounded by rocks. The males would stay with the decoy females and be trapped by the rocks when the tide went out. You can see these precolumbian turtle traps on either end of Manuel Antonio Beach at low tide.

Snorkeling is rewarding at Manuel Antonio. In the dry season, when the water is clear, you'll see iridescent peacock-colored fish, conservative pin-striped fish, outrageous yellow fish with diaphanous capes, all going in and out of the coral rocks. Fins and a mask are all you need, and no snorkeling techniques are necessary. If you burn easily, watch out--you'll

218

lose track of time staring at the fish while the sun is staring at your back. It's best to wear a T-shirt.

The entrance to the park is on the other side of a stream that changes width and depth with the tides. Try to go at low tide, because you have to wade across. Around high tide the water is waist-high.

Camping is no longer allowed within the park. Overcrowding was leading to pollution and destruction of the vegetation, threatening the wildlife.

Do not leave your belongings unattended on the beach. If anyone offers to guide you through remote areas of the park, they should have an official ID card, or be in park service uniform.

Kayaking, biking, and horseback-riding tours in the area are available through Ríos Tropicales (33-6655) and Unicorn Adventures (77-0489). For tours by **sailboat,** call 77-0424.

Manuel Antonio has many lovely places to stay, most of which are on the hill between Quepos and the park. The older, funkier cabinas are on the beach. If you're on a budget, low-cost lodging in the town of Quepos is cleaner and more comfortable than the cheapest rooms near the beach. **Hotel Ceciliano**, about 50m west of the SANSA office in Quepos, has light, airy rooms, immaculate tiled bathrooms, closets, and a tranquil, plant-filled atmosphere (C, pb; D with cb, cf, cw, 77-0192). The **Hotel Quepos** (C, pb, D, cb, cf, cw, 77-0274) is also a good, clean place to stay. It's above the SANSA airline office, about 300m from the oceanfront. **Hotel Mar y Luna** (E, pb, less with cb, cw, tf, 77-0394) is cheap and fairly clean. Upper rooms have windows and shared baths. Lower rooms have private baths and no windows. **Hotel Malinche** (D, pb, tf, cw, 77-0093) has some nice touches in its decor and **Hotel Ramus** (E, pb, cw, tf, 77-0245) is okay too. The above three are located in the block west of the bus terminal. The market at the terminal is a good place to grab a quick bite to eat and to stock up on fruits and veggies.

La Buena Nota, a beachwear and gift shop, is the official information center for Manuel Antonio. It's on the oceanfront after the bridge at the entrance to Quepos. The **Soda Ana** and **Soda Isabel** in the next block on the waterfront have good, cheap *casados*, and the **Quepoa** on the south side of the market has tasty seafood. Our favorite place to stop for a *refresco* in Quepos is **El Kiosko,** on the oceanfront three blocks from La

Buena Nota. If you like wild all-night fiestas with dancing in the streets, Quepos has its annual **Festival del Mar** around the end of January at the full moon.

We will mention hotels in order of their appearance on the road between Quepos and Manuel Antonio. **Cabinas Pedro Miguel** are funky rooms in a tranquil setting 6km from Quepos and 100m from the main road (C, pb, cw, cf, B with kitchens, over-priced, very hospitable, 77-0035). The European-owned **Hotel Plinio,** across the road, has comfortable, wood-panelled rooms off a wide veranda with hammocks, surrounded by lush foliage (A, incl. breakfast, pb, tf, cw, 77-0055, Apdo. 71, Quepos, CR). It has one of the most popular dinner restaurants in Manuel Antonio, featuring delicious pasta, lasagne, eggplant parmigiana and pizza. Their homemade bread is worth a trip in itself. Open for breakfast and dinner only, closed Weds. Call for reservations. Farther down the road on your right is **Bahías,** a bar/restaurant featuring seafood, 46 varieties of tropical cocktails and wonderful music: tangos, vintage jazz, good stuff. Open evenings year round, all day during the high season. Next on the left is the entrance to **El Salto,** cabinas on a hilltop with an inland view. Overpriced (LL, pb, tf, cw, pool, horses, bar/rest, 77-0130, Apdo. 119, Quepos, CR). At the crest of the hill on the left is the Canadian-owned **El Lirio,** spacious, well-designed rooms with a sea view (LL, pb, hw, cf, breakfast incl., 77-0403, Apdo. 123 Quepos, CR). The **Divisamar** (LL, pool, rest, hw, cf, a/c, friendly, helpful staff, 77-0371, fax: 77-0525) is across from the **Barba Roja,** a favorite with visitors because of its gringo-style lunches and dinners: burgers, nachos, BLT's, surf and turf, etc., and its varied and inexpensive breakfast menu. Open 7am-midnight, closed Mon. Above the Barba Roja is the **Mamaya Gallery,** with tasteful exhibits of local artisanry. Just before the main road heads down toward Manuel Antonio are the elegant villas of the **Hotel Mariposa,** with pool, beautiful views from private balconies, and excellent service (XL, hw, cf, gourmet breakfast and dinner incl, no children under 15, 77-0355, 77-0456, fax: (506) 77-0050). Down a steep dirt road, 1km from the Mariposa, is **Makanda-by-the-Sea,** secluded villas with a sunset ocean view in a reserve-like atmosphere (XL, hw, kitchens, 77-0442, Apdo. 29, Quepos, CR.) Back on the main road, is the French-owned **Hotel Byblos,** which rivals the Mariposa for excellent cuisine. Their spacious cabinas are set in a forest below the restaurant (XL, incl. breakfast and dinner, cf, a/c, hw, pool with jacuzzi, 77-0411, fax: (506) 77-0009). Next on the right are the comfortable **Villas Nicolas** (L, hw, kitchens, views, pool, 77-0538, Apdo. 26, Quepos, CR). **La Quinta** (L, pool, cf, cw, LL with view and fridges, 77-0434, Apdo. 76, Quepos, CR) is quiet, with spacious rooms and an ocean view. **Hotel Arboleda** (LL, cf, cw, rest, XL, a/c, hw, 77-0414), has rows of cabinas on a hill, some with ocean views, and others nearer the beach. Poorly managed, not recommended. **Condominios Costa Verde** have kitchens and views (B to LL, 23-7946, 77-0584, fax: (506) 23-9446). The **Karahé** has lovely cabinas with beautiful views, but you have to walk up over 100 steps to get to them (A, pool, cf, hw, fridge, 77-0170, fax: (506) 77-0152). Their restaurant specializes in Uruguayan-style beef and seafood.

Now we're down at the beach, where the less expensive cabinas are. The **Restaurant Mar y Sombra** is the traditional place to eat on Playa Espadilla, still about 1km from the park entrance. Espadilla is known for its dangerous rip currents (see p.74-7). **Cabinas Ramirez** is nextdoor (D, pb, cw, tf, the more secure ones have metal bars and padlocks but are stuffy and dark, others have better ventilation, tend to be noisy, 77-0510). On the way to the park you'll see the **Del Mar Bar** on the beach. They rent surfing and snorkeling equipment. A road to the left goes to the following five places: **Cabinas Espadilla** (C, clean and light, tf, pb, cw, some with hotplates, 77-0416). Across the road is the **Costa Linda** "youth hostel" with small stuffy rooms. The ones in the back have more ventilation (E, cb, nf, shared cooking facilities; B with kitchen, pb, tf, 77-0304). The **Vela Bar** offers food with a Spanish touch. Cabinas in the back have locked wooden security boxes (B to LL, tf, cw, some a/c, some balconies, one with kitchen, hw, 77-0413). The **Grano de Oro** has small, stuffy rooms adjacent to its restaurant (E, nf, cb, noisy, 77-0578). **Cabinas Los Almendros,** on the left at the end of the road, are clean and quiet (B, cf, cw, L, a/c, rest, 77-0225). Coming out again onto the road to the park are two more places: **Hotel Manuel Antonio** on the left (currently closed) and **Cabinas Manuel Antonio,** right on Playa Espadilla (E, run down, tf, cw, pb, 77-0212, 77-0255).

Almost all hotels offer a substantial discount from May through November. Make reservations 3 months in advance during Christmas or Easter, and at least 1 month in advance during the tourist season (December thru May).

If you have more time to spend, you might want to rent a house by the week or month. Accommodations range from a very rustic cabina on a lovely private beach accessible only by foot or 4-wheel drive ($150/wk, no electricity, 28-1811) to a fully-equipped, 2-bedroom house with a breathtaking view of Manuel Antonio ($450/wk during high season, 77-0345, 77-0292).

Getting there: San José-Quepos buses leave from the western end of the Coca Cola at 7 and 10am, 2 and 4pm, returning at 5 and 8am, 2 and 4pm (4 hrs, $3, 23-5567, 77-0263). From Quepos, take a 20-minute bus ride 7 scenic kilometers to the entrance of the park ($.20, 5:45, 8 and 10:30am, 12:30, 3 and 5pm, returning 20-30 min later. Service is continuous on weekends during the dry season).

A **direct** San José-Manuel Antonio bus leaves the Coca Cola at 6am, 12 and 6pm, returning at 6am, 12 and 5pm ($4, tickets in advance on weekends and holidays, purchase return tickets as soon as you arrive. Quepos ticket office is open 7-11 and 1-5; 7-11, 1-4 Sun). This bus will pick you up at your hotel on its way from Manuel Antonio to Quepos, but you must be out on the road to flag it down. Do not let anyone but the bus driver load or unload your baggage. Try to keep it with you if possible. Things have been stolen from the luggage compartment.

Quepos-Puntarenas buses leave at 4:30am and 1:30pm, returning at 4:30am and 2:30pm. All the above buses pass by Playa Jacó, 1.5 hrs from Quepos.

SANSA flies to Quepos Mon thru Sat at 7am returning at 7:35am ($10 one way, 20-min flight, buy tickets at least 2 weeks in advance during dry season, 33-0397, 33-3258, fax: 55-2176, schedules change frequently). There are also 3pm flights, depending on the season. SANSA will transport you from their San José office (c 24, Paseo Colón) to the airport, deliver you to your hotel in Quepos or Manuel Antonio, and pick you up to get you to your return flight.

Sportfishing Costa Rica (see p. 78) has **charter flights** every day to Quepos during the tourist season for about $40 per person (38-2729, 38-2726, 37-5400, fax: (506) 38-4434).

By car, the trip takes about 3.5 hours if you take the Atenas turnoff and drive the narrow, winding road through the Aguacate mountains. This route is scenic and gives you a glimpse of rural life. You can buy sugar cane juice and fruit along the way. If you feel more comfortable with better highways, go all the way to Puntarenas, follow signs to Jacó, and continue on to Quepos. It only takes a half hour longer even though it looks much farther on the map. The last 24 km before Quepos are in the process of being paved. Call La Buena Nota for the latest information (77-0345).

squirrel monkey
(mono tití)

king fisher

THE SOUTHERN ZONE

The Interamerican Highway becomes San José's Central Avenue, crossing the city from west to east, then turning right at Cartago to connect the Central Valley with the southern part of Costa Rica. The road winds into the mountains that surround fog-shrouded Cerro de la Muerte, the highest pass on the Interamerican. Since the late Don Pepe Figueres's farm, *La Lucha Sin Fin* (The Endless Struggle) is off this road, these mountains were the scene of the beginnings of the 1948 Civil War. There is a small monument to those who lost their lives in that conflict in Santa María de Dota, down a road to the right at Empalme.

Day hikers will enjoy a trip to **Copey**, a small town in the mountains above Santa María, about an hour south of Cartago. Its fresh, brisk climate at 7000 ft. makes for an exhilarating walk through hills of native oak. Treat yourself to a trout lunch at William Rodríguez' *soda* and buy tart, crispy local apples for dessert. You can visit Don Fernando Elizondo's well-developed trout farm and rent horses from Chema, his nextdoor neighbor. Chema rents one room with a beautiful stained-glass window (F incl. breakfast, cb) and might know of other houses to rent. Ask him about **hiking, biking** and **horseback** tours around Copey, and to Manuel Antonio National Park, Río Macho Reserve, and the high altitude plateau of Cerro de las Vueltas.

Take a San Isidro bus (c 16, a 1/3) to Cañón del Guarco, Km 58 on the Interamerican highway. You'll see the little yellow markers on the side of the road that tell you how many km you are from San José. From Cañón it's 7km downhill on a dirt road to Copey. Santa María is another 7km downhill. It's customary in that region for drivers to offer rides to people on the road. Buses return to San José from the main square in Santa María at 6am, 9am, 1pm and 4pm. There are a couple of cheap hotels in Santa María. You can catch the bus to Santa María from San José at 6 and 9am, 12:30, 3 and 5pm ($1, c 21, a 16B, 27-3597).

To the left from the Cañón del Guarco church on the Interamerican is the road leading to **Genesis II**, a private cloud forest reserve 7500' (2360m) above sea level, where quetzals can be observed. Visitors stay in rooms under the owner's house (XL, incl. three healthy meals, minimum 3-day stay, D for students with valid ID). Volunteers who spend 5 hours a day constructing nature trails pay $50/week for room and board and stay in primitive cabins (bathrooms in main house, min 6 week commitment). Fax Steve and Paula Friedman, (506) 23-3873.

Out on the highway again, going south from Cañón, is the new **Albergue Tapantí** (B, restaurant, good beds, pb, hw, fax: (506) 22-0436). Soon you'll see the lush vegetation become stunted and then diminish as you wind around the Cerro de la Muerte. When taking this trip, dress in layers and try to go early in the day, before fog and rain reduce visibility to zero. This can happen even in the dry season. Landslides are a very real danger also during heavy rains.

In **San Gerardo de Dota,** Don Efraín Chacón and his family rent cabinas and provide delicious homemade meals for fishermen and nature lovers (C per person, including 3 meals, pb, hw, 71-1732). Trout abound in the chilly waters of the Río Savegre which passes the finca. At 1900m (6300 feet), temperature averages 10°C (50-55°F) in this narrow mountain valley. Don Efraín takes advantage of the crisp weather to grow apples and peaches. *Quetzales* can be observed there, especially during their nesting season in April and May. Be sure to call ahead for reservations. To get there, take a San Isidro bus from San José and ask to be let off at the *"entrada a San Gerardo"*. The turnoff is at the 80-km mark on the Interamerican Highway. The Finca Chacón is a 9-km downhill hike from there. Don Efraín can pick you up if you call him ($12 round trip). If you travel by car, have 4-wheel drive or at least a powerful engine, because the road is extremely steep and narrow.

The Valle de El General is one of Costa Rica's jewels of nature. When the fog clears after Cerro de la Muerte, **San**

225

Isidro and surrounding small towns offer beautiful flowers and a lovely climate. San Isidro is the gateway to Chirripó National Park and Playa Dominical. The **Bar Chirripó** and **El Tenedor** on the Parque Central are good places to eat. There are several clean and inexpensive hotels in town, like **Hotel Chirripó** (E, pb; cheaper with cb, hw, nf, 71-0529) and **Hotel Amaneli** (D, pb, hw, tf, 71-0352). Make sure your room is not facing the Interamerican highway as trucks and buses pass all night. Six km S of San Isidro, on the left, is the large, comfortable **Hotel del Sur**, with gardens, pools, tennis courts and playground equipment (C, pb, a/c, optional TVs, restaurant, 71-0233).

Comfortable buses leave San José for San Isidro once an hour from three bus companies along the same block (c 16, a 1/3, 23-3577, 22-2422, 23-0686, tickets in advance, especially on weekends and holidays, $2.50, 3-hr trip). Buses back to San José leave hourly.

Most people I talked with before venturing off to **Chirripó** told me about their own experiences on the mountain. Many Costa Ricans have climbed it once but won't ever go again. True, the trek can be painful, tiring, frustrating and freezing, but it's so satisfying to reach the summit, which as the highest peak in southern Central America, is really the top of this part of the world.

If you don't feel up to the Chirripó climb, **San Gerardo de Rivas**, the gateway to **Chirripó National Park,** has much to offer. There is a two-person natural **hot spring** less than a kilometer from San Gerardo and you can hike to lovely nearby **waterfalls**.

Francisco Elizondo Badilla offers bunkbeds in his newly-constructed **Posada del Descanso,** 100m past the ranger station in San Gerardo. He also rents horses for the trip up the mountain during the dry season and can take you exploring the San Gerardo area at any time of year. He is a wealth of information. His brother Rafael creates wonderful folk art by carving pieces of wood he finds into all kinds of creatures. Don Francisco's wife serves three meals a day family-style on their covered porch. The views are great and the price is right: about $10 for bunk and meals. There are also some cabinas with double beds. To reserve yourself a space, call 71-0433, ext. 106, and leave a message for Francisco Elizondo saying at what time you'll call back. He'll be at the phone at that time. There are other cheap rooms for rent in the town--ask for info at the same number, the only phone in town.

To climb Chirripó, check in at the ranger station, near the final bus stop. There you register and pay the nominal entrance and overnight fees. They give you two very basic maps. If you want to be able to know exactly where you are or if you're planning to explore any of the neighboring peaks or valleys, we recommend you buy a good, large-scale, topographical map (see p. 83).

The first day is long and grueling. Hikers make the 14 straight uphill kilometers to the huts in anywhere from seven hours to two days. It took us 11 hours. We left at 4:30am, while it was still dark. We took the Thermometer short cut, which is supposed to shorten the trip by an hour. You walk up the road from San Gerardo, veering right at the forks passing over two bridges. It's about 500 meters to a sign that says *Sendero al Cerro Chirripó* and points up--you climb over the fence and head straight up through the steep pasture. Stay to the left of the forest, pass through an opening in the fence at the top of one false summit, and continue along a ridge until you get to the next fence. The whole climb should take half an hour or 45 minutes.

Black-faced solitaire (jilguero)

There you are on the trail. It's well-marked. Signs every 2km give you the altitude and distance to the summit. Subtract 4km for your distance to the huts. You will be slapping flies, sweating and slipping on your long haul, but if you can take your mind off the strain, you'll really enjoy where you are. The trail climbs through a dense cloud forest where *jilgueros* sing their amazing song which sounds like blowing through a flute made from glass. The song is simple, but very fine. Since the bird likes to stay up in the highest treetops, it's difficult to spot. The jilguero's natural habitat is the cloud forest. Sadly, as people are destroying cloud forests in Costa Rica, they destroy the jilguero too.

The first opportunity to get water is at a stream off the trail from a point 15 minutes past Llano Bonito. Since this is four or five hours into the hike, be sure to bring plenty of water.

After the water comes *La Cuesta del Agua* which is the longest haul of them all--it took us three hours to climb. It ends at *Monte Sin Fé* (Faithless Mountain), where you walk into a new kind of forest. It's drier and the trees are shorter with less green foliage. Green, orange, and yellow moss hangs from the grey lichen-covered branches and wags in the wind like furry beards.

The next major landmark is the *refugio natural*--a big cave where five people could sleep if it's raining, up to ten if it's not. A stream next to the cave was dry when we were there in February. This cave is only 1.5 hours from the huts, so try to make it. You have to climb *La Cuesta de los Arrepentidos* (Repentants' Hill), then the trail traces around the side of a mountain. When the view opens up you can see *Los Crestones* on the top of a ridge straight ahead. These are huge sharp rocks that look like they were folded accordion-style. The huts are in the valley just below them.

Arriving at the huts is a relief. The third, the yellow one, is where you should try to stay. There's a wood floor and a good wood stove. If you're lucky, someone will have a pot of water boiling and will offer you a hot cup of tea.

Mornings are clear in the summer until 9 or so, then the valley fills with fog. Wisps of fog drift in until they crowd together and form dense clouds. Visibility minimizes, and at 2 or 3 it rains for about 45 minutes, so be on the trail by dawn. Besides avoiding the fog and rain, it's a pretty hour to be outside. As the sun touches the frost-covered leaves and grasses, the ice melts, the plants stretch and whole meadows squeak softly.

There are many places to explore. Of course you should go to the summit of Chirripó, an hour and a half up the same trail. You pass through the *Valle de los Conejos,* where no rabbit has lived since a destructive fire in 1976. *Lagartijas*, little lizards, have occupied the valley. Each lizard has a different sheen that perfectly matches the rock it suns itself on. On the top of Chirripó you can see both oceans if the clouds haven't rolled in by the time you get there. There's a register to sign in a metal container wedged between the rocks in the summit cairn. Right below Chirripó is the *Lago San Juan.* You can swing by it on your way down. It's fun to take a quick swim and there are ideal sunning rocks on the lake's banks.

The lake-filled *Valle de las Morenas* is on the other side of the peak, with a hut where you can stay. Ask for its key at the

San Gerardo park station. If you want to continue hiking in that direction, you can pass over *Cerro Urán* and continue along the *Camino de los Indios,* a trail known and used almost solely by the local Indians. Talk to Parques Nacionales in San José and hire a guide for this hike. You can also climb Urán and take the Camino de los Indios back through another valley to San Gerardo. Talk to Parques and take a good map.

Other day-hike possibilities are *Cerro Ventisqueres,* the second highest mountain in Southern Central America, whose trail takes off from the main trail a bit below the Valle de los Conejos. It is supposed to be a relatively easy hike. You can also hike from the huts to Los Crestones. The top of the ridge is reached by going up to the left of Los Crestones. Follow the ridge left to *Cerro Terbi,* a mild half hour. There's a register in the cairn stones there, too. To make it a round trip, continue on the ridge a few hundred meters and descend on a trail that goes through a steep chimney and ends up in Valle de los Conejos. You can also continue walking along Terbi's curving ridge, ascending and descending the peaks it includes, going down into Valle de los Conejos when you get tired.

When you go on your day hikes take a map and compass, a sweater, a rainjacket and water. Since the whole area is above timberline, you can always see where you are as long as inclement weather and fog do not envelop you. Watch out for lightning. Some people have gotten lost and died there, so be careful. Be sure to bring:

1) warm clothes and a warm sleeping bag. It is very cold up there. If the ranger is around he can lend you blankets. I slept in a polarguard sleeping bag with one blanket inside it, another on top, another underneath, all my clothes on, and a friend beside me. I was almost warm.

2) binoculars to look for birds and to look out into the distance from the top of mountains and ridges.

3) munchies for the hikes. Dried bananas and peanuts are good for energy when you're climbing. Carrots proved to be our lifesaver on the Cuesta de Agua. They quench your thirst and give you something to do slowly and steadily as you climb that never-ending hill.

4) a poncho to keep you dry during the multiple rainshowers that occur daily.

5) a water bottle, at least one liter per person, to replenish all the liquid you'll lose sweating.

The week before Easter is the *ticos'* favorite time to climb Chirripó, because they are on vacation and the weather is usually dry. At any time of year, call Parques Nacionales (33-4160) three days in advance to "reserve" a spot.

Getting there: From the market in San Isidro, buses leave for San Gerardo de Rivas at 5am and 2pm. The trip takes 1.5 hours. When asking which of the many buses to take, specify San Gerardo de *Rivas,* because there's another San Gerardo. To be able to start your hike before dawn, arrive a day early and spend the night there. The 10:30am bus from San José will get you to San Isidro in time to catch the 2pm bus to San Gerardo.

By car, take the paved road which you'll see going uphill on your left just south of San Isidro. It's 9km to the town of Rivas. San Gerardo is 11km on gravel roads from Rivas.

The scenery along the unfinished Costanera Sur Highway south of **Playa Dominical** is reminiscent of California's Big Sur coast--with lush tropical vegetation, of course. Someday the highway will connect Dominical with Palmar Norte near the Osa Península. Swimming at the long beach at the village of Dominical is quite dangerous. As you enter the village, **Cabinas Wili** on the right are cheap, clean, basic and peaceful (E, cb and pb, cw, nf, on the estuary), **Cabinas Coco** are clean, small, with a disco on weekends (E, fans, cb, 71-2555). **Cabinas Nayarit**, down a road to the right are clean and on the beach (D, pb, cw, cf, 71-1878, A and B for houses). **Cabinas Costa Brava** (E, funky, pb, tf, rest) are about 1 km S of the village.

About 4km S are **Cabinas Punta Dominical**, on a rocky point overlooking the ocean (C, screens, hammocks, hw, pb, cf, fanned by ocean breezes, restaurant, horses, 25-5328). They are well-designed, private, comfortable, tranquil, and the views are great. If you have the time and can get reservations in advance, it is really worth the trip (about 4 hours from San José including rest stops). There's a lovely beach north of the point. Swimming is best at low tide when you can get beyond the coral rocks. Camping is allowed. If you are camping, bring fresh fruits and vegetables from the plentiful market in San Isidro, as they are usually not available on the coast. About 3.5 km south of Punta Dominical on the left are **Cabinas Escondidas** (C incl. breakfast, cooking facilities, pb, secluded, natural, open design, beautiful ocean views, nature trails, nearby tidepools and waterfalls, Apdo. 364, San Isidro de El General, CR).

Buses leave San Isidro de El General at 7am and 3pm daily for Uvita, passing through Dominical 1.5 hours later. The return bus passes Dominical around 7:30am. You can also take a 7am or 1:30pm bus from San Isidro through Dominical and up the coast to Quepos (4 hours). Buses leave Quepos for San Isidro at 5am and 1:30pm. Check local bus schedules by calling Memo's Restaurant in Dominical (71-0866). By car, Dominical is about 45min from San Isidro on paved road with potholes. The Costanera Sur is still unpaved but in good condition, although the rough gravel is hard on tires. Roads between Quepos and Dominical are unpaved but in good condition.

Boruca is a small indigenous town cradled in a green valley in the southwestern part of Costa Rica. The countryside is beautiful--you can walk up the red dirt trails for views across mountains, valleys and rivers.

The Borucas traditionally celebrate the new year with the *Fiesta de los Diablitos,* a dramatic reenactment of the war between the Spanish *conquistadores* and the Indians in which the Indians win. Indians throughout America share the Diablitos tradition, though usually their drama represents a war between the Spanish and the Moors. In Boruca the Diablitos are men disguised as devils. One man is the bull. Costumes are fashioned from burlap sacks and the balsa wood masks that Borucan artisans carve. The Diablitos taunt the bull with sticks and he prances around and chases them.

The group, accompanied by a drummer and a flute player, meets on a hill the night of the 30th of December. At midnight, a conch shell sounds and they run down the hill into town. They spend the whole night going from house to house, giving a short performance at each house and then relaxing to enjoy the *chicha* and *tamales* they are offered. The group visits most houses in town that night and during the next three days. The third day of the fiesta the Diablitos symbolically kill the bull. A huge bonfire reduces the bull to ashes.

Except for the occasional traditional fiestas, the pace of life in Boruca is slow and steady. Men leave town early in the morning to work small *fincas* in the nearby hills. Women usually stay at home. They weave naturally-dyed cotton yarn on simple looms they tie around their waists, making belts, purses, and little table cloths. Men carve expressive masks out of balsa wood. Both men and women carve elaborate scenes into the shells of large *jícaras* (gourds). If you are interested in these traditions or just in getting to know the life of this small town, you would probably enjoy visiting Boruca. Opportunities abound for joining soccer games, teaching new games to children, etc. You should know Spanish and be willing to conform to small town life for the duration of your visit. Many families are willing to take in visitors for a few days. Ask the people on the bus, then ask around town. Expect a lot of curiosity about yourself and your gear. Beware of becoming a gringo Santa Claus. Showering gifts is not a good precedent to set for future visitors nor for the people of the town, who learn to expect undue generosity from gringos they barely know.

Getting there: It takes a whole day to get to Boruca from San José. Take the 8:30am bus from the Zona Sur station (a 18, c 4, 21-4214) to Buenos Aires or to the *bomba* (gas station) along the Interamerican, 1 km out of town. A school-bus leaves Buenos Aires at 1:30, stops at the bomba soon after, and arrives in Boruca (18 km up and down a mountainous dirt road) at 3:30 or so. Or you can get off the Zona Sur bus at the *Entrada de Boruca* about 30 min past the bomba, and walk 8 km up the path that takes off to the right of the highway. The hike takes about 2 hours.

The port of **Golfito** has a gorgeous setting, with lush, forested hills surrounding a deep bay on the Golfo Dulce, the misty outline of the Península de Osa in the distance.

The major player in Golfito's recent history has been the United Fruit Company. United moved to the Golfito region in 1938 after banana diseases, depletion of good soil, and massive labor strikes led it to abandon its plantations in Limón. Golfito became the company's headquarters and main port. The company constructed a veritable town for its employees: homes, schools, a hospital, stores, a dairy farm, etc. They built a huge loading dock that could handle 4000 bunches of bananas per hour and a 246-km railway from the plantations in the nearby Diquis and Coto valleys. About 15,000 people migrated from Guanacaste and other provinces to work for United. In its heyday, Golfito was an archetypical crowded, steamy banana port.

United stopped production in the early eighties and finally moved out in 1985, after deciding that its profit-making potential was exhausted. Production costs were high, there were some violent labor conflicts in the early 80's, the Costa Rican government raised its export tax on bananas, and the Pacific banana market of California and Japan was too small. Most of the facilities United had constructed were left to the state.

After United left, many people migrated to other parts of the country. Some have settled in the Osa. If you can get them started, former banana workers will talk to you about *la Yunai,* as they call United, with nostalgia or resentment, sometimes in the English they learned from their employers.

Now the government has been negotiating with a Venezuelan company to raise bananas on 4000 hectares of land in the Zona Sur. Some of the land would be owned by cooperatives.

The former use of copper sulfides in pesticides in the banana plantations has made it impossible to grow rice and other traditional food crops in the area, due to the high levels of chemicals that persist in the soil.

In an effort to pump new life into Golfito, the Costa Rican government established the town as a duty-free port in 1990. Ticos are allowed to buy $400 worth of merchandise every 6 months. The imported items will still be sold with a hefty tax, which will not make them of much interest to tourists, but does make them cheaper than imported goods in San José. If consumer fever infects you, know that foreigners are allowed to buy as much as they want, but anything beyond the $400 limit will be transported by free port authorities to the customs station of your choice.

The town is stretched along one main road squeezed between the Gulf and tree-covered mountains, which have been made into a wildlife and watershed reserve. The northern part of town was the Zona Americana. United Fruit administrators lived in this quiet neighborhood with big wooden houses on stilts, surrounded by large lawns and gardens. The farthest area north is the airport, built within a golfcourse planted with exotic trees and bushes that United imported from Africa and Asia, now completely overgrown. Near the airport is the free port, the *depósito libre*, a huge outdoor mall with air-conditioned shops filled with *electrodomésticos* (household appliances) and luxury items such as smoked salmon, butter cookies, and Old Milwaukee beer.

Buses run along the road between the north and south parts of town, stopping at both the *depósito* and near the airport. The south part of town is called the Pueblo Civil, a noisy collection of bars, restaurants, brothels and hotels. It feels much more like a crowded, active port than the tranquil, distinguished Zona Americana; it's hard to imagine that the two sectors form the same town.

As of this writing, all hotels are in the Pueblo Civil, but new hotels are being built to accommodate the influx of shoppers from other parts of the country. The earlier in the day you can check in, the more luck you will have finding a room. **El Uno**, (F, pb) 25m north of the municipal dock, is very basic and inexpensive. Rooms do not have windows. **Hotel Golfito**, 25 m. south of the dock, seems to be the best deal in town (E, pb, cf, cw, 75-0047). **Hotel Delfina**, 200m south of the dock, is divided in two. If you stay in the cheaper south half (F, cb), try to get a room with windows and be aware that almost everyone wakes up at 4 am to catch a bus. The other half is more modern and probably more quiet (E, pb, cw, tf; D with a/c, 75-0043). Off of the coastal road, in the heart of the Pueblo Civil, is **Hotel Costa Rica Surf**, proclaiming itself the "Gringo Aid Station". Restaurant/bar down below, real estate office and souvenir shop, American Legion meetings the first Tuesday of every month. Rooms are dark (D, pb, tf, some with a/c, 75-0034). **Las Gaviotas** at the entrance to town (the town bus makes its last stop here) is by far the nicest place to stay. Right on the water's edge with a dock for visitors' boats. Scarlet macaws preen themselves in the gardens. There is an outdoor covered restaurant specializing in seafood, and cabinas with private porches (B, hw, pb, a/c; A w/kitchens, fans, 75-0062).

Across the water from Las Gaviotas on Puntarenitas Spit is the **Jungle Club**, which is reputed to serve good, moderately-priced meals. Many yachts are anchored in the restaurant's little bay, attesting to its popularity. If you're not a yachtee, hire a boat at the municipal dock for the short ride. Also consider taking a boat-taxi to **Captain Tom's Place,** on the other side of the bay at Playa Cacao. Captain Tom is a one-legged expatriate whose boat broke down a few decades ago. He still lives in his remodeled boat, which is carefully strewn with chunks of sea lore: magic realism at its best. It's worth visiting him just to check out the quarters. His wife Rocío serves up Jungle Burgers for a reasonable price. They also run a hotel in a beached 62-foot trawler (E per person, baths in Tom and Rocío's house 50 m. away, cw, nf, kitchen facilities), each "room" with its own creative design and paperback library. They will rent you a tent for camping in their front yard.

Getting there: Golfito buses leave San José (c 4, a 18, 21-4214, 7 hours) at 6:30 ($4, indirect), 11am and 3pm ($5, direct) or take any Zona Sur bus to Río Claro, where the road to Golfito leaves the Interamerican. Villa Neilly-Golfito buses pass through Río Claro hourly (1/2 hour trip).

You can avoid the long, winding (though scenic) bus ride by flying SANSA to Golfito Mon thru Sat at 8am. There is also a flight on Mon, Thurs and Fri leaving San José at 12:30pm, stopping in Palmar Sur at 1:05, then landing in Golfito at 1:40pm (flights return at 9am and 1:55pm; $20 one way, make reservations and buy tickets in advance, schedules change often, 33-0397, 33-3258, 21-9414).

Pavones is highly publicized in surfer magazines for having the longest wave in the world. It draws throngs during the rainy season, when the waves are largest. On peak days, expect between 50 and 80 surfers in the water. If you don't surf, try another beach (such as nearby Zancudo). Pavones is crowded and not suited to body surfing or swimming. The area has been the site of some wild west-like confrontations involving drug trafficking and land disputes.

To get to Pavones, take a bus at 2pm near the municipal dock in Golfito, or hire a jeep-taxi ($50-60). The ride, along bumpy dirt roads and across the Río Coto by ferry, can take up to 2.5 hours, depending on the state of the road and your means of transportation. Buses leave Pavones for Golfito at 5 am.

In Pavones, there are 4 simple rooms above the cantina, the **Pavón Tico** (F, cb, nf). They sometimes annex rooms in other houses across the street. The pulpería next to the soccer field also rents a few rooms (F). Doña María Jiménez, who lives 400 meters east of the school (which is 200 m north of the cantina), has two cabinas and rents horses.

Two km south of Pavones, along the dirt road that follows the coast all the way to the border with Panama, is **Bahía Pavones Lodge**. The lodge is well situated 50 meters from the shore, with a wooden deck built onto the top of a towering rock right on the beach. Rooms in the main building are simple and small with screens (cb). The cabinas are a bit larger, with their own porches (pb). Rates are D per person, including breakfast; the kitchen serves dinner and prepares cold lunches. Make arrangements to stay there through the Tsunami Surf

Shop on Avenida Central in Los Yoses, San José, next to Aza-frán. They are sometimes willing to rent rooms to people who just show up, but don't count on it.

Three km south of Bahía Pavones Lodge, high up on a jungle-covered hillside, is **Tiskita Lodge** (L per person, double, including 3 meals, pb). The rustic but comfortable cabins all have superb views of the ocean and are cooled by sea breezes. They would be our choice for the perfect honeymoon spot. Agronomist Peter Aspinall has planted 100 varieties of tropical fruits there from around the world, which attract many birds and monkeys. Trails wind up and down the mountain backdrop and there is a 20-meter waterfall close to the cabinsites. Packages including charter flights and guided nature walks are available through Costa Rica Sun Tours, 55-3518, 55-3418, fax: (506) 55-4410.

From Pavones, one can take a boat to Playa Zancudo, about an hour away by sea (several hours by land, if it is dry season and the roads are passable). Walter Jiménez, who anchors his boats and himself near the school, will take passengers ($35 per boatload to Zancudo, varied and negotiable rates for other destinations).

Playa Zancudo, on a strip between the ocean and the Coto river, is one of the Zona Sur's most popular beaches during the dry season, though you'd never know it during the rainy season, when adjectives to describe the place range from peaceful to boring. The fine black sand beach stretches for kilometers and the surf is gentle. Good fishing attracts many North American visitors and residents.

Hotels and cabinas are plentiful. At the center of town, across the road from the dock, is **Estero Mar**. It is a lively bar during rainy season, and has the only public telephone in town (75-0056). Estero Mar has been known to rent rooms when other places are full. **El Coquito**, 200m. to the south rents small cabinas with windows that unfortunately are not oriented towards the sea and therefore miss the cool breezes (E, nf, pb, cw). **Los Almendros**, 400m north of Estero Mar, has comfortable cabinas and a good restaurant that cater to the middle class (D, pb, cw, cf, good screens, nightlamps, 75-0515). River, bay, and ocean fishing trips can be arranged in their boats. Nearby, Steve and Dee Lino run a charter fishing business with the latest equipment and a 29-foot sportfishing boat. Call them at

75-0268 or make reservations through Los Almendros. North of Los Almendros is **Río Mar** (E, pb, fans), pleasant, inexpensive cabinas well-placed between ocean and river. **Cabinas Zancudo** are simple and pleasant with good screens, and windows facing the beach (E, pb, cf, cw, 77-3027). Other cabinas which have been highly recommended for friendliness, good food, tranquility, and creative design are **Sol y Mar**, a 25 minute walk south of Zancudo (D, pb, cf; a bit more for secluded "honeymoon suites", restaurant, 75-0353). They also provide boat service from Golfito. The **Soda Tranquilo** rents two rooms and has a menagerie of animals.

Getting there: There is a Golfito-Zancudo bus (2.5 hours) during the dry season. Ask around in Golfito's Pueblo Civil for time and location. Mondays and Fridays, boatloads leave Zancudo for Golfito at 6am and return from the municipal dock at Golfito around noon, usually with the high tide. Passage is $2-3 per person. Other days, hire a boat at the municipal dock of Golfito ($15-20 per boatload). Local boats provide transportation from Zancudo to Golfito for $1-2. They either go via the sea, or take a short cut through the Atrocha, a natural canal through mangroves in which many birds and sometimes alligators can be seen.

American crocodile (cocodrilo)

The **Península de Osa** reaches out of southwestern Costa Rica into the Pacific Ocean. Its large virgin rainforests receive 4000 milimeters of precipitation per year. For years Osa's incredible wealth of tropical flora and fauna was protected from human destruction by the peninsula's isolation from the rest of the country. Then a lumber company moved in, more settlers came, and sports hunters began killing endangered animals in large numbers. Scientists urged the creation of a national park to protect the peninsula: in 1975, 108,022 acres in the western corner of the Osa were declared **Corcovado National Park.**

Corcovado contains eight unique habitats that range from mountain forests to marshes and swamps. Scientists have identified at least 500 species of trees, 285 birds, 139 mammals, 116 amphibians and reptiles, and 16 kinds of fresh-water fish.

Corcovado used to harbor another kind of inhabitant: *oreros* (gold panners), who lived in the jungle and sifted for their fortunes in the park's rivers. Few struck it rich, but most at least made a living. The Banco Central set up a special office in Puerto Jiménez to buy the gold, which the country used to help pay the interest on its huge foreign debt. But due to massive unemployment in the region, the gold panners' numbers grew so disproportionately that their activity started causing real destruction. The silt from their panning was filling up the rivers and lake in the park's basin. So in 1986, the Park Service and the Costa Rican Civil Guard physically removed all the gold panners, promising them an indemnity for their lost jobs. After a year without payment, the *oreros* camped out in protest in the city parks of San José until the government came through with the checks they had promised. Panning activity has started again, this time in the forest reserve bordering Corcovado. Two thousand families are now making their living in this way. Even though it is destructive, the Park Service has decided to let it go on instead of risking more harm to Corcovado itself.

A surge in human settlers is threatening the delicate ecological balance of the unprotected forests in the Osa. An expanding national population, a shortage of land available elsewhere for cultivation, and the new road with bridges built by the U.S. Army Corps of Engineers in 1989 are factors that encourage settlement. *Campesinos* have moved in and started burning and cutting back the jungle to build their houses and cultivate small plots of land.

The situation on the Osa is a microcosm of what has been happening all over the tropical world. The shortage of available land is so serious that clearing and colonizing land seems like the only alternative to many people. But rainforest soil is very poor when there's no forest covering it: its self-fertilization by dead leaves, plants and animals stops, rendering it infertile. When the rain falls, the soil erodes and silt fills the rivers. Since there is little biomass left to absorb excess moisture, floods are common.

The jungle provides a habitat for thousands of animals which die without it. Its trees produce chemicals that are extracted for use in medicines like morphine, codeine, and quinine. Oxygen is a byproduct of their photosynthesis. The jungle conserves the humidity of the land and protects its watersheds. Visiting the Península de Osa is a good way to learn first-hand about the conflict between conservation of natural resources that humanity needs in the long-term, and the short-term options that many people consider their only means of survival.

Now, thanks to international support for Costa Rica's conservation efforts, the Fundación Neotrópica (see p. 39) is starting to address this problem through its **BOSCOSA** project. Indepth studies have been done of the needs of *precarista* (squatter) communities in the Osa, and strong relationships between BOSCOSA workers and the people are being established. Through studies of animal and plant species that grow in forest reserves, new crops and livestock projects are being experimented with to provide solutions for both human and environmental problems. Costa Rican conservationists are realizing that they must create their own models for sustained development, rather than relying on techniques developed in countries with different cultural and economic patterns. They are forging a new understanding of human and environmental issues as one and the same. For more information about BOSCOSA, call 33-0003.

Puerto Jiménez is a small, friendly town, and the gateway to Corcovado. There are good white sand beaches south of town, beyond the second point that juts out into the gulf. The throbbing meeting place in Puerto Jiménez is **La Carolina,** a small outdoor soda right on the main street. Go there to look for anyone in town, as the owners are sure to know where they are. The most comfortable place to stay in Jiménez is **Cabinas Manglares** (F, cf, pb, rest., shared cooking area, 78-5002), with a monkey and alligator in permanent residence. It's a 5 minute walk from downtown, near the airport. Go 300m down the main street from the soccer field then make a left before the church, past Cabinas Marcelina two blocks. Make a right, cross the little bridge (look for the alligator in the water on the left), and Manglares is around the bend. **Cabinas Marcelina** (F, pb, tf) is simple now, but might expand in the future with more luxurious cabinas. Friendly owners can set guests up with horses, gold panning expeditions, fishing trips, etc. **Cabinas Brisas del Mar,**

on the way into town from the dock, windows facing the gulf, is simple (F, pb, tf). **Agua Luna** is a well-appointed restaurant next to the dock in a series of *ranchitos* (round, indigenous-style buildings with pointy, thatched roofs). More expensive than the simpler restaurants in town, but food is good.

Getting to Puerto Jiménez: Buses leave San Isidro de El General at 5:30am and 12 noon for Puerto Jiménez (5 hrs). You can also intercept the Villa Neilly-Puerto Jiménez bus at 7am or 3pm at Chacarita (Piedras Blancas) on the Interamerican highway, by taking any Zona Sur bus from San José.

An old **launch** leaves the municipal dock (*muelle*) in Golfito for Puerto Jiménez every day at noon. The enjoyable ride across the gulf takes an hour and a half. Dolphins often swim and jump alongside the boat. The launch returns to Golfito from the dock below the bus station in Puerto Jiménez at 6am. You can buy coffee from the cook and watch the early birds dive for their fish breakfasts.

If you're susceptible to car- and seasickness, you might want to fly to Jiménez from Golfito with Aeronaves de Costa Rica (75-0278, $110 per 5-person planeload).

Corcovado National Park's administration office is at the south end of the main street in Puerto Jiménez. Several days before you plan to visit Corcovado, you must call the office (78-5036). Tell them how long you want to stay and whether you will need meals and lodging (all guard and research stations within the park can provide rooms and meals if you give sufficient notice). During the dry season you can camp fairly comfortably, but be aware that the beaches are infested with *purrujas*, perhaps the most aggravating of Costa Rican insects. So do not plan to just sack out on the beach; bring a tent. Fees to camp or stay at the stations are both minimal. Bring mosquito nets, repellent, long socks, several changes of cotton clothing, a swimsuit, a flashlight, a water bottle, snacks and two pairs of hiking or running shoes, or rubber boots.

Getting there: There are several ways to get to the park. See p. 235 for info on getting to Golfito by bus or on SANSA.

You can rent a small, **5-passenger plane** that will fly you directly to Sirena, the main research station inside the park (from Golfito: **Aeronaves de Costa Rica**, 75-0278, $110/planeload; from San José: **SAETA**, 32-1474, 32-9514, $400/planeload). Many of the nature tour companies listed on page 49-50 have guided tours to Corcovado.

Hiking: From Puerto Jiménez there are two ways to enter the park. The most convenient entrance is to the north via **La Palma**. Transportation to La Palma from Puerto Jiménez or the Interamerican Highway is quick and easy. A bus leaves Puerto Jiménez at 5:30am for La Palma (hour trip). From La Palma it's a 12 km, 3-hour walk to the park's northeastern entrance at **Los Patos**, crossing the Río Rincón 19 times. The trail in this stretch is a narrow gravel road. When vehicles pass they often offer rides to hikers. The worst stretch of the whole trip is immediately before and after Los Patos, where the trail can be swampy and slippery, especially in the rainy season. Call park headquarters in advance to arrange for room and board at the Los Patos guard station.

After Los Patos, there are 6km of steep trails through high mountain forests, then 14km of flat walking through low, dense rainforest to the research station at Sirena. The trail is clearly marked, but at some river crossings you have to check up- or downstream for where the trail takes off again. Some of the rivers can be thigh-deep in the rainy season.

You might want to bring a machete because the trail is narrow and there are overhanging branches. Be careful not to walk into poisonous spiders, whose webs span the trail, and bring repellent and plenty of patience for the horseflies. Other members of the animal kingdom you might meet are frogs, morpho butterflies, tapirs, ocelots, and monkeys.

The other way to enter Corcovado from Puerto Jiménez is via **Carate**, on the southern coast of the Osa Peninsula. Look for Cirilo Espinosa at the *pulpería* next to La Carolina in Puerto Jiménez. He drives a truck to Carate Monday and Saturday mornings ($4.50, returning any time after 10am). Have patience if something goes awry, and hold on tight--the road gets progressively worse as the trip goes on. If you'd rather walk, it's about an eight-hour trip, with no stores along the way. On other days, the taxi can be rented for $45-60 per carload. Make arrangements through the park office.

At Carate, turn right and walk along the soft sand beach about 45 minutes to the **La Leona** ranger station. You can eat and spend the night here if you check with the Park administration office beforehand. Don't swim--there are sharks and the current is strong.

The walk from La Leona to Sirena spans 15 km and takes about 4 or 5 hours. It is almost entirely along the soft sand beach. You must do it at low tide, because you walk around a couple of rocky points that are covered at high tide. There is a rusty shipwreck at Punta Chancha, with huge engines scattered around the rocks. A bit later you reach Salsipuedes (Get-out-if-you-can) Point, with a pretty cave hollowed out of the coast. At some of the rock points there are trails that cut inland for a few hundred meters. The best way to find them is to start looking as soon as the coast looks impassable. The Salsipuedes trail gives you a break from the soft sand for a km or two, but lather yourself up with repellent before starting into the jungle. There are many monkeys along this trail. You will probably see scarlet macaws awkwardly winging and raucously singing through the sky. *Pizotes* (coatimundis) also come to the coast frequently. If you bring a machete you can take a break along the way to open up a coconut for a refreshing *agua de pipa*. After you cross the Río Claro, cut in either on the Sirena trail, or at the airstrip a bit further down.

Sirena is a large research station populated by biological researchers mostly from the States and Europe, and eco-tourists. There are several km of nature trails around Sirena that unfortunately are becoming severely eroded due to overuse and poor maintenance. Do not bathe in the ocean, as there are sharks, but as long as you look out for crocodiles you can swim in the nearby Río Claro and Río Sirena.

If you want to reward yourself after your wet, buggy time in Corcovado, consider spending a night or two in one of the resorts at Bahía Drake (see below), half an hour by boat from **San Pedrillo**, the northwestern entrance station. The resorts will pick you up there.

The walk from Sirena to San Pedrillo is 25 km, 15 of which are along wide, flat, hard beach, 7 through rainforest, and 3 weaving between beach and coastal jungle. The entire walk can take 6 to 7 hours. Make sure you walk the beaches at low tide. We hiked the first stretch, along the beach, at night. If you want to sleep comfortably, bring a tent, as the *purrujas* are really terrible there.

One km from the Sirena research station is the Río Sirena, the deepest (3-4 feet in the rainy season) river with the strongest current that you'll have to cross on this hike. After that, it's about 2 hours to the Río Corcovado, which has a sandy bottom and is 2 feet deep at low tide. Two hours later is the Río Llorona, comparable to the Corcovado. If you walk at night as we did, you'll note some mysterious fog there. A couple of hundred meters later is the Piedra Arco, a huge rock arch covered with greenery. Soon after, a poorly-marked trail cuts off into the jungle. Around the rocky point you'll find La Llorona, a 100-foot waterfall which cascades onto the beach. Don't be fooled by the tiny waterfall that you see immediately after leaving the sandy beach; continue on another 15 minutes. Do not attempt this except at low tide.

The trail through the rainforest climbs steeply at first then rises and descends to creeks along the way. Much of it is level, winding through the jungle. For the most part it is a wide, good path, but watch the ascents and descents because the trail is eroded and slippery. A couple of hours later, you descend back to a beach. It's another hour to the Río San Pedrillo. With long legs you can jump it near the mouth; otherwise, test the waters and wade. If you want to keep walking, take the trail that follows the coast to Bahia Drake, 10 km away.

Marenco Biological Station, about 5km north of Corcovado on the Pacific, is dedicated to "conservation, education, tourism and adventure". Naturalists enjoy Marenco because they have a chance to see rainforest, river and sea wildlife all in the same area. Some of them even take off their binoculars long enough to enjoy snorkeling. A half-hour hike through a series of lovely rocky coves ends at the Río Claro where a deep natural pool lends itself to a refreshing fresh-water swim. One of

Costa Rica's first ecotourism projects, it has resident biologists to help visitors understand the intricate ecological relationships there. The cabinas, not luxurious, but simple and well-designed (4 beds to a room, cold water, shared baths), overlook the Pacific and the Isla del Caño. Meals are delicious and wholesome, served family-style. Marenco offers tours to the northern part of Corcovado, hiking from San Pedrillo to La Llorona waterfall.

Because of Marenco's isolated location, transportation is coordinated through their office in San José (21-1594, Apdo. 4025, 1000 San José, fax: 55-4513). A 3-night tour costs around $555, including food, lodging, air and boat transport from San José and guides. Guided day trips are extra.

Drake Bay, purported to be where Sir Francis Drake anchored and set foot in Costa Rica in 1579, is about 10 minutes north of Marenco by boat. The bay is calm, and many sailboats and yachts anchor there. Four types of whales visit the bay. Fishing is excellent along the coast. There are three North American-run lodges on Drake Bay.

Drake Bay Wilderness Camp is right on the beach with nice cabinas and good American-Tico-style food (L/person incl. 3 meals, pb, solar hw, cf, trips and transportation extra but reasonably priced, shady campground, charter flights available, ph/fax: 71-2436). Snorkeling is good right at the camp and 10 minutes away at Punta San Josesito. Owner Herb Michaud can lend you masks and fins. The camp is right at the mouth of the Río Agujitas, known for its needlefish. You can canoe up it in search of monkeys. Visitors can take guided tours of Corcovado or the Isla del Caño, do some ocean fishing, or relax in the giant tidepools near the lodge.

Across the Río Agujitas from Drake Bay Wilderness Camp is **Phantom Isle Lodge**, which specializes in scuba diving and sportfishing. They have a 34-foot diving boat and a 24-foot fishing boat. Scuba divers must bring their own bcs and regulators, but they supply the tanks and weights (B/person incl. meals, pb or cb, cold water, no fans, (713) 489-9156 in USA). Owner Richard Ray can obtain discounted airline tickets for guests coming through Houston, Texas.

La Paloma Lodge is built on top of a hill overlooking the Atlantic Ocean (around the corner from Drake Bay). Family-size cabinas with thatched roofs, perched on stilts, are breezy and have porches, lofts, and bathtubs, L/person incl. meals, 39-2801.

244

These lodges will arrange transport for you from San José. If you want to get there on your own, take a bus or a SANSA plane to Palmar (Mon, Th, Fri, 12:30pm, $20, 33-0397, 33-3258, fax: 55-2176), then a bus or taxi to Sierpe, a village on the Sierpe River 20 min. away. You have to go down the river a couple of hours and out into the ocean to get to Drake Bay. The crossing from the wide river mouth into the ocean is dangerous and must be done according to the tides by an experienced skipper. The lodges will send one to pick you up in Sierpe. There are dugouts that take local people in and out inexpensively, but they are usually overloaded and have been known to capsize at the river mouth. If you want to risk it, ask around at the sleepy port of Sierpe. If you need to spend the night there, the **Hotel Margarita** is clean and cheap (F, cb); it's in a big white house near the dock.

If you would like to stay in the town of Drake, Cecilia rents a room and can cook for you. An alternative way to get to Drake is to walk there from the town of **Rancho Quemado** on the Osa Peninsula; it's a 3-4 hour walk along a dirt road (often impassable by car). You can get to Rancho Quemado by jeep or truck from the town of Rincón, which is on the road to Puerto Jiménez from the Interamerican.

The Villa Neilly-San Vito road was built in 1945 before the end of World War II by the USA as a strategic protection point since the area is due west of the Panama Canal. The gravel road rises so sharply that in 20 minutes, Villa Neilly's heat is forgotten in the cool, misty mountains that lead to **San Vito** (3150'above sea level). The trip takes 2.5 hours in a crowded, aging bus, but the countryside is lush and not as deforested as in other areas. Immigrants from post-war Italy founded San Vito in the early 50's. In the last few years its population has doubled to 37,000. It's a clean, modern town nestled in a high mountain valley.

The **Wilson Botanical Gardens**, 6km uphill from San Vito on the Villa Neilly road, is a center for botanical, agro-ecological, and horticultural research, scientific training and public education. Plant species threatened with habitat loss and extinction are maintained in greenhouses and in the wild for future reforestation efforts. The main collections in the 25-acres of cultivated grounds are of tropical palms, aroids, bromeliads, ferns, heliconias and marantas, though many other plants are also featured in the lush design of the gardens, inspired in part by the great Brazilian horticulturist, Burle-Marx. Some 278 species of birds inhabit the gardens and the 342-acre forest reserve surrounding them. Five miles of trails offer vistas to the mountains, overlooks into close rainforest canopy, and hikes to the lovely, rocky pools of the Río Java.

The administration building contains dormitory-style accommodations and 2 rooms with private baths ($45/day incl. meals, no children under 6). Reservations must be made in advance through the Organization for Tropical Studies (40-6696, fax: (506) 40-6783). For more information write Gail Hewson Gómez, Jardín Botánico Wilson, Apdo. 73, San Vito, Coto Brus 8257, CR).

Getting there: You can take the San Vito-Villa Neilly bus to the gardens at 7am and 1:30pm, or take the Villa Neilly-San Vito bus at 6am, 1pm or 3pm. A taxi from San Vito is about $3.50.

Direct buses to San Vito leave San José at 7am and 1:45pm from Empresa Alfaro (c 14, a 5, 22-2750, $6.50, 5 hours, tickets in advance, 7-hour indirect buses at 5:30 and 9:30am). This route is paved all the way, and crosses the Río Térraba on a ferry (5 min.) at Paso Real, east of Palmar Norte. Most of these buses pass the Botanical Gardens after a stop in San Vito. Check with the driver.

You can charter a 5-passenger plane to San Vito (see p. 240), or take the SANSA flight to Golfito ($20) and take a taxi to the Gardens ($40).

Hotels: Cabinas Las Mirlas, next to the Ministry of Agriculture office (E, hw, 77-3054) are perched among fruit trees overlooking a creek. **Hotel Pitier** (E, pb, hw) and **El Ceibo** (E, pb, hw, good restaurant, 77-3025) are also clean and inexpensive. For maximum peace and quiet, stay at the Botanical Gardens.

Parque Internacional La Amistad extends over the Talamanca mountains from the southern border of Parque Nacional Chirripó down into Panamá. It is the largest park in the country (192,000 hectares). Composed of eight life zones, La Amistad is one of the richest ecological biospheres in Central America.

Preliminary surveys indicate that two thirds of the country's vertebrate species are found in the park. Some animals are not protected anywhere else in Costa Rica. The park is an important refuge for animals that require large areas for hunting, foraging and reproduction, like the jaguar, margay and puma.

Facilities in the park are still being developed, but camping is allowed near the park entrances at Las Mellizas, Aguas Calientes and Helechales. The Las Mellizas area is the best for hiking and the easiest to get to. Take a San Vito-La Lucha bus at 9:30am and walk 6km. A regular car can drive all the way to the park station. There you can get information on trails. Taxis can drive you in from San Vito for about $80 round trip per taxi. Meals can be arranged through the cooks at Las Mellizas farm. Water in the streams is good. Trout fishing is possible, with a permit (see p. 80).

Hiking deeper into the park should only be undertaken by experienced tropical trekkers. There are wild animals, few paths, and the topography is abrupt. North Americans have been known to suffer from hypothermia there. But hiking in the Las Tablas forest reserve at the entrance to the park is safe and rewarding. Horses and guides can be arranged for at Las Mellizas. For current conditions, call Parques Nacionales (22-7911, 33-4070, 33-4118).

Isla del Coco (Coco Island), 500km off the Pacific coast, boasts 200 dramatic waterfalls, many of which fall directly into the sea. Because the island is uninhabited, animals there are not afraid of humans. The fairy terns find humans so interesting that they hover about them curiously.

Although its geological origin remains a mystery, scientists believe Isla del Coco is a volcanic "hot spot" at the center of the Cocos tectonic plates. The Coco Island finch is a sub-species of the finch endemic to the Galapagos Islands which prompted Darwin's questions about evolution. Several species of birds, lizards and fresh water fish are endemic to the island, that is, they are found nowhere else on earth. Whereas on mainland Costa Rica there are so many species that the behavior of each is highly specialized, on Isla del Coco individual birds of the same species will have different feeding habits-- very interesting from an evolutionary standpoint. Some 77 non-endemic species, mainly sea-birds, can also be observed there.

European sailors probably first discovered the island in the 1500's. Many early visitors were pirates who rested and restocked fresh water there during their expeditions. They named the island after its numerous coconut palms, but apparently enjoyed the coconuts so much that there are almost none left today. Passing boats landed pigs, deer and goats on the island to provide meat for return voyages. Having had no predators, these animals now constitute the majority of the wildlife there.

There are two main tales of buried treasure on the island. The Portuguese Benito Bonito, "The One of the Bloody Sword", is said to have buried his fabulous treasure there. At the time of Peru's wars of independence from Spain, the aristocracy and clergy entrusted their gold and jewels to Captain James Thompson, who promised to transport their riches to a safe port. Thompson disappeared with the loot and is supposed to have hidden it on Isla del Coco. Although many treasure hunters have searched the island, no one has found anything yet.

Hunting for gold doubloons might not be rewarding at Isla del Coco, but scuba divers find it rich in natural treasures. The ship **Okeanos** takes scuba divers to the island for a week of heavy-duty diving. A sister vessel, **Temptress**, takes tourists to all the coastal National Parks and Reserves south of Puntarenas with a biologist guide (in US: 800-348-2628, in CR: 20-1679).

Contact Parques Nacionales for current access information (33-4070, 33-4118).

Fairy tern

STAYING LONGER

Options for Residency

Securing permanent residency here is a complicated and increasingly difficult process. Temporary residency can be obtained by students in registered university or language school programs, or by volunteers with US Peace Corps (or its Canadian, European or Japanese equivalents) or church-affiliated service groups.

Retired businessmen can join the International Executive Service Corps, a private, non-profit firm sponsored in part by AID. They have a skills bank in Stamford, Conn. which matches volunteers with third-world companies needing consultants. Volunteers are paid living expenses only. Eight other "developed" countries in addition to the US have similar organizations (IESC, Apdo. 70 Centro Colón, San José, CR (506) 33-9855).

To live here on a permanent basis you must either have a lot of money to invest in starting your own company (*inversionista* status), or apply for *pensionado* or *rentista* status. Pensionados must receive at least $600/month from a qualified pension or retirement plan, or from Social Security. Rentistas must prove that they have investments outside Costa Rica which will guarantee them an income of $1000 per month.

You must apply for these residencies through the nearest Costa Rican consulate in your home country. You must supply the following documents: birth certificates for you and your dependents; all marriage and divorce certificates; naturalization certificates (if applicable); and a letter from your home police department certifying that you have no criminal record.

Pensionados must obtain a letter from their pension or retirement plan company or Social Security stating that the pension is for life and that the stated monthly amount will be paid in Costa Rica. The pension company must have existed for at least 20 years, and must provide a statement of incorporation and economic solvency, certified by a CPA, which in turn must be authenticated by a Costa Rican consul. References from two banks with which the company deals must also be provided.

Rentistas must submit a letter from a bank or recognized investment company stating that the amount of monthly income the candidate receives is stable, permanent and irrevocable and that it will be paid in Costa Rica for no less than five years. The company providing the income must have existed for over three years and must supply statements of incorporation, economic solvency and bank references, as above.

All documents must be authenticated by the Costa Rican consul nearest to the place where they were issued. This costs $40 per document. All documents must be translated into Spanish by a translator approved by the Costa Rican Ministry of Foreign Relations.

In addition, the candidate must submit two copies of his passport, one copy for each dependent and four passport-size photos for each person involved. He must sign a sworn statement that he will live in Costa Rica at least four months a year, and must submit to a chest X-ray for TB, and blood tests for venereal diseases.

Pensionados must provide fingerprints and photos before they receive residency permits, so that their identities can be checked by Interpol, in an effort to eliminate criminals who present falsified police documents.

Both pensionados and rentistas can set up their own businesses, but they cannot be employed by someone else. They must convert their $600 or $1000 into colones each month. There are about 2000 bonafide pensionados and rentistas living in Costa Rica. The best place to get current information is through the 850-member

Asociación de Pensionados y Rentistas
Apdo. 700-1011, San José, Costa Rica
Phone: 33-8068, fax: (506) 22-7862

For $500, they will handle all the paperwork and running around necessary to secure the above residencies in two to four months. Private lawyers can charge up to $1500 or $2000 for the same services and take up to two years. Once you get your residency through the Asociación, you automatically become a full member, and are eligible for many other services, as well as medical insurance offered by the Costa Rican Social Security System. The Asociación offices are in the ICT building mezzanine, a 4, c 5.

Do not plan to do your residency yourself unless you have plenty of patience to deal with the lines, the national holidays, the lunch-breaks, the misunderstandings, the offices that have moved from where they were a month ago, the impossible-to-find phone numbers, etc. If you've got comfortable shoes and love to meditate or read novels while waiting in line, you'll find *trámites* (bureaucratic machinations) just your cup of tea. If you are nervous and impatient or have fallen arches, you will suffer.

The Costa Rican government doesn't want foreigners to take jobs from Costa Ricans. Therefore, most foreigners are not allowed to work unless they are performing a task that Ticos cannot do. But with some thought, you might be able to discover a skill you have which will help you establish residency. Qualified teachers are needed at the English, French, Japanese and German-speaking schools in San José. English teachers are often needed by the various language institutes. The National Symphony needs musicians, The *Tico Times* needs reporters.

Doctors, lawyers, architects and engineers are plentiful here, and are protected by powerful professional associations which make entry difficult for foreigners.

Legal Advice: If you live here and have a business or buy land, etc., sooner or later you will need to hire a lawyer. Here are our guidelines for choosing one in Costa Rica:

1. Shop around. There is usually no charge for meeting and consulting with a lawyer. Find someone you respect and can communicate with easily. Actually, your paperwork will probably be handled by law students working in the lawyer's office, and they will be the ones you end up having to communicate with, so meet them too. Probably the most important person to

have a trusting relationship with is the secretary. Some lawyers are always "not there" or "in a meeting" according to their secretaries. You can call for *weeks* and never get to talk to them.

2. Talk with other residents about whom they would recommend. Find a lawyer with whom people have had positive experiences in the field you are interested in. *Licenciado X* may be a terrific international lawyer, but you can bet his specialty isn't residencies, so don't expect him to be good at it.

3. Don't go to someone because he's a "nice guy" or somebody's friend. "Honest and efficient" is better than nice. Costa Ricans are always nice, even if they are irresponsible and slow.

4. Legal fees vary greatly. Some very good lawyers charge more because they know that what they do is far superior to the run of the mill. If you have the money, it is worth every penny to have a good lawyer here. Of course the mere fact that a lawyer charges more does not mean he is good. Some very reliable lawyers are not all that expensive. Guidelines have been established to govern legal fees. They were published in the *Gaceta* (the legal government newspaper). You can make a copy from the archives of the Biblioteca Nacional, or ask for going rates at the Colegio de Abogados (Bar Association).

5. Most legal work does not get done unless you keep tabs on what your lawyer is doing. It is best if you educate yourself on rules and regulations, etc. Do not sit back and expect that everything is humming along now that *Licenciado X* has your affairs in his capable hands. Check and double check, ask to see receipts, ask to see your *expediente* (file). Watch out if the lawyer tells you *"Tranquilo. No hay problema. No se preocupe."* (Relax. No problem. Don't worry.) This is Costa Rican for "Don't make me think about it".

6. Whether you have a good lawyer or a mediocre one, things still take a long time to get done here. So, as long as you know that things are *en trámite,* enjoy the relaxed pace and go on a couple of long weekends yourself.

Real Estate and Investments: "...the potential investor in Costa Rica should beware of ALL glib, fact-filled English-speaking promoters flogging ANYTHING, whether it's gold mines, beach property, condos, agribusiness, or mutual funds. Unfortunately, Costa Rica has long been a haven for con men, whose favorite targets are trusting newcomers. This doesn't mean, however, that legitimate investment opportunities don't exist, in agribusiness as well as in other areas. They do, and it's unfair to tar all projects with the same brush. Would-be investors here, like everywhere else, are advised simply to move cautiously, ask lots of questions, and check with well-established, reputable companies before parting with any money. That way, they can be confident of making a good choice."

--*The Tico Times*, Apdo. 4632, 1000 San José, CR; weekly, 32pg., $45/year.

Contact the **American Chamber of Commerce of Costa Rica,** Apdo. 4946, 1000 San José, CR, (506) 33-2133.

Renting: Houses and apartments in San José rent from about $200/mo. and up. Suburban and country houses can rent for as little as $150/mo. Luxury condominiums or estates can rent for $1000-$1200 or more. "Unfurnished" usually means without stove or refrigerator as well as without furniture.

Schools: English-language schools are excellent. They follow the U.S. academic year and prepare students for acceptance in foreign as well as Costa Rican universities.

Costa Rica Academy. Prekinder through grade 12. West of Cariari Country Club. Apdo 4941, San José, 39-0376.

Country Day School. Kinder through grade 12. Escazú. Apdo 8-6170, San José, 28-0873, fax: 28-2798.

The European School. Prekinder through grade 6, will expand to high school in the future. Barreal de Heredia. Apdo. 177 Heredia, CR, 37-3709, fax: (506) 31-7583

International Christian School. Prekinder through grade 12. Apdo. 3512, San José, Barrio Escalante, 25-1474.

Marian Baker School. Prekinder through grade 12. Apdo. 4269, SJ. San Ramón de Tres Ríos, east of San José, 34-3426, 34-4609.

253

Bilingual private schools are usually less expensive and also prepare students for U.S. college acceptance. They follow the Costa Rican academic year which begins in March and ends in November.

Anglo-American School. Primary. Apdo 3180, San José, 25-1729.

Blue Valley School. Primary. Apdo. 561, 2050 San Pedro, CR, 25-6703, fax: (506) 53-7708.

Colegio Humbolt. Kinder through grade 12. Classes in German and Spanish. Rohrmoser, 32-0093.

Colegio Internacional SEK. Prekinder through grade 9. Apdo. 963, 2050 San Pedro, CR, 53-1231, fax: (506) 53-9762.

Colegio Metodista. Kinder through high school. Apdo 931, San José, 25-0655.

Escuela Británica. Kinder through grade 10. Located in Pavas. Apdo 8184, San José, 22-0719, fax: 32-7833.

Lincoln School. Kinder through grade 12. Moravia. Apdo 1919, San José, 35-7733.

Saint Anthony School. Primary. Apdo 29, Moravia, 35-1017.

Saint Benedict. Primary. Apdo. 142, 2350, CR, 27-9504.

Saint Clare. Junior high, high school. Moravia, Apdo 2910, San José. 35-7244.

Saint Francis. Kinder through grade 12. Moravia. Apdo 4405, San José, 35-6685.

Saint Joseph's Primary. Apdo 132, Moravia, 35-7214.

Saint Mary's School. Kinder-6th. Apdo. 229 Escazú, CR, 28-2003.

Teocali Academy: Prekinder through grade 9. Apdo. 186, Liberia, Guanacaste, 66-0273.

254

Labor regulations for domestic help: All domestic employees have the right to social security benefits from the *Caja Costarricense de Seguro Social*, maternity benefits set by the Ministry of Labor, the Christmas bonus, and severance pay.

Whether live-in or not, the employee is entitled to the minimum wage set by the Ministry of Labor (23-7166). Live-in help can be required to work no more than 12 hours a day and other employees eight hours. The employee has one half day off each week, a 15-day paid vacation after 50 weeks of continual service, and half-days on January 1, Holy Thursday, Good Friday, May 1, September 15 and December 25. If they work these days, then an additional half-day salary must be paid. Days off should be previously scheduled.

The new employee must be registered with the Caja, in the fifth floor Department of Inspections (23-9890). The employer must bring identification such as a passport or residency *cédula,* the employee's *cédula* and the facts about the job and wages. The employer then receives a computer form which s/he uses to make the monthly payments to the *Caja* (19.5 percent of the monthly wages). The employee receives a paper giving him/her the right to the *Caja's* services (health care, maternity care, pensions). The monthly payment may be made by a messenger. If you lack a messenger, lines at the *Caja* seem shortest between 10:45 and 11:15.

An employee/mother-to-be is entitled to one month off before the birth and three months afterwards, with half of her monthly wage. Pregnancy is not a legal reason for dismissal.

The Christmas bonus (*aguinaldo*) is paid to employees who have worked from December 1 through November 30. It is equivalent to one month's salary. Most employers pay the *aguinaldo* early in December.

If the employer has cause to dismiss an employee, s/he must pay unused vacation time, the proportionate *aguinaldo* and all wages due. S/he must also document the dismissal with the *Caja*. If the employer must lay off help for reasons other than performance, such as leaving the country, s/he must give the employee prior notice, severance pay, unused vacation pay, the *aguinaldo* and wages due. Should the employee decide to leave, the employer is not obligated to pay severance pay.

RECOMMENDED READING

Abrams, Harry. *Between Continents, Between Seas: Precolumbian Art of Costa Rica.* New York, Harry Abrams, 1981.

Bell, John. *Crisis in Costa Rica: The Revolution of 48.* Austin, The University of Texas Press, 1971.

Biesanz, Mavis, Richard and Karen. *The Costa Ricans.* Englewood Cliffs, NJ, Prentice-Hall, Inc. 1987.

Bonilla, Alexander. *La Situación Ambiental de Costa Rica.* San José, Ministerio de Cultura, Juventud y Deportes, 1985.

Boza, Mario. *The National Parks of Costa Rica.* San José, Editorial Heliconia, 1987, softbound, 112 pages, bilingual text, beautiful photographs.

Boza, Mario. *Costa Rica National Parks.* San José, Editorial Heliconia, 1988, hardbound, 271 pages, bilingual text, beautiful photographs.

Carr, Archie. *The Windward Road.* Gainesville Florida State University Press, 1979.

Cornelius, Stephen E. *The Sea Turtles of Santa Rosa National Park.* San José, Fundación de Parques Nacionales, 1985.

DeVries, Philip, *The Butterflies of Costa Rica*, Princeton University Press, 1987, 327 pp., 50 color plates.

Gallo and Mayfield, *The Rivers of Costa Rica*, color photos, maps, hydrographic tables, 1988.

Glassman, Paul. *Costa Rica.* Passport Press, Box 596, Moscow, Vt. 19890.

Golcher Valverde, Federico et al. *Investors Guide to Costa Rica.* San José, Costa Rican-American Chamber of Commerce, 1990.

Gómez, Luis Diego. *Vegetación y Clima en Costa Rica,* San José, UNED. 2 volumes, 21 maps, 1987.

Janzen, Daniel, Editor, *Costa Rican Natural History.* Chicago, University of Chicago Press, 1983.

Mena, Ramón, *Costa Rica,* 130 photos, San José, 1988.

Palmer, Paula. *What Happen, A Folk History of Costa Rica's Talamanca Coast.* San José, Ecodesarrollos, 1977.

Palmer, Paula. *Wa'apin Man.* Editorial Costa Rica, 1986.

Palmer, Sanchez, Mayorga, *Taking Care of Sibo's Gifts, an Environmental Treatise,* Asociación de Desarrollo Integral de la Reserva Indigena Cocles/Kekoldi, San José, 1991, Apdo. 170 Sabanilla Montes de Oca, 24-6090, fax: 53-7524.

Perry, Donald. *Life Above the Jungle Floor,* San José, Don Perro Press, 1991. 170 pages, index, 52 color photos.

Searby, Ellen, *The Costa Rica Traveler.* Windham Bay Press, Box 1198, Occidental, CA 95465.

Skutch, Alexander F., University Press of Texas: *Parent Birds and their Young; Birds of Tropical America; Life Ascending* University of California Press: *A Naturalist on a Tropical Farm; Nature through Tropical Windows* University Presses of Florida: *The Imperative Call* University of Iowa Press: *Helpers at Birds' Nests*, 1987 Ibis Publishing Co, Santa Monica, CA, *Life of the Woodpecker* Crown Publishers: *The Life of the Hummingbird*

Stiles, Gary. *Field Guide to the Birds of Costa Rica,* Cornell University Press, Ithaca, NY, 1988.

Young, Allan. *Field Guide to the Natural History of Costa Rica.* Trejos Hermanos, San José, 1983.

Periodicals:

Mesoamérica. Published monthly by the Institute for Central American Studies, Apdo. 300, 1002 San José, Costa Rica.

The Tico Times. Published weekly. Apdo 4632, San José. (22-8952, 22-0040).

Videos:

Costa Rica: Making the Most of Your Trip. Practical info on travel, shopping tips, health care info, 1 hour, 36 minutes, $35 incl. shipping. In CR: 28-0266, in US: Marshall Productions, P.O. Box 534, Carlsbad, NM 88221.

Costa Rica Video. VHS, 34 minutes, $25 incl. shipping. Megaview Productions, 255 N. El Cielo, Suite 155, Palm Springs, CA 92262

Costa Rica Today. Aspects of Costa Rican life for both tourists and potential residents, 1 hour, $30. In CR: 59-7946, in US: Carlos Thomas, P. O. Box 5042, Dept. TT, New York, NY 10185

This is Costa Rica. 35 minutes, $25. Features all tours offered by Swiss Travel Service, Apdo. 7-1970, 1000 San José, CR, 31-4055.

INDEX

DOWNTOWN SAN JOSE

HOTELS: (See map)

12 Alameda
5 Ambassador
40 L'Ambiance
34 Amstel
38 Astoria
33 Aurola Holiday Inn
35 Balmoral
47 Bellavista
10 Boruca
32 Bougainvillea
4 Cacts
17 Capital
45 Casa Ridgway
7 Castilla
16 Central
24 Centro Continental
9 Cocorí
1 Corobicí
37 Costa Rica Inn
15 Diplomat
49 Aparthotel Don Carlos
39 Don Carlos
31 Dunn Inn
26 Europa
21 Fortuna
44 Galilea
14 Gran Centroamericano
29 Gran Costa Rica
28 Gran Vía
43 Lamm
19 Marlyn
44 Morazán
8 Musoc
3 Napoleón
27 Otoya
42 Pensión de la Cuesta
6 Petit

20 Plaza
36 Presidente
22 Principe
23 Ritz
11 Roma
25 Royal Gardens
46 Aparthotel San José
18 San José Garden Court
30 Santo Tomás
13 Talamanca
2 Torremolinos
48 Toruma Youth Hostel
50 Tres Arcos

BUS TERMINALS

A Monteverde, Tilarán
B Puntarenas
C Guápiles, Río Frío
D San Vito
E Nicoya, Sámara
F Peñas Blancas
G Zarcero
H San Isidro de El General
I Coca Cola
J Santa Cruz, Junquillal, Flamingo
K Liberia
L Alajuela
M Heredia thru la Uruca
N Escazú
O Golfito, Zona Sur
P Sixaola (Cahuita, Puerto Viejo de Talamanca
Q Heredia thru Tibás
R Cartago
S Turrialba
T Santa María de Dota
U Limón